Eating Our Hearts Out

Other Books By Lesléa Newman

Novels
Good Enough To Eat
In Every Laugh A Tear

Short Stories
Secrets
A Letter To Harvey Milk

Non-Fiction
Some<u>Body</u> To Love: A Guide To Loving The Body You Have

Poetry
Just Looking For My Shoes
Love Me Like You Mean It
Sweet Dark Places

Children's Books
Heather Has Two Mommies
Gloria Goes To Gay Pride
Belinda's Bouquet
Saturday Is Pattyday

Eating Our Hearts Out

Personal Accounts of Women's Relationship to Food

Edited by

Lesléa Newman

The Crossing Press, Freedom, CA 95019

Second Printing 1995

Copyright © 1993 by Lesléa Newman
Cover design & photography by Amy Sibiga
Photographic styling by AnneMarie Arnold
Book design & photography © 1993 by Amy Sibiga

Printed in the U.S.A.

Library of Congress Cataloging-in-Publication
Eating our hearts out: personal accounts of women's relationship to food/ edited
by Lesléa Newman
    p.   cm.
  ISBN 0-89594-570-3. --ISBN 0-89594-569-X (pbk.)
  1. American Literature--Women Authors. 2. Women--United States--
Literary Collections. 3. Food Habits--United States--Literary collections.
I. Newman, Lesléa.
PS508.W7E34 1992
810.8'09287--dc20   92-33669
                                   CIP

Acknowledgments

"The Mind Tongue Connection" by Elizabeth Alexander was excerpted in *Women's Glibber* (Crossing Press, 1992). Reprinted with permission of the author.

"Hearts" by Tricia Bauer was originally published by CALYX, A Journal *of Art and Literature By Women*, Volume 14, No. 2, Winter 1992/93. Reprinted with permission of the author.

"Scavenger To Angel" by Gayle Brandeis previously appeared in the Summer 1992 issue of *The Compleat Mother* (Volume 26). Reprinted with permission of the author.

"Ode To A Boardwalk Fry" by Elayne Clift first appeared in *The Leader* (Point Pleasant Beach, NJ, July 1989). Reprinted with permission of the author.

"Fat" by Janice Eidus first appeared in *the George Washinton Review* (1983). Reprinted with permission of the author.

"The Dieter's Daughter" by Anita Endrezze first appeared in *At The Helm Of Twilight* (Broken Moon Press, 1992). Reprinted with permission of the author.

"Cake Walk" by Susan Hauser is reprinted from *Girl To Woman: A Gathering Of Images* with permission of the author and from Astarte Shell Press.

"Literary Weight Loss" by Sibyl James previously appeared in *Hurricane Alice* and appears in *The Adventures of Stout Mama* by Sibyl James (forthcoming, Papier-Maché Press). Reprinted with permission of the author and publisher.

"Lesbian Stew" by Lee Lynch was previously published in *The Amazon Trail* (Naiad Press, 1988) and forthcoming in *Lesbian Culture* (Crossing Press, 1993).

"The Refrigerator" by Tema Nason was previously published in *A Stranger Here, Myself* (Puckerbrush Press, 1977). Reprinted with permission of the author.

"anorexia neurosis" by Sheryl L. Nelms has previously appeared in *Amazon, Womankind, Winewood Woman* and *Soundings East.* Reprinted with permission of the author.

"Song For Ten Scallops" by Lesléa Newman first appeared in *Love Me Like You Mean It,* (HerBooks, Santa Cruz, CA, 1987). Reprinted with permission of the author.

"One Spring" by Lesléa Newman previously appeared as the frontispiece for *Good Enough To Eat* (Firebrand Books, Ithaca, NY 1986) as well as in *Love Me Like You Mean It* (HerBooks, Santa Cruz, CA 1987), and *SomeBody To Love* (Third Side Press, Chicago, 1991). Used with permission of the author.

"throwing laughter" by Naomi Rachel first appeared in *10 point 5* in 1976. Reprinted with permission of the author.

"Bittersweet" by Amber Coverdale Sumrall was previously published in *The Sun* (June 1991, issue #187). Reprinted with permission of the author.

"Losing The Passion To Lose Pounds" by Linda Weltner is reprinted from *The Boston Globe* (July 14, 1989) with permission of the author.

"Tempted By the Demons Of An Eating Disorder" by Linda Weltner is reprinted from *The Boston Globe* (September 6, 1991) with permission of the author.

for hungry women everywhere

Table Of Contents

Introduction

As I sit down to write this introduction, I can't help pondering my own relationship with food. It is ten o'clock in the morning, and before I began writing I enjoyed a light breakfast of a toasted bagel with butter and a glass of orange juice. To many people, that would not be a big deal. But to others, including the 92 contributors to this anthology, the act of actually *enjoying* breakfast, the fact that I ate both halves of the bagel because I was hungry, the fact that I used real butter instead of diet margarine, the fact that I didn't add onto my breakfast a second bagel and then a third and then some ice cream and cookies to boot, and the fact that I didn't stick my finger down my throat to get rid of my food is nothing short of a miracle.

Before you read on, think back to what you ate yesterday. Picture yourself eating at the kitchen table, in a cafeteria or restaurant, at your desk, in your car, on the street or wherever it was you happened to eat. What did you eat and whom did you eat with? Can you remember the foods you chose to nurture and feed yourself with? Did you eat what you were hungry for or did you eat what you thought you should? Were your choices made according to your desire for certain foods, or to change your body size? Were your choices affected by whom you were eating with? Did you say after eating anything in particular, "I shouldn't have eaten that"? Did you eat too much on purpose, vowing to deprive yourself at some later date? Did you eat less than you wanted or needed? Did you spend the day calculating your calorie intake? Did you get rid of your food by vomiting, over-exercising or abusing laxatives or enemas? And lastly, did you *enjoy* your food?

Our culture makes it nearly impossible for us as women to have a healthy, easy relationship with food. On one hand, we are supposed to be the nurturers of the world, perfecting recipes to delight our families, and, on the other hand, we are supposed to deprive ourselves of these delicious meals in order to look the way our society deems it best for us to look, which can be summed up in one four-letter word: thin. Not all of us develop full-blown eating disorders, of course, but most of us have, or at least at one time had, a voice inside us that nags at almost every meal: *you shouldn't eat that, why are you eating that, you don't need that, that's no good for you, you should know better than that, put that back,* stop!

As I write this, an extraordinary memory comes back to me. About thirteen years ago I was sitting in a health food restaurant with a new friend of mine, Anne. It was lunchtime; I ordered miso soup, because I was on yet another diet, and Anne ordered vegetable tempura. The waiter came back with our meal: a pathetic little bowl of broth for me, and a huge dish of batter-dipped, fried vegetables for Anne. Anne did not say, "Oh my God, that's too much," or "I'll never eat all this," or any such comment I was so used to hearing. As I delicately sipped my soup, she used her fingers to dip a big piece of fried yam into some soy sauce and then scrunch the whole thing into her mouth. With great gusto she ate piece after piece of tempura—zucchini, eggplant, potato, broccoli, cauliflower, string beans, *all deep fried*—without once apologizing for the unabashed way she was satisfying her appetite. When she was done, Anne wiped her chin with her napkin and sipped her tea with a quiet look of contentment.

I was astonished. I was pretty sure Anne hadn't just binged, as bingeing was something one did in private like me. Somehow Anne didn't strike me as a woman who was always on and off ridiculous diets. And she, unlike a true dieter out to cheat on her diet, had actually left on her plate a few pieces of mushroom tempura which I coveted but was of course too shy to ask for. No, Anne had actually enjoyed her meal with no pangs of guilt afterwards. I had *never* seen a woman eat like that before.

At this point in my life, I was twenty-four years old and had been on and off a diet (mostly off, wishing I could stay on) since I was twelve years old. For half my life I had monitored every morsel of food that passed between my lips. I, who never was very good in math, kept a running count in my head of how many calories I had consumed and how many I had burned. For twelve years I never ate anything without feeling guilty about it. And here was this woman who had just eaten, in one meal, more calories than I allowed myself to ingest in an entire week, looking as pleased with herself as my cat after she's devoured a saucer of cream.

The image of that lunch stayed with me, though I continued to diet for three more years. At various times in my dieting career I became bulimic, alternating huge binges with days of compulsive over-exercising and fasting. At times the self-deprivation bordered on anorexia; I would eat nothing for weeks at a time, until my exhausted body rebelled with a full scale binge that would also last for weeks. I was involved in a love/hate relationship with food and with my body, which I feared would never end. I was consumed with my food obsession, which in turn was consuming me. I thought about little else except what I couldn't eat, what I shouldn't eat, what I wanted to eat, what I should eat and what I would eat. Being so preoccupied with food was as time consuming as a forty hour a week job.

I am now thirty-seven years old and I can honestly say after ten years without dieting and overeating, that I have a healthy relationship with food. This peace has been hard won. It took a great deal of effort, effort I can now say was well worth it. Ten years ago I began to consider the radical idea that diets don't work. I knew that—in fact I was living proof of it—but I began to consider this notion differently. I started to realize that dieting failed not because I was a failure, but because one can deprive oneself only for so long before the body, in its infinite wisdom, rebels and demands to be fed. The billion dollar diet industry depends on this concept. If diets worked, we'd all go on one for a year or so and then we'd be done with the whole thing. But diets don't work, so after gaining back the lost weight and then some, most women try another diet, and another diet and another diet until we decide to stop dieting once and for all. Until we decide that there is nothing wrong with our bodies. Rather there is something wrong with the message that our society preaches to us, which is basically that we are all supposed to look like hip-less, breast-less, belly-less and buttocks-less teenage boys.

I stopped the overeating-dieting-overeating cycle once and for all in 1983. It was absolutely the hardest thing I'd ever done. When I stopped, I had no idea what would fill the void I had been filling with food for so long. My biggest fear was that deep down inside that bottomless pit of my hunger, there was nothing at all. What I discovered instead was that once my hunger for food was truly satisfied, my other hungers emerged: hunger for meaningful work, hunger for a satisfying relationship, hunger to make a contribution, hunger to know who I am. These new needs of mine were terrifying, and it took every ounce of strength I had not to satisfy these new longings with food.

In 1984 I took the risk of fulfilling a lifelong dream and decided to write full-time for six months. It didn't surprise me that what emerged from my pen was a semi-autobiographical novel about a bulimic woman, entitled *Good Enough To Eat*. What did surprise me, after the novel was published two years later, was the enormous amount of mail I received from women all over the country who felt I had told their story as well. "Have you been following me around for the past ten years?" one woman asked. "How could you possibly know what has been going on inside my head?" another woman demanded. In 1967, when I started my dieting career, the words bulimia and anorexia did not exist. I knew other women dieted, but I truly thought I was the only one who constantly fretted about food and behaved so bizarrely around it.

And so I began leading workshops for women called *What Are You Eating/What's Eating You?* Women would come to my house, sit in a circle and honestly talk and write about what they did with food. It was painful, it was funny, it was healing. Women would look at each other in utter amazement as they told of the Tootsie Rolls they stole out of their kids' lunch boxes, the gallons of ice cream they ate straight out of the freezer at three a.m., the tray of sweet and sour meatballs that never got to the dinner table because "the dog ate it." *You do that, too?* we all said to each other. Why? Why did we eat to the point of literally passing out on some days and starve ourselves to the point of passing out on other days? What did we need? What were we so afraid of?

Of course there were different answers to these questions for all of us. I'll never forget the day a woman who weighed three-hundred pounds said, "I'm afraid to be empty," and the woman next to her who weighed eighty-nine pounds responded, "I'm afraid to be full." I'll never forget the woman who, mid-sentence, realized her first binge occurred the night after she was raped. I'll never forget the woman who started her first diet because her parents threatened to stop paying her college tuition unless she lost ten pounds.

3

In 1991, I published *SomeBody To Love: A Guide To Loving The Body You Have,* a book of writing exercises designed to help women explore their relationship with food and their bodies. The book contains a short anthology of writings by women who have taken workshops with me. Again, I got letters from women who said the writing changed their lives. Again, I wanted to take it one step further.

I decided to compile an anthology of women writing about what they do with food. Many women in my groups said they would rather give a blow-by-blow account of what they did in their bedrooms, than divulge what really goes on in their kitchens. For all the recent attention eating disorders have garnered, there is surprisingly little talk of what we actually do with food.

I sent out a call for manuscripts and read the writings of hundreds of women. I was amazed by the honesty I found in those manila envelopes that crowded my mailbox every day for six months. Teenagers, women in their sixties, housewives, radical lesbians, mothers, grandmothers, secretaries, doctors, construction workers, teachers, dancers, all had something to say about how their relationship with food affected their lives. Some women wrote in their cover letters that they had never told anyone about their "problem with food" before and that "coming out" as a bulimic or anorexic or compulsive overeater was extremely terrifying, and, at the same time, a huge relief. Many women wrote that, even if I couldn't use their piece, they had learned a lot from writing it and were grateful for the opportunity.

I'm sorry I can't share with the general reading public the privilege of reading so many manuscripts from the courageous women who wrote so honestly about their lives. I tried to choose as diverse a selection of writing as I could, and I suspect any woman who picks up this anthology will find something she can relate to.

Lastly, because this is an honest book, it is not a "politcally correct" one. Many women who consider themselves feminists, and radical feminists at that, still feel uneasy with food and with their bodies and with the fact that they are or might become fat (as I write the word I have somehow managed to avoid thus far, I let out a deep, deep sigh). Our culture constantly tells us it is terrible to be fat that being dead is preferable to being fat that fat people, and in particular fat *women* are bad, ugly, stupid, worthless and worse. Of course we know this is nonsense. Of course we know that a woman's appearance has little to do with how wonderful she is inside. And yet, so many intelligent, creative, powerful women cannot stand the thought of gaining five pounds, and live in constant fear of food. Others have conquered the fat-hatred inside themselves. And still others remain ambivalent about it all.

These are our stories. This is what, where, when, with whom, how and why we eat. I wish to thank Elaine Gill of The Crossing Press for taking on this project, and my agent Charlotte Raymond for her support. I am extremely grateful for all the

4

essays, stories and poems I had the opportunity to read and I thank every single woman who sent me a manuscript. I wish all of us could go out for lunch together. I imagine a huge room full of hundreds of hungry women, women of all shapes and sizes. We talk, we laugh, we cry, we rage, we hug each other and we *eat,* each one of us nourishing ourselves with exactly the foods we want, just as we all deserve to be fed.

Lesléa Newman
August, 1992

Queen of the Anorexics

Innocence

by
Ellen Linz

Before guilt
And maybe even pleasure,
When chocolate merely grew on trees
And wasn't made in factories
Like Ghirardelli or Ferrero Rocher—
When greed was good
Or at least understood,
Before calories invented
Gloria Marshall or Jennie Craig—
In a world without Snickers
When passions ran free
Before there was Cosmo or MTV—
And Madison Avenue began messing with our sexuality
After Freud, imitating Adam, took it all away—

Was it really okay to eat?

Tempted by the Demons of an Eating Disorder

by
Linda Weltner

—⟨OOO⟩—

It didn't take an article in the Boston Globe to convince me that the common cold can be brought on by stress. I got the message directly from my body as I lay in bed struggling to breathe through a stuffed nose, keenly aware that after weeks of intense pressure, the first relaxed breath I'd been able to take in a month was beginning to feel like my last.

I hadn't thought meeting the deadline for a magazine article would be a problem until one daughter got meningitis and the other came up from South Carolina for a week's visit. My life caught me up in tiny tendrils of love and obligation while my mind kept repeating, like a refrain, "When am I going to find the time to write?" until my neck was stiff as a board and I'd lost the knack of falling asleep at night. In the end, I spent two precious days of my vacation sitting over my computer in a Vermont library while my husband went fishing without me.

Hours after I put the article in the mail, I came down with one of the worst colds of my life.

That first day, I blew my way through one box of Kleenex and moved on to a roll of toilet paper. I sat up in bed like a limp Raggedy Ann doll, four pillows behind my head, convinced if I ever lay down, I'd drown in my own body fluids. I took the recommended dose of decongestant, and then, two hours later, doubled it. I slipped into neutral, emitting only a low moan when anyone spoke to me. As day became night, I roused myself only long enough to take an occasional sip of water.

I rose after a sleepless night, feeling no better. I felt sunk in gloom, too exhausted to rally. As I tried to brush my teeth without asphyxiating myself, my mind had its first clear thought in 24 hours.

I haven't eaten anything.

My dry lips parted in an involuntary smile. This was the silver lining to my infectious cloud. Something good has to come out of everything, I supposed. Nice to think I might lose a few pounds. I fell back into bed and didn't have another thought until dinner.

My husband called up from the kitchen. Dutifully, I descended to the table. He'd grilled bluefish, baked a potato, boiled some corn and this nutritious fare sat on my plate, looking delicious, though, God knows, not to me. I stared at it for a while, watching my husband chew. We didn't talk. There was a Nazi chattering away in my head, and she required my full attention.

I don't have to eat, she mocked. *I'm in charge of this body, not a slave to it like you.* I knew whom she was addressing—that part of me without will power, the hungry little pig who can't resist a piece of cake if it's set before her, the one who screws up every diet I've ever tried. *I don't have to touch this,* the voice taunted. *I'm not weak. I'm not needy. I can't be tempted.* There was contempt in her words, and barely contained disgust. She reached for the glass of water and took a long drink. *I'm full,* she said. *I don't need anything.*

I excused myself and went upstairs. I was surprised to find how elated I was. I felt complete and powerful in spite of my cold. How easy it was to set yourself against food. Just one powerful *no*, instead of a zillion daily decisions, a zillion daily capitulations. Toast or bagel? Neither. Fish or chicken? Nothing, thank you. No stopping three times a day to fill up that embarrassing empty space, no more guilty feelings after eating a normal amount of food. Until I went forty-eight hours without eating, I hadn't quite realized how compromised I felt after every single meal, no matter how moderately I ate.

I was thick around the middle, wasn't I? My stomach stuck out, didn't it? Eating had taken away the slimness I valued so highly, and that was condemnation enough, even if what I "pigged out" on was a healthy piece of fruit. I'd only been vaguely conscious of it before, but it was obvious now. At some level, I disapproved of my eating. And every meal, three times a day, year after year, was the signal to rally that disapproval against myself.

Unless you cave in, we can have water for breakfast, my storm trooper interrupted. *Give me a week or two. I'll make you thin again.*

I could feel how much I longed to be slim and graceful, how much I hate that every calorie I eat shows up on my body for everyone to see. I was painfully in touch with the shame I attach to my desire to eat. How had I ever come to consider this awful feeling so ordinary and so unremarkable?

I used to think people with eating disorders were different from me. Anorexia was for adolescents caught up in a power struggle with their parents. Bulimia affected people obsessed with their appearance. What person in her right mind would starve herself past gauntness? What kind of woman would stick her fingers down her throat so often the enamel on her teeth rotted?

The Roman philosopher Terrence said, "Nothing human is alien to me," more than 2000 years ago. I wonder what it was he caught a glimpse of inside himself. Here I am middle-aged, married—not at risk for an eating disorder. But now I know that this illness, which has been called the female disorder of our age, lurks within me too.

This morning I ate. And I judged myself. And I forgave myself.

What else can any of us do?

anorexia neurosis

by
Sheryl L. Nelms

sucking ice cubes
instead of eating

she reminds me of that fish

the Egyptian mouth brooder
lips locked
coddling
those
eggs

while her body evaporates

fat reservoirs gone
toothpick ribs
prick
out
against caved-in skin

hovering in a shadowed corner

she savors
her total dedication

The Competition

by
Faithe Glennon

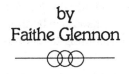

It's 5:58 p.m.—I know this without looking at the clock. I can read it in the faces around me. We all have developed a type of super hearing so that from anywhere in the unit, our ears can detect the roll of the metal wheels. One by one we walk to the cart, search for our last names on the tray, and carry it into the room. We are in this room for a good part of our day. The table is long and the chairs are wooden and wide, so getting ourselves seated is a chore. Tonight there are six of us. The other four have passes, so they are upstairs in the cafeteria where they can practice eating in front of other people. "Practice eating in front of other people"— I turn this phrase over in my mind and half smile. I have been here three weeks but I still have to convince myself that I am really here—and why. This whole block of time seems like an enduring dream. I look around the table. The nurse sitting with us is kind, she tries to make conversation. Carrie, who is on my right, begins to dissect her food. Cutting, mashing, flicking and hiding stray pieces will occupy her for thirty-five out of the next forty minutes. During the last five she will attempt to digest—between long pitiful sighs—a scrap of lettuce or a sip of milk. She is truly a master. I no longer cut my food into tiny pieces. What we don't consume will have to be swallowed in liquid form, called Ensure, and I have no desire to subject myself to that again. They tell us that Ensure is not meant as a punishment, only to supply us with the nutrient and calories that we need. So in essence we can eat our meals or take Ensure; but no one who has been discharged is still drinking dinner. The first night I was here, I had a potato that stared out at me with a million eyes and a piece of chicken with some type of orange sauce. I pictured the chicken as it was being slaughtered, its feathers being plucked and the noise it made when its head was cut off—a bloody mess. I thought of the bit of fat clinging to the meat and imagined it expanding inside me, softening under my skin. The chicken's revenge. I used to make myself imagine things like this when I was first losing weight, to make all food as disgusting as possible. Now I have to fight to think about other things. That first night I didn't even attempt to eat, so my entire meal was Ensure. Drinking that chalky, mock-vanilla concoction, as it coats my throat and fills my stomach with concentrated calories—all designed to make me fat—is more revolting than any image I can invent. So I choke down my food as best as I can. Besides, they note the way we eat in our charts, and eating all your food is a sign of improvement. They chart everything we do in stringent detail, or so we are told. I look across the table at Amira. She is stark white with long dark hair and huge, haunted eyes rimmed with smudges of sleeplessness, and the youngest among us—thirteen. She has been here for three months and before this somewhere else for nine. She doesn't mutilate her meal, but she organizes it according to calories and eats them from lowest to highest. Charlotte is next to her, managing to look elegant in her jewelry and sweats. She is the oldest among us—about thirty-five—and she has a seven year old boy who is deaf. You can tell she is a good mother by the way she talks about him, protective but not overbearing, and her eyes take on a sort of glow. Her ex-husband's a real jerk and I feel bad that she can't be the one to take care of her son, that, like the rest of us, she can't even take care of herself right now. She reminds me of a picture I had when I was little of this sad, painted clown.

7:00 p.m.—We are in the lounge. We have to sit here for 40 minutes, so we can be monitored and so we won't make ourselves throw up. I stare out the window at the parking lot. There are a few people outside walking to and from cars out in the real world. I feel like I'm in a play. A nurse brings in Carrie's glass of Ensure. She drinks it in tiny sips and the nurse is impatient. I glare at the nurse and I feel a little better. Afterwards, Carrie comes over to me and we play Super Pac-Man. I think I'd played Pac-Man maybe twice before I came here. Now I am an expert. Carrie's even better. We are an unlikely pair. She is the sickest here, and I'm usually lamenting about how I want to get well. Carrie doesn't want to get well, even if she has to stay here forever. We are the only ones without weekend passes, which is how we first became friends. Weekends can get very boring. Pac-Man kills time but sometimes he bothers me—chomping on dots and growing bigger and bigger…

6:00 a.m.—My mind wakes in stages. I gain a consciousness that I have to wake up, that I'm late for school or work or something—but I can't remember where I am. A nurse pops her head in and the ignorance of sleep diminishes; we have to be weighed. I hesitate waking up my roommate, Nancy. She looks so peaceful sleeping. We walk down the corridor to the scale. When it is my turn, I step on backwards, so I don't know what the number reads. They like it when you do this—it shows you are less focused on weight. I can usually predict my weight to the exact quarter of a pound, anyway. Carrie never gets on backwards. She doesn't care what they write on her chart. When she gets off the scale she storms into her room and slams the door. I have a feeling she's punching her stomach—she does that if she has gained—but her roommate, Lisa, will inform us of all the details later. Lisa is short and sly and prides herself on being the eyes and ears (and mouth) of the unit. I go back and get ready for breakfast. I pass the little Chinese man who empties our trash and we nod at each other in the way people do when they are trying to be friendly but don't know a word of the other person's language. "I hope they take us outside today for Recreational Activity," I say to Nancy. She looks at me and laughs. "This place is like a kennel," she says. "They feed us, they take us for walks, they clean our cages…It's not a hospital, it's a kennel." We laugh. It does not take much to get us laughing here—anything to slice through the thick haze of hospital depression that clouds our days.

9:00 a.m.—Recreational activity. This is actually a mini-aerobics class. It is the only time we are allowed to exercise; otherwise, if we are caught we get Ensure, no questions asked. Sometimes, we get to go outside for a walk instead, but not today. I know because I see Patti, our leader, all suited up in her aerobic gear. We can't stand her. She wears a nervous smile and we, like dogs, sense her fear. It makes me feel powerful and angry at the same time—that she is afraid of us. At first, I think it's funny, almost like she thinks we are contagious, but then I picture her sitting around her dinner table in her normal life, talking with her friends about her job and how weird we are and I feel small and alien. But we do our best to make her job as difficult as possible. We imitate her behind her back and when she asks for volunteers to lead exercise, she is greeted with stone silence. I feel immature— like we are in grade school torturing a substitute teacher. She picks Michelle, the easiest choice. Michelle is blond and pretty and so full of energy I have trouble believing she is one of us. She has been here for two months but is leaving at the end of the week. I think that this daily routine is the most bizarre part of the program. Patti's cassette recorder is blasting "Fame," and we are on all fours, doing leg lifts. Patti is counting out loud in her peppy voice and Charlotte is muttering "Go to hell," under her breath. Some of us were compulsive exercisers in our pre-hospital days but this ritual is quite different, quite humiliating. Most of us can't do the exercises well. We have no energy—our muscles have diminished. I think the reason Patti bugs us so much is that she can't seem to comprehend why we don't enjoy this. She thinks we should be having fun. After class is over she sulks and scribbles comments on our charts.

10:00 a.m.—My medical doctor comes in to see me. He has a high-pitched voice and a silly nose. He makes me smile. He says that he has been hearing good things, that I have been doing well. He thinks that maybe next weekend I might get a four-hour pass. He talks with Nancy longer. I can hear their conversation through the curtain. We have no privacy here, but we are lucky that we get along. Like sisters, there is very little we conceal from one another. Nancy does not have Anorexia. She is Atypical. This (she has to explain to everyone) is like a flu-bug that never goes away. She throws up whenever she eats but it's not intentional. The doctors are baffled, and everyone has a different theory about what causes it, if it's physical or psychological or both. I know it started happening after her mother got killed in a car accident. I really hope they find a purely physical explanation. I'd like to see the looks on the faces of those who have been blaming her for her illness when they find out they have been wrong the entire time—especially her father. Her dad is banned from the unit for a while. I am relieved. He is short and round, like a mushroom with a moustache, and I feel violated when he comes in our room. He sits and watches sports on our TV. I don't really watch television, so I don't care, but I think it's pretty presumptuous of him. He usually spends about an hour lecturing her. When he leaves, she sometimes has one of her attacks where she can't breathe, and it takes about an hour for her to calm down. I wish he would disappear forever; maybe then she'd have a chance of getting better. She's been here four times.

      10:23 a.m.—Carrie enters our room looking strange. She has heard from her roommate that last night Amy Hastings was admitted to the medical unit. Though we have all heard of her, only Carrie's roommate knows her. She is a legend among us—the Queen of the Anorexics. She lives on the edge of death at sixty lbs. I want to see her, I want to talk to her. But the medical unit is past the blue carpet. We can't go beyond the blue carpet. Sometimes I stand at the edge of the orange carpet and touch my foot on the blue. Nothing happens. I expect an electric shock or something. It's the only rule I have broken. Carrie leaves in a rush and I figure she wants to be alone.

      11:12 a.m.—A candy-striper brings us our mail. I have a letter from Cindy, my friend from school. She moved to Detroit the week before I was admitted. I consider throwing the letter away, but I am curious, so I open it. It's full of ramblings about her new house and weather and ballet classes. A little further down she mentions her weight and working out and losing more. I am amazed that she is writing this to me, here, but the words are right in front of me. I know that she is sick, too, except she's in Detroit spreading more of her diet-gospel and I am here and I'm glad that I'm getting better and all, but sometimes I have to wonder where I'd be if I hadn't met her. She tells me to write back. Sure. I also have a letter from my grandmother—a cheery note telling me about her neighbors and golf and how she hopes that I will just start eating and stop worrying my poor mother. She tells my mom that she's not a bit surprised I'm here—I always was a picky eater. Carrie and I exchange the letters we get from our relatives. She has this uncle whom she barely knows, a preacher. He sends her cards full of scripture and advice like "Don't think you are a mistake." I guess he's thought this through and decided that this is the root of her problem. He closes with "Write me—you have the time!" Neither of us believe in God.

2:00 p.m.—We are back in the room, but the table is gone and the chairs are arranged in a circle. I save a seat for Carrie but she hasn't come in yet. This is Psychotherapy—usually an uneventful experience. It is our group and we are supposed to discuss whatever we choose. Sometimes we just sit and stare at each other. We have Multi-family Therapy on Thursday nights. The only difference is we sit and stare at each other's family members. The doctor starts each group the same. We've all memorized his litany. If Carrie were here, she and I would mouth the words to each other as he recites them in his boring monotone. "This is Psycho-(Multi-family)-Therapy. This is your group. There is no format. Some of the topics we have discussed in the past are 'what it's like going into the hospital' or 'what it's like getting ready to leave the hospital.' What will we talk about today?" he questions and then adds a thoughtful pause. "I don't know," he concludes, "but I suspect I am about to find out." For the past week our subject has seemed to be "what it's like getting ready to leave the hospital," since Michelle is arranging her discharge plans and no one else really feels like talking. It's nice to have her save us from the silence but hearing about her fears of the outside world is beginning to get old. I can't even picture the outside world clearly, and the idea of leaving here terrifies me. Sometimes Psychotherapy can be entertaining—if someone is having roommate problems or there is something else to complain about. Today we start talking about Amy Hastings. We all feel her presence. I know that it bothers Carrie, but she probably wouldn't say anything about it, even if she were here. She can be extremely competitive, and up until now she has been known as the most hopeless case on the unit. Not a title most people would desire, but it's the basis of Carrie's identity. Lisa starts talking and I block her out. When she speaks, it's always in a dry whisper, like something's caught in her throat and it is an effort to form words. She has esophagus damage, and she never lets anyone forget it. She is interrupted by a nurse who calls the doctor out into the hall. He returns looking quite calm. "I'm afraid we've had some rather distressing news," he announces in his monotone, "and I don't want any rumors to emerge among us." (We all look at Lisa.) "It seems that Carrie Jenkins has injured herself."

4:30 p.m.—They are moving Carrie upstairs. Upstairs is not like here. It is locked and it is not an eating disorder program. They are putting her there because she cut up her own stomach with scissors. They let me help her pack, because I am her best friend. Her wounds aren't deep, more like cat scratches. She didn't even need stitches. I am afraid for her but I have this stupid smile stuck on my face. I keep saying "Don't worry—it will be OK." I don't know why I say this, it will probably be horrible. I tell her I will visit, when I get off-floor privileges. She smiles back at me. A nurse comes to get her and they go away. I sit in her room for a while, thinking. I remember in high school, we had this demented guidance counselor giving our honors class a "pep-talk" about going to college. She said, "You might think you are a good student now, you might even be the first in your class, but just wait until you get to college. You'll be surrounded by valedictorians, and suddenly you won't be number one anymore—you'll have to fight to keep your place." I guess that's how it is here sometimes, for people like Carrie. I hear the sound of metal scraping and I catch a glimpse of the cart passing by. It's 5:58.

An Autobiography of a Psychiatric Technician in an Eating Disorders Clinic

by
Cynthia M. Stacey

————⬤⬤⬤————

At 10:15 p.m. each evening I work, I watch an anorexic patient eat her nighttime snack. Because it is critical that she ingest these nutrients, and has been found, at times, to have hidden her food in one of several cosmetic boxes at her nightstand, it is necessary that I observe her carefully. Sometime her methodical manner of eating can take over half an hour, so I use the time to try to talk about her day, or something interesting that is not associated with food or feelings. It is important that I help create a comfortable atmosphere around mealtime, because the intake of food is my main objective. And conversing also helps to diffuse the anxiety I feel in being her guard, and in finding the consolation that works. Sometimes I sense that this anxiety level is increased during our conversation, as though she would prefer to eat quietly, so I will pick up a magazine, or talk with her roommate, all the time focusing on her.

This woman's roommate has needs of a completely different nature. Although she has bulimic tendencies, she has for the moment changed her behavior (or so she says) and is interested not only in working on the problems underlying it, but in understanding larger social problems as well. I see her dissatisfaction with the "system" as perhaps a manifestation of her discomfort with herself, i.e., her body (We can discuss intellectually the idea that changing world politics begins with oneself, but not in the context of her changing her own life—she's not quite there yet.) I sense her sincerity, remembering that stage in my life, and give in with pleasure to philosophical debate and discourse. This young woman needs nurturance on a rarer plane, as a supplement and means, perhaps, toward understanding her illness. This could also be how she manifests her denial of her body, so I find myself bringing the larger to the more personal.

Thus, during those times when the anorexic woman prefers to be quiet and my conversation with her roommate reaches heightened moments, I gain a keen sense of both their processes and the stages of denial of their bodies and the role I play in attempting to lessen it. For as I'm discussing Jean-Paul Sartre with one

19

woman, steering the conversation out of the rut of outside blame to responsibility to oneself, I'm watching the other slide further into ritualized behavior and out of my psychic grasp. I maintain a silence with her not only because I see our goal being accomplished, that she is eating her snack, but more so because I am in awe; I cannot speak.

I watch her take a bite of her cracker and peanut butter (I can feel her cringe at the sound of "crunch" in the rarefied air), and, as she chews, I watch her reach into a large basket of cosmetics for her dental floss. After carefully measuring out a piece of floss, she breaks it and places it upon her bedside table. She takes a drink of her supplement and, after carefully swallowing, prepares her toothbrush with toothpaste and pours water into her dental tray. Another bite of her cracker. She then finds a denture tablet in her basket and opens the metal foil packet and places it inside a denture cup, where she will soak her retainer after she cleans it. Another drink of her supplement. She then finds her nail strengthening polish and dabs each nail precisely and carefully. Another bite, another drink. She finds her mouthwash at her nightstand and turns it upside down to fill its handy measuring pouch, and then upright again. She places it on the bedside table and begins the chemistry involved in maintaining her contact lenses.

Meanwhile, my conversation with her roommate has branched into a multitude of possibilities and our excitement level increases with this knowledge. However it is time to make closure. We finalize with a topic that encompasses all of the possiblities we have raised, that it is very important to keep oneself open to life, and we agree that, regardless of the pain inherent in living consciously, it is well worth it. The anorexic woman places her empty glass on the bedside table.

I say goodnight to her roommate and retrieve the empty glass and plate. I must help this woman prepare herself for bed because her illness involves complete bed rest. I prepare the commode for her use, empty it, measure out her nightly glass of water, empty and clean her dental tray, wet a washcloth for her to wash her hands and face, and find a johnnie. I then give her a hug and tell her that I think she's getting better and wish her pleasant dreams.

And as I close the door behind me, I can't help wondering what a large circle it is to make whole and what I must do to contribute to that process.

Contemplating Sweets

by
Karyn Bauer

─── ◯◯◯ ───

She walks into the brightly lit diner, squinting slightly for it is gray and rainy outside, making the vibrating fluorescent lights that much more irritating. She blinks her eyes tightly for a quick second, then opens them wide, an exercise she hopes will cause the disturbance to fade, though it merely causes her to trip slightly over the not-so-even rug that loosely covers the cold tile floor built for hungry sheet metal workers clad in overweight shoes and hats coming in from the blistering heat of the factory; their appetites seemed to match the heavy duty strength of their uniforms. Now it's a diner, cheaply renovated and overpriced with lights that make your head spin. With her eyes aimed at the sweet glazed pastries lining the counter, she makes her way to a small booth and slides across the cool vinyl couch until her cheek nearly touches the damp window. Her brother slides down next to her. He sits a bit too close to her, making her somewhat uncomfortable. But even more disturbing than his proximity to her is the calm and self assured way he speaks with his parents, who are incidentally hers as well, seated directly across from the two of them.

Squashed in the corner, eyes dancing in her head, her tongue nearly licking the condensation off the window, she stares at the formica table top, losing herself in the miniscule nooks and crannies which are so well hidden that the table appears perfectly smooth. She absorbs herself into the table, wishing she could squeeze inside those shallow cracks and lose herself inside them, forgetting altogether where she is and why. She snaps out of her trance-like state when a plastic laminated menu slides under her fingers. The movement shocks her, causing her stomach to tighten. Along with the menu wafts a warm, thick odor of hot hamburger grease which envelopes her and reminds her that, yes, she is here to eat. She was taken from her bedroom, stolen away from her tiny attic room for the sole purpose of eating in the company of her family and hot hamburger grease. The thought of food is so remote at this point that the words on the menu seem to say absolutely nothing. A knot wells up in her throat—the first sign that her tolerance is nonexistent right now; perhaps even ordering the toast would be a bad idea.

Believing that the decision is too much to bear, she looks up at her family; maybe by some magical twist of fate they will actually calm her down. She looks first at her mom, who is, as usual, mid-sentence, talking about her brother, whose math teacher recently told her what a good worker he's been this year, even though he still refuses to quiet down during class discussion and occasionally creates a serious disturbance. While her mother is talking, a short, slightly chunky waitress in a brown polyester skirted suit strolls over to the table. With pad in hand, the waitress writes down her mother's order—a bacon cheeseburger with fries—which her father insists on declaring to allow her mother to continue talking uninterrupted. Her brother, on the other hand, by now giddy and fidgety and proud of his rambunctious reputation, is only barely listening to his mother and proceeds to shout that he, too, will have the bacon cheeseburger. Her father looks at her expectantly, wondering what she is going to order. He looks her straight in the eye, which, in combination with the stale smoky and greasy smell of the place, has literally upset her stomach. As if he is yanking the words out of her without her consent, she finds herself ordering an open-faced turkey breast sandwich which will undoubtedly be served on mushy white bread dripping in canned, oily gravy to conceal the cheap cut of turkey fat they consider breast meat. He orders pancakes.

The thought of all this food makes her gag, and her palms begin to sweat slightly. At this point, the thought of swallowing anything, even water, is utterly repulsive. Nevertheless, she tips a small sip of water into her mouth. She forgets how to swallow. The muscles just won't work. It's just water, and eventually, force of nature wills it down. Though she's made every effort to conceal it, her discomfort is undoubtedly evident on her face; she senses her parents' prolonged stares of disgust and impatience. She wonders how long this ordeal is going to last, as she's already anxious to leave.

As expected, the food arrives on a thick white plate with deep gray grooves from years of people trying, with a dull butter knife to slice through the shoe-leather-like sirloin that is the specialty of the house. Gravy is dripping over the side of the plate, mixing with the excess flow of syrup from her father's pancakes and oozing into the bacon grease from those burgers. She can do nothing but think about how this will all congeal in her stomach and form a thick waxy knot that will gnaw at her for hours. She is certain that the knot will never actually decrease, for she has never quite learned how to digest the food before she expels it. It's all one extended, unsatisfying experience.

She sinks the side of her fork into the rounded corner of bread and gravy. The turkey is too small to reach the edge which is just as well because it is nearly petrified anyway. She lifts the fork and bends her chin down in one smooth motion so as to avoid having the gravy slip through the teeth of the fork before it reaches her mouth. Her timing is good, but the gravy manages to ooze down her chin anyway, dripping onto the letter "c" on her old Cosmos soccer t-shirt. She continues to work her fork around and around the edges of the turkey, swallowing mouthfuls of pasty bread and salty gravy. Occasionally her throat clenches up and she has to stop and stare at her plate for a while until she sees nothing, tastes nothing, and hears nothing so the food can drift down her throat by sheer force of nature. She washes it down with a tiny sip of water, just enough to ease the process.

After what seems like hours, she finishes half of the sandwich and looks up to see how she is pacing herself. She is always the last one to stop eating; she has never finished an entire meal. Of course, everyone has finished theirs. Her mother and brother sit with grins on their faces, soaking their fries with the last of the grease that has oozed out of their burgers. Just as she was disturbed by the ease with which her brother spoke to her parents, she is equally distressed by his ability to eat that damn cheeseburger, a meal that would have given her a more severe case of motion sickness than any shaky boat ride at sea. She wants desperately to run screaming into the cold rain where the cold water hitting her face and streaming into her mouth and eyes would cleanse her of the stench that has crawled under her skin. It would wash the suffocating smell of the restaurant out of her hair and her clothes and she could dash secretly into the trees to hide, and to wish with all her might that she could vomit up all of this horrible, horrible food.

She sits. She continues to put smaller and smaller mouthfuls of what seem like dog meat into her mouth. Her parents nudge her to clean off her plate for once because they are tired of paying for her to pick at her food and why can't she eat a full meal like her brother and isn't she too skinny anyway… She stops eating with four bits left on her plate which her mother forces her to eat "at least the turkey, you can leave the bread over if you'd like."

She eats the last bits of turkey. It makes her teeth hurt and her fingers shake. She shuffles her feet back and forth on the floor and thinks about the cold hard tile that supported the heavy steps of those sheet metal workers with their hearty appetites and she thinks about how hard and tight her stomach is—just like the heavy duty plastic hats they wore. She delights in knowing that she has that same hard hat deep down inside her belly. It cannot be penetrated no matter how many turkey sandwiches she is forced to eat.

One Spring

by
Lesléa Newman

The air was thick with the promise
of lilacs and rain that evening
and the clouds hovered about my shoulders
like the mink stole in my mother's closet
I tried on from time to time.
I was sixteen and I knew it.
I tossed my head like a proud pony
my hair rippling down my back in one black wave
as I walked down the sultry street
my bare feet barely touching the ground
past the sounds of a television
a dog barking
a mother calling her child,
my body slicing through the heavy air
like a sailboat gliding on lazy water.

When the blue car slowed alongside me
I took no notice
until two faces leaned out the open window.
"Nice tits you got there, honey."
"Hey sweetheart, shine those headlights over here."
"Wanna go for a ride?"
I stopped,
dazed as a fish thrust out of water
into sunlight so bright it burns my eyes.
I turn and walk away fast
head down, arms folded,
feet slapping the ground.

I hear, "Nice ass, too,"
then laughter
the screech of tires
silence.

All at once I am ashamed of my new breasts
round as May apples,
I want to slice them off with a knife
sharp as a guillotine.
All at once I am mortified by my widening hips,
I want to pare them down with a vegetable peeler
until they are slim and boyish.
All at once I want to yank out my hair by the roots
like persistent weeds that must not grow wild.
But I am a sensible girl.
I do none of these things.

Instead I go home, watch TV with my parents,
brush my teeth and braid my hair for the night.
And the next day I skip breakfast,
eat only an apple for lunch
and buy a calorie counter,
vowing to get thinner and thinner
until I am so slim I can slip
through the cracks in the sidewalk
and disappear. And I do.

My Hero, Myself

by
Kimberly Sender

———— ⟨⟨⟨ ————

I learned at a very young age that food could be used as a weapon. I remember being victimized with food, routinely, throughout my early childhood, setting me up for a lifetime of nutritional misuse and eating disorders.

I had little interest in food with the exception of the almighty cookie, not unlike other five-year-olds. Breakfast was never a bother, though, as morning is still my preferred time of day.

At noon I had a standing lunch reservation with the gang from Sesame Street. Salami and potato chips couldn't fail in the company of Ernie and Bert.

Supper, however, opened the gates to hell. Not a minute past five o'clock, Mom rang the triangle, my sister skipped into the kitchen, and Dad returned from doing whatever Dad did at work. I never knew what that was and frankly, I did not care. He was home and geared up for the kitchen table battle, and that was all I needed to know. It wasn't much of a battle, though, seeing how I could never hope to win.

Supper failed to be appetizing, even if Mom made my favorite entree, because each supper included that incarcerating vegetable. I loathed vegetables entirely, as Dad inadvertently taught me.

His firm religious beliefs compelled him to take stands as the king of his castle. The family behaved as Dad instructed for the sake of a proper Catholic upbringing and his status. The kitchen table was more often than not his podium.

I shrank into my kitchen chair, hoping I would keep shrinking into obscurity. My sister, the good-for-nothing vegetable-eater popped into her chair. Mom filled my sister's plate to her liking, unlike mine which was always handed to me with one threatening brussel sprout or green bean or pea.

"Now you're not leaving that chair until you eat that!" Mom and Dad would holler.

And they meant it. The impact of their words petrified me. They kept on me from beginning to end, reinforcing their words, poking and prodding.

26

Twenty minutes later, my sister was out the door playing in summer's gifts. And there I was, still at the table, unwillingly joining Mom and Dad for coffee. Except my coffee was still a vegetable.

I made feeble attempts at eating it, without results. The odor sickened me. It was alien and odd and its blazing color intimidated me.

Pleading for deliverance was as unsuccessful as attempting to eat the horrid thing. I resorted to crying, effortlessly. With each glance at my plate, the thing turned more revolting. I refused to recognize that looking out the window and staring at my lap was not about to make it disappear.

After several more glances, looks, and stares, I raised my white flag half-heartedly. I gripped the fork but made one last request to Mom and Dad to overlook this inane scene and let me go play. Besides, I had cleaned the rest of my plate, and my tears were painfully sincere. I was only a little girl without any control or voice.

Mom never answered but kept her eyes down. Dad glared at me domi-nantly and ordered me to just eat it. I sank in my chair, crushed, feeling rejection they never knew.

With countless sour faces and gag reflexes, I ate the now dismembered vegetable. Offered some dessert, I said no, and quickly left the table with enough resentment to last me my whole life.

The kitchen table battles continued up until my preteens when my parents began to separate. Dad wasn't home for supper as much, and although Mom still tried to feed us right, she realized the absurdity and harshness of making her daughter cry every night for the sake of discipline. One single pea can't make a nutritional difference.

At age fifteen, I was in charge of my own meal planning. My hedonistic eating regimen was reflected in my growing shape. The ample calories caught up to me as TV tag died and made way for MTV. Hours and hours of MTV. I was too busy bowing down to Duran Duran to notice my increasing size.

By age sixteen, it had increased to 135 pounds—on the pudgy side for a girl measuring 5'1". Not that it bothered me, though. Though I have not seen better days since, and my mind has yet to be so healthy again. Food meant pleasure, then. My self-esteem was roaring. I felt beautiful, attractive, and equal to any Barbie doll, regardless of physical appearance.

My sister and I shaped a sacred world for us both filled with laughter, silly antics, and inside jokes that pushed the limits. We were beyond content. We snickered with our little brother as Mom, now a divorced woman, went on dates.

We were introduced to the Fat Man, Mom's one of three choices from a dating service. A very large man in all directions, the nickname my brother, sister and I gave him was fitting. We giggled each time he picked up Mom for a date and began our carefree evening as soon as the door shut behind them.

They dated frequently and for long periods of time, leaving our evenings carefree. Before we could ask questions or even blink for that matter, Mom announced her engagement after only two months of dating a man whose last name we did not know. Equally as shocking, the wedding date was set to be on her birthday—next month.

Speechless and scared, my sister and I trickled off to our bedroom in search of air. We discussed it in few words, unsure of too much.

Nothing was said to Mom for a day and a half, until anxiety forced it out of me. Numbed and monotone in voice, I asked what she was going to do with the house.

"I'm putting it up for sale and we'll live in his house," she answered in a comparable flat tone, but with more arrogance.

I nodded slowly and looked away, protectively aloof. Confused by her answer, I asked where we, the kids, were going to live.

She gave an indifferent sigh, which indicated the lack of vacancies at the Fat Man's house. My little brother would go with her, she said. My sister was to live with our aunt in California. My mother was not concerned whether that was even possible. Entering my senior year in high school, I was told to move into a friend's one-bedroom, deteriorating apartment which she shared with her mother in a bad neighborhood. I would finish school later.

Bordering on catalepsy, I took the lump in my throat to my bedroom, shut the door and let the flowered bedspread absorb my tears. Round One had begun, but we weren't down for the count.

The next day, my sister and I shared our information with our army reserve, our dad. Friends and family sympathized with us and over-extended their kindness, which made it all the more shameful to ask if we could live with them.

We used every tactic from probing psychology to secretly tossing out business cards from realtors. Weeks of brutal insecurity and brewing hostility swelled within the home. How could she be so ignorant and cold? Didn't she feel responsibility for us? Was this legal?

Nothing could penetrate her selfishness, until I finally made a break-through. I petitioned for a postponement of selling the house until I graduated seven months later—anything just to hold onto our house. She agreed. My sanity restored, I quietly spread the news, relieved.

In the meantime, my heart had been snatched by a very special young man. A flamboyant, postmodern type, Stephen stood roughly 5'8" and was bone thin. He ate very little, apart from his excessive intake of alcohol. An overactive thyroid was to blame for his weightlessness, not an intended goal. Stephen was full of life and love and was my passport to unforgettable evenings. I pursued romance in our every encounter, but we always remained friends.

I was an impressionable eighteen years old and irrationally in love with him. My society-programmed mind convinced me that Stephen's potential girlfriend would have to be even thinner than he was, and I intended to be just that.

Over the last few months, my weight had dropped to 115 pounds. But the fat still showed and was magnified in the presence of Stephen. I cut my calories to 900 a day, while studying the supermodels from head to toe. My visits to the bathroom became more and more exciting as I dropped from 113 pounds to 112 to 110, day by day. I went on shopping sprees every week in honor of Stephen and out of need for clothes that fit my beautifully minimizing size. I was enthralled by it all.

There had been word that Mom had been in touch with various realtors and there was to be a "For Sale" sign on our front yard within the week. We were losing our home, despite Mom's seven-month promise. But I quickly denied it and sought the comfort of my size-four body, trying obstinately for size two.

As promised, four days later an ugly, yellow, metal sign was hammered into the lawn, right next to the gorgeous exploding maple tree. The sign looked so out of place, not only because of its clash with nature, but because it was in our lawn. Our lawn! Good lord, our house was being sold and there wasn't a thing we could do to stop it. And my sister and I still had no place to live. Would it be sold that month? That week? Oh, no, not that day.

Once again, I was fighting the kitchen table. My control was repossessed and my voice was unheard.

I could not cope with the loss of security and foundation, let alone the loss of shelter. Subconsciously, I chose to escape for psychological salvation. My subconscious chose Anorexia Nervosa.

Mom had metamorphosized into a heartless stranger, apparent the afternoon my sister and I opened the floodgates to our emotions. I slid off the couch and onto my knees, sobbing and pleading, hands clasped.

"Please!" I screamed at her, "Please don't do this."

She rolled her eyes, clicked her tongue and looked at me so condescendingly, I can still feel it rip through me today.

"Knock this off already. I am not changing my plans again so you better get used to it," she said.

The bathroom scale became my sanctuary after that. I devoted all my thoughts and energy to food, or the lack thereof. By the end of the week, I had dropped to 95 pounds, now adhering to 600 calories a day, tops. My days were spent with eyes fixed on the clock, anxious for my next permitted meal. In raving pursuit of thinness, I stopped chewing gum as dessert after learning it had eight calories a stick. I had allowed myself half a stick at one time, but the guilt remained.

My friendship with Stephen deepened, putting more demands on my weight. He had introduced me to his closest confidant, beer, and insisted on raising my alcohol tolerance to compete with his. Torn between impressing Stephen and losing weight, I tightened my caloric restriction further to allow the extra beer calories without getting fat.

Now checking in at ninety-one pounds, I thrived on hunger, uneased when it was satiated with my one hundred calorie meal. I felt weightless, hollow, as if I could pass through tangible objects like a ghost. I was supernatural; removed from the cruel world, untouched by reality. I had conquered reality. Menstruation ceased; my breasts were deflated. I was numb to all pain, including the bruises which appeared so easily.

Yet, I was hurting inside. My soul ached out of confusion and hopelessness when I refused food even though I was zealously hungry. This was my jumbled statement and I would not be swayed.

People began staring when I hit eighty-nine pounds, I assumed out of envy and admiration for achieving such a goal. My rude mother insisted on letting me know I looked like a concentration camp prisoner. I tuned her out as I did each time she told me I was getting anorexic. It only made me work harder...scream louder.

I lost all interest in my mother and the rest of my family. Stephen became obsolete. There was no time to think of them or the house or my residential limbo or the fact that I was covered with hair and had no sex drive. I was thin, goddammit. And I could be thinner. I didn't care if it killed me. At least then, everyone would know that I died because I was so thin. What a final exit!

At 86 pounds, my mood began to change. Now at 200 calories a day, I couldn't shake off any more fat. Depression pulled me away from social activities. I realized my state of starvation and researched anorexia at the library, looking for mercy but also for new tricks to lose more weight. I was tortured with obsessive thoughts of food and thinness. I wanted my mind rescued from this hell, but I feared the weight gain of therapy. Learning I was anorexic didn't shock me into recovery but rather confirmed the fact that I was very thin and very special. I was proud of my disease.

The next month, Dad and I arranged for me to move in with him immediately, removing me from the deadly influence of that once happy home. It broke my heart.

While Dad was at work, I was left alone unmonitored too often. I didn't know how to eat or how to feed myself. He had no scale or diet food—no guide. Bite by bite, appetite overrode the mind. All control was obliterated and I recognized an incredible hunger within. I ate and ate and ate until panic stopped me. What had I done? The pattern was broken, irreversible. Or was it?

Finger down my throat, I discovered magic and absolvement. A new pattern to live with, as bleak as it was. Ten laxatives and four diuretics a day left me in poor shape. Drained of all my nutrients and strength. I acquired mononucleosis, and calmly hoped for death.

Through a frigid winter and two months of recovery from mono., I twice visited with a psychologist at my mother's expense. She vowed to pay for my mental help but seemed irked, nonetheless, by the imposition. I declined to pester her for a third visit.

February 21, 1990 was the final day I was able to walk into our house on Lincoln Avenue. The new owners were due to move in the next morning. The house was vacant, apart from the big, beige recliner chair in the corner of what used to be my room. Closets were empty, walls were blank. Even that wicked kitchen table was gone. Nothing was in the basement. All our toys had been thrown in the garbage; Fisher-Price toys, board games, my two-hundred item stuffed animal collection. All my teddy bears, kitties, doggies and little bunnies were gone, as if a terrible fire had destroyed them all. My childhood was gone. My roots had been erased.

I walked back upstairs to my bedroom and curled up in the recliner. I hugged the chair as if it was a huge teddy bear, and tears rolled down my face and arms. It was over.

Goodbye, I said in a whimper. Goodbye, chair. Goodbye, room. Goodbye, my precious little house. Goodbye, family of four.

Goodbye, anorexia.

Howl

by
Heather Stephenson

I.

I saw the best bodies of my generation destroyed by self-control, starving deter-
    mined well-heeled,
jogging through suburban streets at noon looking for a set of scales,
slimhipped sweethearts burning for the ancient physical connection to the lean
    discipline of the empty dawn,
who affluence and goals and perfect and nude nibbled celery before full-lengths
    floating through remembered recipes contemplating eggs,
who bent like nun nurses over pure white porcelain to count pieces of carrot in a
    gastric sea,
who passed through universities with mute clouded eyes hallucinating hamburgers
    and makeovers among the arbiters of success
who picked kernels off rice cakes, doled out curds of cottage cheese, chewed 50
    times a side,
who spent lunch money on cigarettes and clothes to shrink into,
who deathgripped dance barres, whispering the mantra "I'm so fat I can't do this
    I'm so fat I can't do this I'm so fat I can't do this" until their thin blood
    swished to the beat,
who stepped like shy antelope on swollen toes before Mischa's framed inscrutable
    stare,
who clenched and released their buttocks while riding the bus or purgatoried their
    torsos night after night
with movies, with candy, with popcorn, fingers and throats and endless abdomens,
calorie clouds of refrigerators, kitchen white knives hospital dawns, Metamucil and
    raw fruit bursting over the sink, drugstore families and aspirinhead denial
    inches pounds cholesterol counts and RDAs for pigs in the soap opera
    afternoons, poolside calculations and harsh daughter's control of mind,

who sized up every woman they saw, x-ray eyes blazing through the subterfuges of
    bold prints and vertical lines,

who mixed powders in shotglasses of blue milk, popped pills and gloried in the
    banquet,

who leapt from bed to toilet to scales dropping their nightgowns snipping nails and
    shaving legs to make the wand wave lower,

who meditated on glasses of stylish sexy water and eight times a day drank the
    cleansing draught,

who weaned themselves on the wizard's tit of sugarfree lifesavers,

who rocked 'til they dropped at the dance-a-thon in ecstatic communion with
    dissolving thighs,

who tweezered pubic hair, toothpicked vomit from braces and walked the beach
    once a year in throat-to-ankle raincoats,

who treadmilled their minds into lockstep obsession pared themselves like potatoes
    and apologized for every inch of earth they occupied,

who struggled with snaps in department store dressing rooms as the discreet and
    polished toes of size 2 salesladies clicked up and down the numbered
    aisles,

who served seven-course meals on fine china while violins oozed butter in their ears
    and fat-fingered CEOs reached for non-existent asses,

who broke down crying in white gymnasiums naked and trembling before the
    machinery of other skeletons,

who scribbled "my body, my choice" on the stretcher sheets in their own blood the
    stink of rotting cells and stomach lining leaking from their lips,

who hid huge weights in rectum and vagina to show the smocked irrational judges
    how much they'd gained,

who yanked IVs and bubbling nostril tubes with chopstick arms in the fluorescent
    stroke of midnight,

who corseted their skulls with celluloid and silicon,

who dried up like apricots, asexual Alices singing happy good-byes to their
    monthlies

    ah, Mandy, Bella, Rosalie, while you are not safe I am not safe

You chose from the few roles available
that of the most perfect subject for poetry (a beautiful woman dying)
played it to perfection so the audience gasped.

    Were we right? Is heaven clouds of whipped cream?
    Are you angels lighter than air?

always hungry   always hungry

Orgy For One

by
Ellie Mamber

Many of my friends live
on supermarket shelves;
they call to me
colors flashing, cellophane crackling
as I press firmly past,
eyes averted
carting skim milk, cottage cheese.
For Triscuits, and Mallobars
Oreos, Gauchos and Crax,
Chocolate Chip and Fudge Bars
are not the friends
I should choose.
I tend to fall in
with the wrong crowd.

I avoid bad neighborhoods:
M&M's, Rolo's, Hershey
with Almonds, Sky Bars
and Nestle's Crunch.
Some days I look them
in the eye
and tell them to bug off.
Other times I stay away.

The best/worst days
are when I submit.
Calmly I know
I will let myself

have my way with them
(or they, with me).
Coolly I select my favorites
while they display themselves

two M&M's with peanuts,
to start; add a Rolo
for the chew (the cost
if I lose a filling!)
throw in a Sky Bar,
and for sustained delight,
a Milky Way.
I require privacy
for my gluttony,
retire to my room
possibly my car
crumpling the papers
fingers eager to begin.
My juices flow, everything
is in readiness as I
lift the exposed bar,
chocolate deep and rich
caramel or peanut secretly within;
part my lips and close on the first
present of my teeth
to tongue.
Each lifting of hand to mouth
supplies fresh treasure;
teeth meet, close, chew
heavily, richly,
grinding glory.

This is so deeply satisfying
that I do not care
if it stands for something else,
am content to crave
the readily accessible.
Later, distressed, distended,
I cup my aching belly with empty hands
and could cry for reasons
I cannot fathom.

The Refrigerator

by
Tema Nason

She walked into the kitchen and paused. The refrigerator winked at her. Hesitating, she turned around and stared back. Some women, she thought, dream of fur, of jewels, of a beautiful house or a wild love affair. Not me. Or rather, those too. But all she wanted right now, two hours after a big dinner, was food, food, something sweet and luscious.

And something sweet and luscious was right in there. For she knew the refrigerator's contents like a book. Hadn't she stored the fragrant chicken soup in a Pyrex bowl on the lowest shelf, the leftover chicken shredded and mixed with celery and mayonnaise ready for the children's sandwiches on the next to bottom shelf, and all the cheese, cream, cottage, cheddar and muenster, on the top next to the olives, sour cream, and pickled herring? The meat tray she knew held some leftover hamburger meat for the dog, and a half-pound of kosher salami.

A slice of salami—just one? She touched the refrigerator door, absent-mindedly stroking it, debating. No, nothing doing, it wasn't legal, not on the list. Reluctantly she withdrew her hand, yet knew instantly that the image in her fat brain was of the chocolate refrigerator cake that she had had to sit and watch the family eat and never touch a single crumb herself. The cake now lovingly protected in saran was shoved clear to the back of the refrigerator, concealed from view by a large bunch of leafy broccoli and a dozen oranges deliberately arranged so as to hide the treasure, the prize from the enemy...herself.

No. That's it. Just say no politely and walk out of the room. And she steered herself into the living room, a large pleasant room filled with books, plants, and a baby grand piano. Someone had left the stereo on, though the record had finished long ago. Vaguely she remembered asking Danny to please turn it down, it's too loud, and he had groaned, "Jeezus, Mom, why?"

I should have noticed it sooner, it's not good for the set, she thought, as she turned the power knob to the OFF position. And look at the pile of records on top of the stereo, the kids never return them to the folders. I keep reminding them, but it doesn't do any good. Sure, other mothers seem to know how to get results, but not me. I make requests—like a lady—and then they do whatever the hell they want to.

Her growing anger stabbed at her throat and she swallowed hard, meanwhile restlessly roaming around the large, pleasant room. But to her, only its flaws stuck out, like typographical errors. A scratch on the coffee table, a small rip in a pillow on the couch nagged at her. With an impatient twitch, she straightened a drapery hem, and then, after one more swift critical glance around, she relaxed into a lounge chair picking up a book, its yellow dust jacket still unsullied. She read the first page, started to turn to the next, looked up, and abruptly slammed it down on the end table. The sharp sound echoed hollowly through the empty house. The silence was unnatural. For a change, no one was home. Dave had taken the boys to a Western. "Not for me," she had said, "but you go." And Phyl was out on a date, one she had bitched about, he's too short, too dull, too everything, but she had gone anyhow. Why do I even listen to them, she asked herself, it only upsets me.

Now though, the house was too quiet. Even the phone had not rung once…too quiet. She'd never realized how much she liked the sounds of human occupancy. She listened to the silence. Only the hum of the refrigerator off there. Much too quiet.

So where were her reading glasses? Where had she left them? Probably upstairs in the bedroom. Oh, the devil with it, too much effort to climb the stairs. She picked up the book, then laid it down again. She might as well water the plants. When the leaves drooped, who else was there to blame.

Back in the kitchen, she bent down to get the watering can and hesitated. Just a taste. One little taste. That flush of excitement, and her mouth swelled with desire. Quickly swinging open the door, as though to pass over the action before it was recorded somewhere, she unpiled the oranges and put them haphazardly on the pink counter, along with the sharp green broccoli. Then, only then, did she reach in and lovingly lift out the cake, a shimmering mound of chocolate mousse ringed by lady fingers and crowned by deft swirls of whipped cream. Truly a confection fit for a king…and noshers like herself.

But she had reason to be proud of herself. For this was one time when she hadn't even tasted it, not in the preparation, not in the serving. Not one lick. So now one teeny taste was coming to her.

Languidly, her index finger sank into the whipped cream as far as it could go and only then did she carefully lift it out. Chocolate tipped to the first joint, the next joint down to the knuckle was swathed in a succulent creamy fluff. Into her mouth went her finger; first she licked and then she sucked. So-oo delicious. Soon she was satisfied.

Only briefly. Sitting on the kitchen stool, she eyed the cake with renewed lust, but the phone rang, a reprimanding voice. A momentary shudder passed through her stocky frame. Like someone abruptly awakened from a dream, hastily she shoved the cake back into the refrigerator like a thief hearing voices at the door. Then she picked up the receiver.

For a moment she listened, then spoke briefly into the phone. "No, this is 3-4-0-5, not 3-4-9-5. That's all right, you're welcome," and she quickly replaced the phone.

Back at the counter, she touched the plastic wrapping, forgotten in her haste to return the cake, and again opened the refrigerator door. Again she lifted the cake out, this time slowly shaking her head at herself, and set it back on the counter...

Five separate trips to the kitchen finished off the cake, each time with a bigger and bigger serving until the last time she just picked up what remained on the platter, perhaps a third of the whole, and sloppily dropped it from the cake server onto her plate. This time, she didn't even pretend to look at the newspaper while eating. Just one rapid bite after another, no longer savouring each spoonful, quickly, purposefully, fanatically. The nausea in her throat grew and she almost retched but she kept on. Then...so quickly it seemed, the cake was finished. All gone. No more left. Only the sticky empty plate, catching the sharp overhead light, glinted back at her disapprovingly. The whipped cream stuck in her throat. Yet deep within her, the emptiness grew larger, consuming.

Later that night, after the family had come home, the boys talking a mile a minute about how great the movie was, Dave couldn't understand her sudden tears when they went to bed. "What's the matter?" he pleaded. "Is something wrong? Anything happen while we were gone? Tell me, don't just lie there sobbing like a baby."

"It's nothing, it's nothing," she sobbed and turned away from him, from his love and his caring, lying in a fat heap on her side of the bed. Another day loused up, she thought.

The Midnight Prowl

by
Nina Silver

I'm hungry. The clock says midnight but that's a minor detail. Time is a human construct anyway, a delineation of made-up units, and therefore not real. My hunger is. My stomach's moaning and scrunching, whoosh, quiver, clamped down on itself. There's nothing for it to digest. Or is that my small intestine? A minor detail. The entire space down there is one, big, empty cavity waiting to be filled. Hungering to be filled. Urging me to fill it.

What shall I eat? There's the leftover chicken from yesterday's dinner. No, not the chicken—too bland and unimaginative. Spaghetti in cream sauce with capers? No, it'll give me an upset stomach. Much too rich so late at night.

What about the chocolate cake? I didn't tell Paul about the chocolate cake. I just had to have it one day, and after scarfing almost half, I hid the remainder in the freezer behind the spare ribs for times precisely such as this. Dare I?

No. All that sugar will rot my teeth and make my jeans fit even tighter. Maybe I should set my sights a little lower—in calories.

How about the tuna? Ugh. That's two days old. Better leave it for Paul. He's such a sweetie, he eats all the leftovers. He knows how sensitive I am to food. If it's more than a day old I won't touch it. Except the cake. I froze that as soon as I got it home, so it's all right.

But is it really all right? Do I really want to expand to the size of a baby blimp? Paul told me he doesn't care what I look like, that no matter how full and bloated and disgusting I feel, I'm the sexiest woman he's ever known and it makes no difference to him how much I weigh. But I can't quite accept this. He must need glasses. Or maybe he's losing his mind. Besides, he only went out with one woman in his whole life—so how would he know? Still, it's hard not to believe him. He sounds so sincere when he tells me.

Like Nancy. She said the same things when I was dating her. Maybe they're right. Maybe I do exude sensuality and passion. But if I'm so wonderful and desired, what am I doing roaming the house in the middle of the night like some animal in gastronomical heat, scavenging my own refrigerator as quietly as a thief?

I'd better go back to bed. Maybe it's not food I want, after all. There's Paul, sleeping peacefully—undisturbed by hunger or dreams of pineapple pizza. His skin's so warm and soft, it makes me want to curl up right next to him. Now that might be almost as good as chocolate.

Eating Cake

by
Moira E. Casey

———— ⟠ ————

I hate Thanksgiving. I don't hate it because I have to cook. I hate it because
I have to eat. With all the others. I actually like the cooking. I have been preparing
the food for several days. Everything is perfect, as usual. The fat turkey is turning
golden brown in the oven; another hour and it should be done. The peas, the baby
carrots, the mashed potatoes are all heating up on the stove while my husband mixes
up the gravy. I am bustling about and I feel very important and in charge. The kids
are in the basement playing video games, just waiting for the call to the table. Most
of the relatives are watching football games in the living room, probably munching
on the hors d'oeuvres. I wonder if there are any left. My brother is here in the
kitchen, talking with my husband as he stirs. Both have had several glasses of wine
already, and their round Irish faces have a rosy tint. My mother-in-law sits on a stool
at the kitchen counter and throws her opinion in now and then. I am quiet, mostly.
I don't talk because I want them to know I'm too busy with the meal. Of course, I'm
not really too busy; everything is right on schedule.

I put the dinner rolls in the oven to warm up a bit. Then I take out the
desserts: an apple pie, a pumpkin pie, and the very famous chocolate raisin cake.
One by one, I cut in between my husband and brother in order to set the treats on the
kitchen table. They don't really need to be set out—at least not yet—but I do it
anyway because the cake is such a conversation piece. The cake is from an old
family recipe, but everyone tells me that mine is the best. As I set it down carefully,
I feel the urge to run away with it. Or to lie and say I forgot to put some necessary
ingredients in it so I can save it for myself. As soon as I turn away from it I expect
my sons to run up and hijack it before anyone (me) can have even a slice. Or worse,
my brother. He would eat it just to spite me. I'm not being paranoid—he would.
Even now, he makes some comment about how I never want anyone to eat too
much cake because I want all that is left over. "Heh, heh, heh," he laughs, "I know
my sister!" I smile too, but I'm pissed because he's right. My husband sees the
exchange and changes the subject. "Hon, the gravy's done." "O.K., I'll take care of

43

it." Taking charge, I pour the thick liquid into a gravy boat and light the candle beneath it to keep it warm. Out of the corner of my eye, I follow my husband as he takes another tray of hors d'oeuvres out of the oven and disappears into the living room. I didn't get to try any hors d'oeuvres.

My brother starts talking to me as he pours himself another glass of wine. How much wine is he going to drink? He has no tolerance; he better not be drunk at the table. I start scooping the vegetables into the china bowls and serving dishes, trying to ignore my brother's chatter. He is talking about food and all the preparation. Blah, blah, blah. I don't want to discuss the food. I want to make it, I want to sit and eat it, and then I want everyone to leave. When they're gone it's mine.

My mother-in-law hobbles to the bathroom, brushing by my husband returning from the living room. "The Giants are winning," he declares. Great, talk about sports, not food. But I know my brother isn't into sports. I'm right. The sports conversation ends at the beginning and my brother starts talking about some book he's reading. It's better than having him watch me cook. I take the rolls out of the oven, dump them in a woven basket, and cover it with a linen napkin. The turkey is almost ready. I timed everything just perfectly. The table has been set for hours. I am ready to give the call.

"O.K., get the kids, and we can all sit down." My brother claps his hands and does a little hop, obviously he has been waiting for this. I bet he wishes the leftovers were his. My husband takes the turkey out and carves a plateful of meat. Slowly, everyone filters into the dining room. I don't think anyone did call the kids, but here they are anyway. I bustle into the dining room before everyone else. They can't sit down until I tell them where. Everyone has a particular spot. I designate the seats; mine is right next to the kitchen entrance, where I can command the feast. My husband sits next to me, and my sons sit next to me and on the other side of my husband. My brother (whose wife stayed home to care for her elderly mother) and his children are at the opposite side of the table, while the older folks have easy-access seats, near the entrance to the foyer. I stand as everyone gets settled, and survey the scene. Everything and everyone seems to be in place. The food begins to be passed around. I make sure everyone is served before I fill my own plate. Appearances. Hypocrite, I think to myself. I smile at someone's joke, and silently note how fast each dish is disappearing. I gulp some champagne. I don't eat too much—as if my example will be followed by the guests. Of course no one notices. My husband and brother heap mounds of mashed potatoes and turkey on their plates and cover it all with warm gravy. I watch them and nibble on a roll. I can't really enjoy myself, not here. Not in front of them.

When the meal is over, I clear the table. Everyone offers to help but I urge them back into the living room. Put them in front of the TV where they can't see me snack. I'm not really hungry but I'm not really full either. I can see that everyone else is. They compliment me on my cooking, pat their stomachs and stroll slowly into the living room. I cover up the food with plastic wrap, sneaking a spoonful of this and a forkful of that. Brusquely, I return everything to the safety of the refrigerator. My refrigerator.

After the dishes are scraped, my attentions turn to dessert. Not yet, I think. They'll have to wait a bit for dessert. Not too long, though. I want them to still be a little full from dinner. Nevertheless, just to have something to do, I take the pies from the boxes and set them on serving dishes. The cake, majestic on its stemmed plate, looks luscious. Carefully, I carry it into the dining room and place it in the center of the table. A bit of icing plops down on my finger. Almost automatically, I suck it off. The rich mocha-chocolate flavor melts all over my tongue and I want to gobble the whole thing up now and tell them the dog ate it. Maybe, I think, no one will want any. After all, there are lots of other desserts. Well, two pies, some ice cream, and a plateful of bakery cookies. No, that's silly, someone will want a piece of cake—at least one. I realize I need to get away from the food. So I sneak into the garage and smoke a cigarette. It helps a bit. I wish I had that cake out here with me, though. I check my watch. Dragging on the cigarette, I wonder if I ought to serve the dessert now. I drop the cigarette, only half-smoked, and crush it under my heel. Yeah, I think, now is as good a time as ever. Back in the house, I hear noise and scores being shouted about. I peer in the dining room only to find my brother snatching a couple of chocolate cookies from the plate. He looks up sheepishly.

"I couldn't wait," he winks. I smile, the phony Princess-of-Patience smile.

"That's all right, we're going to have dessert soon anyway."

"Great!" he says, and sits down at his appointed seat with three more cookies. Everyone except you, I want to say. You've already had your dessert. He'll have a piece of cake, I know. Maybe two, or three even. The kids will have some too, at least the ones who eat raisins will. I have to stop myself before I make a mental calculation as to how many pieces could possibly be eaten.

Once again, without being told, everyone starts to return for dessert. This has to be handled systematically. I serve the cake; my husband serves the pie and ice cream. The cookies have already begun serving themselves. Each person passes their plate down and requests a dessert. I do this beginning with my sons sitting next to me and then work farther down the table. My brother's plate gets passed last. I watch as the cake grows smaller and smaller. My brother jokes about not making his piece too small. I am not amused and I cut him a large slab to be contrary. Only three people are having cake, I notice gleefully. I slice a small piece for myself and eat it daintily, in small forkfuls. Glancing up, I see my brother has greedily finished his piece already and is passing his plate for some pie. Good, I think, eat all the rotten pie you want. One of the kids wants some more cake, but just a small piece. I slice it, probably a little too small, and pass the plate back. Now there is a little less than half of the cake left. Perfect. Unexpectedly, though, my husband slices himself a large piece. Inwardly I cringe. I want to hiss the word "traitor" in his ear. But fortunately, everyone else seems to be full. The kids excuse themselves and run back downstairs. In the kitchen, I lovingly wrap the remaining hunk of cake. As I place it on the counter, my brother steps into the kitchen.

"What do you say to wrapping up some leftovers so I can bring a doggie bag home to Kathy? She was really looking forward to your wonderful cooking before her mother got sick."

What can I say? No? That would be ridiculous. "Of course. Here," I start throwing things in tupperware, "take some turkey, some potatoes, some turnips—how's that?"

"Is there any cake left?" he looks around. "You know how Kathy loves that cake. It wouldn't be Thanksgiving without it."

No it wouldn't. "Sure!" My voice sounds a little too generous. "Here, there's only a couple pieces left. You take it and tell Kathy I said Happy Thanksgiving!"

"Thanks, hon." He takes the container and goes back to the dining room. I think he looked at me a little strangely, but maybe it's my imagination. I grab the bowl of mashed potatoes and a fork. I slip back out into the garage and gorge myself on the creamy potatoes, my tears dripping down into the bowl.

Cake Walk

by
Susan Hauser

———— ⦿⦿⦿ ————

I call it wedding cake. My friend Debbie calls it birthday cake. Some
people call it bakery cake, and that's what it is, white bakery cake with white
frosting. I know it has no egg yolks, and I know the frosting is made with lard—
that's why it is so utterly white. But I don't know what the addictive ingredient is.
Maybe it's some subtle combination of sugar and fat.

I do know that I am addicted to it. They say that alcoholics remember their
first drink and I remember my first white bakery cake. It wasn't exactly mine. Well,
it wasn't supposed to be. It was in the dining room—a room reserved for very
special occasions. There was some grown-up event in preparation. I was little. I
could barely reach onto the table. There was a silver tray full of little white cakes.
Petit fours, I know now. They were so incredibly pretty: pure white, each one a little
handful, and decorated with the sweetest little flowers and leaves.

Only an addict would have defied the order: don't touch. I did touch. And
I ate, too. More than one. I don't remember the ultimate consequence, but I do
remember my mother's skirt appearing at my side.

The next cake I remember was at a birthday party. This time it was a two-
layer cake. But it had the magic combination: white cake, white frosting, and it
came from a bakery. At the mother's instruction, a dime had been stirred into the
batter. Whoever got it in her piece would get a prize. I didn't care about the dime or
the prize. I just wanted more cake.

Of course, it is not unusual for children to abandon restraint in the face of a
favorite food. I did not begin to recognize the trouble I was in until my older sister
got married, and I had my first piece of wedding cake. I was a teenager at the time.
I knew about restraint.

It was that first bite that did it. With it still in my mouth, I found myself
sidling back toward the cake table. I had a second piece, and then a third. Only the
attendant there noticed, and he seemed to enjoy my passion. He did put an end to it,

though, when I started eyeing the topmost piece of cake, the one with the little bride and groom on it. The one my sister was supposed to have.

She got it. But only because the waiter was so stubborn. Anyway, I was getting full. And I was beginning to experience another craving, this time for milk. As my habit refined itself, cold, cold milk became a necessary complement to a good white cake binge.

Binge is the right word for my cake eating behavior. I could go months, even years, without bakery cake. But as soon as it was in my presence...And I never have learned restraint. I have, in fact, embarrassed myself. Some years ago I was at a reception. I had wondered a few days before if there might not be some white bakery cake with white frosting. If so, it would probably be a sheet cake—long, wide, single layer, with plenty of extra frosting available in the borders, flowers and letters. My mouth began to moisten. Maybe I would go early.

The reception was important, and fun: a gathering of old friends, some I hadn't seen for years. At first the cake was nowhere in sight. Then they brought it out, and a little ceremony was held over it...not for the cake, but for the friends gathered. I was in an adjoining room. "The cake is out," I said hopefully to the group I was with. No one cared. They wanted to know about my kids.

People started going by us with little white paper plates with white cake on it. White frosting. Flowers. I excused myself, came back with a plate and nibbled while we talked. "I think there's plenty of cake," I suggested. No one cared. I had to go back alone for seconds. Very shortly I was ready for my third helping. I had pretty much lost the drift of the group's conversation, so this time I just hung around the cake table. Really should talk to some other people too, I told myself.

I don't think anyone actually noticed my cake-driven behavior. But I did. I knew that I had chosen my addiction over the solid food of good conversation. The next step was inevitable: public humiliation.

It was a number of years later. We were at a dinner party, with friends. Just a small group, eight of us at one table. Debbie, the hostess, also liked white bakery cake with white frosting. And she taught me a dangerous lesson: there is no rule against having it for an ordinary dinner gathering. It didn't have to be a wedding or a birthday or an anniversary.

We had it that night, in fact, and I had two generous pieces. So far so good. The cake sat in the middle of the table. I could have just cut another piece. But the conversation was good, too, and I was so comfortable, so at home. I didn't even know what I had done until I felt my husband nudging against me. I looked at him. He had a look of disbelief and not a little horror on his face. I had been dipping into the cake itself, nonchalantly breaking off one forkful at a time and eating and talking. One side of the cake was all broken down.

Debbie understood. Now we occasionally have a cake-lunch, where we just sit at a table with forks and the cake between us and a gallon of milk alongside. It is sort of like having your cake and eating it too.

Those planned indulgences may be the reason I have developed a bit of control over my cake craving. Now I shop at a grocery that has a bakery right there. They always have whole cakes ready to buy. That's too much for my husband and me, and I do resist. But they also have four-packs of cupcakes with frosting that doubles the height. Perfect for dinner for two. I've bought them many times. Someday maybe they'll make it home to the dinner table.

Mint Cookie Trilogy

by
Nina Rapoport

———∞———

Mint Cookies I

I walk into the kitchen and stare at the Chocolate Mint Girl Scout Cookies sitting in a box on the counter to the left of the refrigerator.

No. No cookies. Cookies will make me fat.

Something healthy instead. I open the refrigerator. Apple and cheese—that's healthy. I grab an apple hastily, not bothering to wash it, stab a knife into the block of cheddar, while already munching on the apple. I have succeeded in procuring myself a chunk of cheddar, and I am alternating: cheese, apple, cheese, apple, cheese, apple, without taking the time to finish working on one before I take another portion of the other. Cheese, apple, cheese, apple, cheese, apple, cheese. Done.

Done? Hardly? I want more. I hear Mom's voice ringing in my ears: "Wait fifteen minutes after eating something and then see if you're still hungry," but I ignore it. I tear open the box of stoned wheat thins that is sitting on the counter, take out four. No. Five. Might as well finish the entire wax-paper package. I stuff the crackers into my mouth one after the other. No time to finish chewing and swallowing before taking the next bite.

Finishing the fifth cracker, I decide that a couple more can't hurt. I shake the box to get the next package, rip away the paper, and stuff another two in my mouth. Then one more. Then one more. I leave one in the package, fold up the paper, close the box and throw it on top of the refrigerator.

But now my mouth is dry. I need something to moisten it. An orange. An orange would be the perfect thing. The fruit basket is to the left of the refrigerator and the cutlery drawer directly under it. The orange is quartered and in my mouth in no time.

Damn it! I still want those cookies.

No. No, not the cookies. The cookies will make me fat.

What can I substitute for a chocolate mint Girl Scout cookie, though?

Peanut butter? Peanut butter is almost as tasty as chocolate, and Laura Scudder's 100% Natural Peanut Butter (Crunchy) has *no added sugar.*

O.K. Half a peanut butter and Blackberry "Reserves" (also sugarless) sandwich on Branola wheat bread. That can't be too bad. But I'll need something to wash it down. Milk. Milk goes well with peanut butter. Two thirds of a glass of milk.

I have finished the half-sandwich. My hand is moving toward the cookies. Oh, fuck it. O.K. O.K. I'll have a couple of cookies. But just two. Just two. I fill up my milk glass—I need more to balance out the cookies. The two are gone in no time. O.K. Another two. But just two more—that's all. And two more. And two more. Until half the package is gone.

I knew I should have just eaten those cookies to begin with!

Mint Cookies II

Apples. Banana. Spinach. Zucchini. Cauliflower. Carrots. I round the produce aisle, and am faced with a wall of cookies and crackers.

I'm not a big junk food purchaser, but I am fond of figuring out exactly what it is my stomach is craving and satisfying that.

I have been a big Cheez-It fan lately. I even went so far as to send in two proof-of-purchase stamps and a coupon to get my "FREE" box of Cheez-Its in the mail. I am sort of hoping this Cheez-It phase will peter out, but so far it hasn't, so I put another box in my cart.

Today, though, it's not just salt I crave. No. I want something sweet. I turn my eyes to the cookie section. Lorna Doone Shortbread. Chips Ahoy. Mother's Assorted Cookies. Oreo. Double Oreo. Ah ha! Mystic Mint. Yes, Mystic Mint Cookies are exactly what I want.

I get home, unload the groceries, pour myself a large glass of milk, open the box of Mystic Mint Cookies, take out two, and put them on a plate. Two cookies seem so insubstantial. All right—three then. After all, they're *small.* All right—four. To make an even number.

I sit down, eat my cookies, drink my milk. *How sweet.* A nice, all-American afternoon snack.

I open the refrigerator to put the milk away. I pick up the cookie box, planning to put it on top of the refrigerator, but change my mind.

I take out another two. Six really isn't that many. Two more. Eight?! Well…getting there. Two more. Ten! That's really pushing it.

I don't want to eat any more of these cookies!!! But I can't stand having a half-full box of Mystic Mints within reach. My housemates Sue and Zoe would be glad to help me out, but I don't have the patience to wait until they return. No. I'm just going to have to get rid of these cookies. I'm just going to have to throw them away.

Opening the back door, I stare at the bucket where we keep the compost. This'll never work. I'll throw them in and then take them right back out and eat them.

Annoyed, but determined, I throw the cookies on the porch and stomp on them until the chocolate coating has cracked into a thousand pieces, the mint filling has doubled in diameter, and what remains resembles balls of playdough flattened into pancakes.

The Mystic Mints no longer look so appetizing. But just to be sure, I scoop the mashed morsels off the porch and walk over to the garden. I grab a handful of dirt and knead the cookies and soil together with zest.

I return to the compost, drop the mixture in the bucket, and mix the contents of the entire bucket: Mystic Mint mush, banana peels, and burnt rice are no longer individual items, but one conglomerate smelly mess. Brushing the crumbs off my hands, I return to the kitchen, grinning victory from ear to ear.

Mint Cookies III

The potluck started at 6:30 p.m. It is now 7:15 and it will take me thirty minutes to walk there. So much for my elaborate plans of butternut squash stuffed with rice pilaf. I need something cash-down quick: chips, juice, cookies…

Cookies. Scanning the shelves of the Seven-Eleven, my eyes rest on a box of Pepperidge Farm Brussels mint cookies. I grab a package and make my way to the cash register. Inside my head, an all too familiar voice is nagging:

"One package of cookies? That's all?! Under three dollars?!"

But I know if it were two packages of cookies and a bottle of ginger ale, the voice would still hound me. "Junk food?! Lazy!" it would sneer disgustedly. Knowing that I cannot please, I remember not to waste my time trying.

I arrive to find three women and two men, all somewhere in their twenties, sitting on the carpet with paper plates and paper cups, engaged in a philosophical debate about the nature of reality, while Joni Mitchell, oblivious to the discussion, sings "They took all the trees, and put them in a tree museum…"

I put the Brussels Mints on the table in between the lasagna and the fruit salad, load my paper plate full of various salads and entrees, pour a cup full of Martinelli's Sparkling Apple Cider and sit down.

It is such an effort for me to get myself to any kind of social gathering that I have started to shower myself with praise for the most meager accomplishment. For instance, if I go to a party and just sit there the whole time without uttering a word to anyone, I consider it an astounding success. I went, didn't I?

I can talk about the nature of reality, though, so I am in and out of the conversation. During the out periods, I make second and third trips to the table. I want a Brussels Mint cookie, but I refuse to be the first to open the package, and everyone else seems too intent on philosophy to pay any attention to food.

Finally, the party seems to be disbanding. I get up to leave.

"Here, take your cookies," the hostess smiles.

"Oh, that's O.K. You have them."

"But they're completely unopened," she pauses. "Bring them to the next potluck." She smiles again and pushes them into my hands.

I walk out the door, and down the road a couple of blocks. I sit on the curb in the dark.

I give up. I give up on Mint cookies. I refuse to fight anymore. I surrender. I open the package, and eat them all.

Losing It

by
Patricia J. Washburn

———— ⬡ ————

I swore I wouldn't eat after 8:00 p.m. It's 8:05. I'm at work and I'm fighting the food fairy.

"I'm *hungry*," she wails. "No, you're not," I say. "You've had plenty to eat today."

"But my shift doesn't end till ten! I'm stuck here at this desk! I don't *want* to write this headline! Maybe if I eat I'll feel better about it." She's got a million of 'em.

"They need that headline for tomorrow's newspaper, and you're being paid to write it, so just do it." I am trying not to think about the Reese's Peanut Butter Cups that can be mine with just a few coins in the machine. But she knows about them.

"Mmmmm, that would be good! C'mon, let's go get one!" She gets my wallet out of my bag. I drop it on the desk.

"No, and that's final. You're on deadline, you've had your dinner and you're trying to lose more weight, or have you forgotten?"

"I've already lost a hundred pounds! That's a lot! I *deserve* a reward—a chocolate reward!"

"Isn't life rewarding enough already? You've got a good job, an interesting life, and the most wonderful man waiting at home for you."

"I want to be with him now! These people are boring." But they're not. In fact, some of them are just as interested in food as I am. One of them, Jan, shouts at me to look at a wire story she's found about dieting. Apparently they did a study and found that people who lose weight have fewer heart attacks, but more deaths due to violence, accidents and suicide.

"By now, I should be entitled to kill someone," I say to Jan. The rest of the editors chip in with suggestions for my victim. Most of them say I should start with management, but a few say I should assassinate someone important so we'll have a story for the front page. Gallows humor keeps newspaper people from going insane amid deadlines and destruction. It also keeps our minds off food—but not for long.

"What the hell are you eating?" snaps Ken, who would absolutely hate to be called "gruff but lovable." He hates the smell of melted cheese for some reason, and the man next to me has Wisconsin cheddar soup. It smells divine. The food fairy notices it, too.

"Oooh, doesn't that smell good." But even she knows I can't eat Tim's soup. Jan has a more practical suggestion. "Anyone for Ben and Jerry's?" This den of ice cream sin lies a mere half-block from the newspaper building. "Come on, a raspberry sherbet won't be so bad," the food fairy urges. "You can have it with chocolate sprinkles on top…"

"Can't, Jan, I've got a lot to do." This business of being strong is a pain. I've been doing it for two years. I've lost a lot of weight—I had a lot to lose—and learned a few things about why and when I eat.

Nights are the worst. So, of course, are days. And weekends. And work-days. And vacations. And Christmas.

As it is, I'm not that healthy. I still eat burgers, pizza, chocolate (the words themselves are making me hungry, and I just had breakfast). I just try to eat in moderation over the course of a day. My weight loss has really come with exercise. Occasionally the food fairy gets involved in that, too, trying to convince me that I really don't feel like putting on my gym clothes and driving half an hour to the aerobics class. But I always feel worse if I don't go than if I do.

If I *did* kill someone, it would probably be anyone who ever said to me, "You could be so pretty if you'd just drop a few pounds." Or "Do you really need that cookie?" Remarks like that always made me want to kneel at the end of a Twinkie production line with my mouth open.

I started losing weight when I started feeling good about myself. I had moved to a beautiful city, jettisoning a high-stress job and a problem-plagued relationship at the same time. When no one was telling me to lose weight, I found I wanted to do it for myself.

I now weigh 212 pounds. I've got a ways to go before they'll let me be an airline stewardess. Still, this is the smallest I've been since sixth grade. I no longer have to shop at Lane Bryant. And I've started to get a lot of compliments on my appearance. One of them arrives at my desk, distracting me from the raspberry sherbet.

"You've lost so much weight!" The speaker is a colleague with whom I seldom deal directly. "I just had to tell you how good you're looking these days."

"Thank you. It's been a lot of hard work," I say.

"And it shows! Congratulations!" She stays by my desk for a few minutes, and we chat about food and weight loss, the twin subjects which American women always have in common.

I'm glad I've lost weight, learning to nourish my body instead of my emotions, treating food more as sustenance and less as a substitute for love, success and security. But the changes haven't been all positive.

A couple of larger friends have distanced themselves from me, somehow feeling betrayal or failure at my success. I miss them and want to tell them they're beautiful the way they are.

A few people have revealed their hypocrisy. I'm thinking in particular of a man I'd known for a while, who suddenly decided to ask me out after I'd lost weight. I've gotten a lot more attention from men as I've grown closer to the conventional idea of beauty. The skinny me, apparently, has a "great personality" that the fat me somehow lacked.

The man who lives with me now is loving and supportive, cheering when I tell him I've lost weight and saying nothing when I reach for a couple of his Pecan Sandies. Yet early in our courtship (and in my weight loss), he said, "I don't understand. What is it about women and food? To me, it's just fuel."

On the most basic level, women *are* food. Our breasts have the capability to nourish children. How natural, when we can satisfy a baby so completely with our food-bodies, to think that we can satisfy our own unmet needs by feeding ourselves.

The conflict comes when we are asked to maintain the unnatural thinness expected of women today. Women's magazines give us luscious cake recipes for our families and diet tips for ourselves.

Some of us rebel. We eat too much. We exercise too little. We become large, huge, overweight, chunky, obese—in a word, fat. I was one of them. In this world, that's considered ugly. Yet I was able to change only when I began to think of myself as attractive.

As a child, I took guilty pleasure in sneaking lumps of sugar from the bowl. I started early, drowning my first grade sorrows in chocolate syrup. In high school, I had no dates. I had good friends (and still have some of them), but many people rejected me because of the way I looked. I kept my nose in a book, and my hand in a bag of cheese popcorn. The food fairy had to do little to convince me to eat.

If misery loves company, so does food. My sister was my partner in eating. After school, we'd pool our financial resources and I'd drive (walking would have defeated the purpose) to the convenience store for potato chips, popcorn, choco-late—the fat-filled foods that advertisers and vendors continually thrust in America's face. I didn't succumb to temptation—I chased it.

College was another food fest, but this time I grew secretive. "Helpful" dorm-mates were always trying to put me on diets. But once again, the convenience store came to my rescue, putting my junk food in nice anonymous paper bags. I got through finals on cheese-flavored Chex Mix the way other people used coffee.

Later, I grew increasingly frustrated when I tried to find acceptable office clothing to fit my jumbo body. When a man moved in with me, I felt good about myself and ate better for a few months. At first, he accepted me the way I was. Then he changed, began criticizing my weight and revealed the extent to which he was using me. I began consuming huge bowls of onion dip just to spite him.

I moved away from him, to a better job and a better life. I felt more valued at work, more peaceful at home. I did volunteer work, and saw that I had the power to make other people's lives better. And I signed up for an exercise class.

At first, my goal was simply to go to the class and exercise three times a week. That was hard enough. I had fought any form of exertion for years. I would leave class and head straight for the junk food aisle of the nearby supermarket. But gradually, after about six months, I found myself looking forward to class, making a habit of it, buying clothes for it, building friendships in it. I knew it was time to take the next step.

Slowly, I began revamping my diet. I still don't eat what the government says I should, all those servings of vegetables, fruits and whole grains. But I do eat less fat, and I do balance my meals across the course of a day or week. Restaurant lunches are followed by Weight Watchers dinners. A few days of "being good" can earn me a piece of candy.

A few months later, I had lost about thirty pounds. But I felt the achievement was a tenuous one, that it might come back at any time. Once again, I took a plunge, this time into a therapy group on food issues.

The women in the group were an education to me. The law student whose mother criticized anyone with a double-digit dress size; the group home resident trying to fight her inner demons along with her food issues; the nurse's aide who defiantly claimed "Fat's beautiful"; the advocate for the mentally ill, whose eating was a way of telling her father to let her be herself. I learned from each one of them, and from the knowledge that all of us were dealing with the same friend/enemy.

By succumbing to cultural pressure to lose weight, I sometimes feel I've betrayed my feminist self, bought into the "beauty myth," failed to rebel against patriarchal standards of what woman should be. Yet I know I'm healthier than when I couldn't haul a bag of (fattening) groceries up the stairs without running out of breath.

Food is still my friend and my enemy. When I'm feeling stressed or unloved, my first thought is "What is there to eat?" This isn't necessarily bad, as long as I realize what I'm doing. Before, I would eat and not know why, then hate myself for it. Now, I try to examine what's wrong and what I can do about it. Then, if I really think it will help, I feed myself.

The food fairy, of course, finds this process unpleasant. She wants to skip straight to the eating part. "Criticism from the boss? Make yourself feel better with that Hershey bar!" The man next to me is eating a chocolate doughnut.

It's going to be a long night.

Elise

by
Dana Lauren Ramos

—⚬⚬⚬—

Elise was watching a late-night rerun of "Cheers." What does Sam see in Diane anyway, she thought. She's always mean to him. Why do guys always go for girls like that? The tunnel of light coming from the TV flashed colors on Elise's wide legs beneath her terrycloth robe.

A commercial came on and Elise clicked on a lamp which stood beside the old, worn sofa. She hoisted herself up and a deep, depressed spot remained on the cushion where she had sat, as if it had sighed and given up the battle to remain lively long ago. As she walked into the kitchen, Elise heard that idiotic commercial, where the two old ladies argue about nothing, for Denny's restaurant. "Lenny's," one of the ladies called it; "Denny's," the other corrected her.

On her way home that evening, Elise had popped into Ralphs and bought a frozen pizza, some Coke, a small loaf of white French bread, margarine, and because it was on sale—only two-forty-nine—a box of six jelly donuts—her favorite kind with the powdered sugar covering that drifted into her nose and stuck on her fingers so she had to lick it off. She had sworn that she'd allow herself *one*—just one—jelly donut if she only ate half of the large pizza and only a piece of bread for dinner. She didn't get the donut. But that was many hours ago; was she supposed to stay hungry until breakfast in the morning? And don't most diets these days say you should not go too long between meals because it actually lowers your metabolism and can *cause* weight gain? Elise opened the box of jelly donuts.

No, no, no. Stop! You do not have to do this, a voice inside her said. She ignored it and took a large bite of a donut, then another and another, so fast that she was barely chewing or tasting before swallowing. There! she yelled back to the voice; There and there and there! She gobbled up another donut, and another and carried the last one into the den with her when she heard the music of "Cheers" return, meaning that the commercial break was over. She put her feet up on the couch and lay back, savoring the final donut, rolling it around in her mouth—on the gums above her teeth, under her tongue—chewing each bite into a fine paste before

58

slowly swallowing. I win, she thought as she licked her fingers. She felt a wave of nausea, so she shut her eyes. I win, I win.

The twang of guitar music coming from the apartment next door stirred her awake. How can that idiot stand to listen to music like that every morning? she thought. Morning! Elise snapped her eyes open. Light was leaking through the mini-blinds and her wristwatch confirmed it: ten minutes to eight. She had less than forty-five minutes to be at work.

No time to shower. Damn. She'd fallen asleep on the sofa again and missed her shower, just as she had the night before. Elise threw her bathrobe on the floor and ran a wet washcloth over her face and under her arms. She rinsed her mouth twice with Lavoris and brushed her greasy brown hair back off her face, securing it haphazardly with bobby pins. It was going to be hot today, but she had no lightweight clothing hanging in the closet. She rummaged through the two plastic laundry baskets in the corner of her room (she had meant to do the laundry yesterday, too), and came up with a long, flowery caftan—one of her least favorites, but it was only slightly rumpled and didn't smell too badly. She hated that dress— a fat lady's dress—but it would have to do, she thought as she lifted the dress high and spritzed Tabou in a mist around it.

There was no time for breakfast. Good, she thought, I'm not going to eat today anyway—to make up for last night. Her stomach grumbled at the thought. Tough—no eating today, that's final. She grabbed her battered purse, locked the apartment door behind her, plodded down two flights of stairs to the garage, squeezed into her little Dodge Colt and started for the preschool where she worked as a bookkeeper. I've heard that people get more energy when they are hungry, she thought. They say they feel in control when they are fasting, and by being busy, they don't notice the hunger. Well, that's me from now on. I'll stay busy and won't even think about food. After work, I'll do the laundry and clean the bathroom. I'll take a walk. I'll call my mother and tell her I'm losing weight, really losing weight.

Elise made it to work with five minutes to spare. She shook her office key loose and unlocked the door. After hanging her purse on a hook on the door, she lifted a metal folding chair, set it up outside the gates of the preschool and sat down. Part of her job was to greet the parents and children at the gate each morning, and to inspect the kids for any signs of a cold. The rules said you couldn't bring a sick child, but some mothers were so desperate for a morning off that they'd try to sneak a runny-nosed kid in anyway before dashing home and taking the phone off the hook so they wouldn't get the call to come retrieve their child.

Elise shifted her large bottom side to side on the metal chair, trying to get comfortable and to balance her weight; she always felt as if she was tipping one way or the other. The first car pulled up, then another and another; they seemed to come in a flood, as if they'd all waited just around the corner until one minute before eight-forty-five so that they could zoom up at exactly the opening time and participate in the parade.

"Good morning, Elise!"

"Good morning, Mrs. Bannon. Hi, Jennifer. Hello, Mrs. Potnik, Mrs. Bates. Jason, could you come here a minute please and let me look at you?"

"How are you, Elise?"

"Fine, Mrs. Gregg. Mrs. Potnik, Jason looks a little flushed."

"Oh, it's just allergies."

And then came the one Elise hated the most, pulling up in her peach-colored Mercedes. She got out of the car and went around to the passenger side. Her caramel-colored long legs were topped by lemon-yellow shorts, and even when she bent inside the car to unbelt her little girl, you couldn't see a ripple or dimple. Now she approached Elise, holding her daughter in one hand and carrying a white box in the other.

"Good morning, Elise. Going to be another hot one today!" she said, all fake-perky as usual and made up in eyeshadow and blush as if she had someplace important to go.

"Hello, Mrs. Bennett. How's little Darla today?" Elise struggled with a smile and her eyes narrowed uncontrollably like they always did around this woman; as if Elise could block out the vision of her—or somehow protect herself from her—by squinting.

"Oh, fine as ever. And I brought a little something for you and the teachers today. I had to stop at the bakery to pick up some desserts for a little dinner party I'm having tonight—"

I hate you.

"—and I just grabbed a few extra pastries that I thought you all could share."

I hate you, I hate you, I hate you. "How nice," Elise said, her eyes avoiding the box.

"So, could I just give you the box and let you pass it around?"

Elise hesitated. "Well, I'm certainly not going to have any; but sure, I'll give them to the others." There. That'll show her. Shows up here like a devil-bitch to tempt me, but she won't win.

"Oh, great! I hope you like them." Then Mrs. Bennett handed the box to Elise, gave her little girl a quick hug and headed back to her Mercedes. Elise glared at her back. Hear that? "I hope *you* like them," she said, even after I told her I wasn't going to have any, Elise thought. So wrapped up in her own world that she doesn't hear what other people are saying.

As Elise carried the pastry box toward her office, her stomach gurgled, reminding her that she hadn't had any breakfast. She glanced over her shoulder and saw Mrs. Bennett pull away in her peach-colored Mercedes. She'll never know if I eat one of these, Elise thought. I might not even tell the teachers that she brought these in. Elise scratched under the tape on the box's lid. She lifted the top and sniffed. I win. I win.

Lynn Eats

by
Gwynne Garfinkle

Hot fudge sundae   love
spaghetti w/tomato sauce   love
hard boiled egg   love
vegetable soup   love
fudge ripple ice cream   love
molasses cookies   love
bowl of blueberries   love
Chunky beef stroganoff love
piece of cheese   love
Lipton's tea w/sugar & milk   love
almond coffee cake w/icing   love
tuna on rye   love
chocolate chip cookies   love
peanut butter cookies   love
apple   love
sectioned orange   love
instant orange cappuccino   love
peach walnut muffin   love
always hungry   always hungry   love

A Separation of Self

by
Pamela S. Gross

"Do you really need that?" my husband Alan asked.

His tone had been more solicitous than cruel, but I ignored him and shut the refrigerator door. I ran the apple under water and polished it with a dishtowel.

He breathed in and out slowly. "When was the last time you looked in the mirror?" This time there was no kindness in his voice.

I raised the plump, green Granny Smith to my lips. The spray from the juicy crack reached across to him through the filtered sunshine like a shower of saliva. He blinked several times but restrained himself from wiping his face.

"It's only an apple," I said.

I hated the predictability of this scene. His comments, my juvenile response. It wasn't that I didn't want to put the apple back or the crackers or the left over chocolate chip cookies, the handful of potato chips, the few licks of chocolate fudge icing on the deep double dutch chocolate seven layer cake. I just wanted to never *have* to put those things back or to never want them in the first place.

He stood in front of me, jaw set, chin jutting, like he'd just swallowed something not quite right and was too polite to spit it on the floor. Why wasn't he intelligent enough to understand that every time he reprimanded me, every time he looked at me with disgust, every time he ate steak while I picked through my fish, I went berserk.

"You'd better lose weight," my father said. "Believe me, sweetheart, Alan will look elsewhere. No one wants to go to bed with a baby elephant."

My father sat in the Queen Anne chair in the middle of my living room, puffing in between words on an old olive wood pipe, his legs spread wide to support the layers of stomach that swelled and receded with each labored breath. My mother hummed in my kitchen to a recent Kenny Rogers single, making batches of oatmeal cookies for the children. Her hips swayed in time with the melody, almost brushing the walls of the tiny room with each dip and jiggle. Her long gold chains bounced up and down on her ample breasts that spilled out of her 38D bra.

"I thought there was more to marriage than just looks," I mumbled. "Besides, Alan loves me; what's inside of me."

My father edged his way off the chair and in a final puff of smoke said, "He has to be able to get to the inside first, you know."

My parents left after watching my two children demolish a platter of cookies and milk. I walked back and forth preparing dinner, my eye on the remaining cookies, proud of myself that I had not touched them.

Alan sat at the dinner table wiping a fifth slice of white bread in the gravy from his pot roast. He pushed the remnants of his green beans and mashed potatoes between the crust and his fork, sucking the contents into his moist pink mouth. Stretching his long thin legs the length of the table, dislodging mine from their resting place, he leaned back in his cane chair, belched politely and asked, "what's for dessert?"

"Mom made cookies today," I said, anticipating the skin wriggling its way up his nose. Cookies were a snack; something to eat before dinner, or munch during a hockey game, certainly not *dessert*. I came back to the table with a thick slab of jelly roll filled with mocha, topped with whipped cream and chocolate sprinkles. I watched him eat mouthful after mouthful as I nursed a cup of hot water and lemon. He finished, leaving a minute portion of cake and cream, and rose, his lean six-foot-two frame towering over me. I waited until he'd left the room before clearing his dessert plate. On the way to the sink, I rolled my finger in leftover cream and sucked it in quickly, letting it roll across my tongue and slide down the back of my throat.

There are days when something unexpected happens; a sudden snowstorm in May when the flowers are frozen solid; being at the top of the escalator and feeling as if the ground was leaving you behind; standing in front of the crazy mirrors in the fun house and appearing miraculously thin. It was one of those deceptive mornings when the sun shone strongly but it was actually bitter cold outside. I was packing the children's lunches, debating whether to force-feed them hot oatmeal or let them get away with their routine sugared cereal. Inadvertently, I took three Hershey bars from the cupboard. I placed two of them in the lunch bags while the other stared at me from the countertop. After Alan left and the kids were busy brushing their teeth, I grabbed the bar, stuffed the wrapping into the bottom of the waste can and ate half in one bite. It tasted like soap. I smelled my hands to see if any dishwashing liquid had not been rinsed off. Tentatively, I took another bite, but the soap taste was still there, stronger than ever. I spit the candy into the sink and rinsed my mouth.

I was sick to my stomach all day and felt guilty that I had not called the school to warn the children. When they came home, I asked them how their lunch was and how they felt. They both grinned that it was great, and the younger one handed me back his bag with a smashed banana, already bursting and rotting. I barely made it to the bathroom.

It must be the flu, I thought. I was queasy for a week until I realized I was fine except when it was time to eat. Thank God, I said and watched five pounds subtract themselves from the scale. The next five months were a paradoxical nightmare. The spaghetti noodles turned to worms crawling across my plate, the pizza cheese was inundated with bugs, anything chocolate reeked of soap. The pounds kept coming off; I was shrinking.

Everyone was so happy with my metamorphosis that no one seemed to mind the garbage oozing out of the kitchen into the bedrooms. Not only could my intestines not bear the disgusting job of eating, they were wrenched by the thought of scraping dishes, cleaning the kitchen, anything to do with food made me feel lightheaded and quivery. Alan had to take over the shopping for me when, after several trips to the supermarket, I was blinded by the fluorescent lights and my heart thudded hard in my chest. It seemed my sole occupation was becoming thin.

Some mornings when everyone had gone and the house was quiet, I would stand and stare at the person in the full-length mirror. There, on the plush maroon carpet of her art-deco bedroom stood an emaciated young woman in a puddle of reflecting glass being stared at by a woman the size of a balloon at Macy's Thanksgiving Day parade, with very thin emotions and very thin thoughts. I felt like an amputee who was certain he still felt his missing limbs.

The more the clothes hung, the more the compliments grew. What kind of diet are you on; you haven't looked this good in ages; why, you look like you've lost ten years. But my skin, parchment thin and tight along my cheekbones made it very difficult to smile. My lips lost their warm, voluptuous geniality and lay a long line across my lower face above a new, very pointed chin.

Our king-sized bed grew enormous, and I was quite frightened at night searching for Alan amid the endless sheets and blankets. In the dark, I was frail, small and trembling to him. He was not able to dominate our loving with his weight and height. I wondered why he wanted to touch my breasts that looked like popped balloons, with nipples like blistered berries.

I grew smaller and smaller, quieter and quieter. The house became larger and larger; the laundry, Mount Everest, capped with snow-white underwear. Alan loomed in thresholds, towered over the dining table, vaulted over any fragment of emotion or energy I had left. The children ate candy bars, fruit bars, ice cream, potato chips instead of supper, realizing that I wouldn't come within fifteen feet of them when they were eating and my voice was so thin they could pretend not to hear me.

"She's much too thin," my father said. "Has she seen a doctor?"

Alan smiled down at me and patted my hand. "Why she's never looked better. She's thinner now than when I married her. Soon she'll run off with a younger man." He chuckled to himself.

"Well," my mother said, sniffing, "If you ask me she looks terrible. Everything hangs on her." She grabbed a foot of fabric from the side of my plaid skirt. "See!" she said.

A few nights later Alan searched for me across the expanse of the large bed. He ran his hands over my stomach, down my legs and pulled me toward him. "You feel so good," he muttered into the pillow under my head.

"I can't," I whispered.

"Hmm?" He questioned back, placing his knee between my legs.

"I can't," I said again, trying to speak a little louder.

"Too tired?" he asked, sounding considerate but continuing to massage my depleted breasts.

"I'm too small," I said.

I sat in the doctor's waiting room while Alan conferred with the doctor balancing my body by holding tight to the arms of the green leather chair. I had been needled, prodded, pinched, weighed, examined outside and barely in for the last two hours.

"You may go in now," the nurse smiled and glided me through the reception door down the hall to the dark muskiness of the conference room. She planted me firmly in another green leather chair. Alan and the doctor continued their conversation.

"You're certain she doesn't need professional help?" Alan asked.

"I'm positive," the doctor said, smiling over at me. "She's just lost much too much weight too soon. This is obviously not a good weight for her, physically or emotionally. She should put on a little. Come back and see me after she's gained five to ten pounds. I'm sure things will improve."

Alan drove directly to a Haagen Dazs ice cream store from the doctor's office. He left me alone, tucked into a corner of the front seat and returned with a quart of mocha chocolate chip and a plastic spoon.

"Eat," he commanded.

"I can't," I said, wondering what nightmarish thing the ice cream could taste like.

"Eat!" he repeated. "Doctor's orders."

Meekly I took the spoon and placed the cool, sweet dessert on my tongue and let it sit there for a minute, testing my response. My stomach lay calm like open arms waiting to receive a cool surprise on a hot day. My tongue tingled with cold and recognition. The chips crunched musically against my teeth. Alan watched and smiled and nodded with every bite. He pushed the container closer to my mouth, holding the bottom with his hand. His eyes followed the spoon as every last morsel entered the cavernous recesses of my body. At the last mouthful, he took the spoon and scraped every last drop into my mouth.

"Feel better?" he asked.

During the ride home a small smile began to creep to the edge of my lips, my cheeks softened. My shoulders spread and relaxed against the car seat as I listened to my stomach enthusiastically greet the treat. My eyelids fluttered in sated exhaustion and my body started to hum as the little chips and cream spread their way, puffing out a wrinkle here, a breast there.

Alan parked the car in front of the house and turned to look at me, his face still showing concern.

"Everything okay?"

He was used to my recent quiet so he wasn't annoyed when I didn't answer right away. I waited until I had sprung my feet out the door and felt myself on solid ground once more.

"Better. Fine," I said, searching out the last remnant of cream from the corner of my mouth with my tongue.

throwing laughter

by
Naomi Rachel

*"My husband wears the pants in our family,
and when he told me to stop wearing the
pounds, I knew he wasn't kidding."*
        —Jack LaLanne ad in the L.A. Times

i bought all the rich
red
juicy
fat foods.
the ripest watermelons
the darkest chocolates
& those dangerous soft
white potatoes,
creams
& breads.
i put them on the floor,
carpeted white
& i opened the cartons,
broke the wrappers
& split the skins.
one by one
i threw the rich
fat foods
against our white
bedroom walls
& i laughed.
i threw

& i laughed.
the juice
fat
foam
cream
& mush
was everywhere
& i laughed.
the cat howled
& i threw
the cheese cake.
my husband's picture
fell off the wall
& shattered
into the oozing
chocolate
& i laughed
& i threw
& i laughed
& i threw
& i left.

Red, White and No Longer Blue

by
Lesléa Newman

⎯⎯⎯⎯⎯ ◯◯◯ ⎯⎯⎯⎯⎯

You want to know why I'm eating blue spaghetti with tomato sauce and tofu all by myself on the fourth of July? There's a simple, logical, one word explanation: Margaret.

She left me. I was looking forward to spending a whole day with her smack dab in the middle of the week. You know, we'd get up late, make love, hang out, drink coffee, go back to bed, have a picnic, watch the fireworks. Well, that was the plan, but it seems my Margaret was off somewhere making fireworks of her own. With someone else. And like a poorly written soap opera, I was the last to know.

So, while the rest of Boston was celebrating the birth of our nation (or protesting it, whatever turns you on), I was alone. All by myself with no picnic ingredients, no party to go to, no one to *ooh* and *aah* with down at the Esplanade when it got dark and they shot those babies up in the air.

I moped around most of the day, and then around five o'clock I snapped out of it. I had no right to feel sorry for myself. I was young, healthy, employed and reasonably good looking, with a roof over my head and food on the table. That's when I decided, what the heck, I'd make myself a festive meal and have a private celebration. Hell, I'm a woman of the nineties. I don't need anyone else, right? I can take care of myself.

So, due to the day being what it was, and me being the cornball that I am, the meal had to be red, white and blue. I opened the refrigerator and immediately saw red: a jar of Paul Newman's tomato sauce. Perfect. Red was for blood, anger, revenge; how dare that bitch leave me for somebody else? I'm the best thing that ever happened to her. And she knew it, too. Or used to know it.

Now I was feeling blue. Blue food was trickier. I didn't have any blueberries in the fridge. On to the pantry. Would navy beans count? Hardly. How about a can of green beans? Almost, but not quite. Although some people have trouble telling the difference between blue and green and some people don't even think there is a difference. I found that out a few years ago when I was waiting for the T at Harvard Square. A music student from Japan struck up a conversation with me, pointing at my sweater with her flute case. "That's a nice green sweater," she said, though my sweater happened to be blue. When I told her that, she smiled and said there was only one word for blue and green in Japanese, which sounded quite lovely and meant the color of the water. I started wishing that train would never come, but of course it did, and off I went, only to meet Margaret three days later as a matter of fact. But I refuse to think about that now. Anyway, the point is, if I was Japanese the green beans would do just fine, but then again if I was Japanese, I'm sure I wouldn't give a flying fuck about the fourth of July.

Back to the pantry. That's when I spotted those little bottles full of food coloring: red, green, yellow and blue. I'd gotten them last year for St. Patrick's Day, to make bona fide green mashed potatoes for Margaret. The blue bottle was still full. What could I dye with it?

Why, spaghetti of course. We used to color spaghetti when I taught day care. We'd save this special activity for a freezing Friday in February when the kids were off the wall from being cooped up all week, and the teachers were going bananas from five days of dealing with seventeen pairs of mittens, boots, snowsuits, scarves, sweaters, hats and jackets. To while away the afternoon, we'd cook up a huge vat of spaghetti, dye it different colors and throw it against the wall, where it would stick, making a mural I'm sure Picasso himself would have been proud of.

I put up a pot of water, contemplating blue: sadness, an ocean of tears, Lady Day singing the blues, red roses for a blue lady, that was me all right. Sigh.

Two down, one to go. White. Like every good dyke, I didn't have any white bread, white flour, white sugar or white rice in my cupboard, but I did have that handy dandy item that no lesbian household is complete without: a virgin block of tofu sitting on the top shelf of the fridge in a bowl of water. I chopped it up, thinking about white: a blank page, empty space, tabula rasa, clean sheets, starting over, yeah.

So I set the table and sat down with my very own red, white and blue meal, feeling angry, empty and sad. To tell you the truth, the plate in front of me wasn't very appealing. I took a bite anyway and smiled. Not too bad, actually. A little chewy maybe, but other than that, okay. After I forced four bites down past the lump in my throat, it hit me: it wasn't just the Fourth of July I was celebrating; it was Independence Day. I was celebrating my independence by eating a completely ridiculous meal and the best part about it was I didn't have to explain it or justify it or defend it or hide it or even share it with anyone. I tell you, the fifth bite was delicious and after that the food just started tasting better and better. As a matter of fact, I don't remember spaghetti ever tasting so good. I had seconds and then thirds. I ate it with my fingers, I let the sauce drip down my chin, I picked up the plate, and licked it clean. Yum, yum, yum. My country 'tis of me.

Food Is My Life Sentence

Eating

by
Ariadne Northstar

—⊙⊙⊙—

I eat to be redeemed, and I eat out of fear that there is no redemption. I eat out of frustration that all those tears, which would dissolve if they fell, have turned to fat cells and glued themselves to my body. I eat to remember my past and to deny my future. I eat because I hate the world I live in, and am afraid I can neither fit into it nor change it. I eat because I love the world I live in, and am afraid it will be taken away from me. I eat when I see injustice and when I see beauty. I eat to be alone, and I eat because I am alone. I eat because I am passing one of my houses of worship (McDonalds, Ben and Jerry's, Taco Bell) and want to pay homage. I eat because I am passing a health club and want to protest the way women must discipline their bodies. I eat because, damn it, the stuff just tastes good and life is too short not to eat what tastes good. I eat to be rewarded and to be punished. I eat so the guys on the corner will shut up with their wolf whistles. I eat to find out whether my mother, and my friends, and my lovers really love me unconditionally. I eat because my desires will not be denied. I eat because my desires terrify me.

I eat for every possible reason except bodily hunger.

I eat when I look up from my work and it strikes me that somehow things used to be better. I eat to reconnect to moments of freedom when I was on my own and no one could hurt me, when I had not yet discovered how deep the horrors of the world go. I eat and remind myself of how little it took to let me feel good as a child, how filled with wonder I was. Today, when I bite into a Yodel, I know better than to expect the same momentary rush of deliciousness that I experienced when I was younger, and yet I expect it every time. And am disappointed every time. And nonetheless keep trying, looking for the perfect Yodel, the perfect egg cream, the perfect pizzaburger.

I eat when I look up from my work and face my terrors about the future. I eat because I don't know what's going to happen next, because I want to avoid making important decisions as long as I can, because time stops when I eat and I desperately want time to stop. Just for a little while, until I get my life in order. Just for a little while, until I make peace with myself. Just for a little while, until I learn how to maneuver in the world without sacrificing my integrity, until I accept the burden and the delight of my abilities, until I am able to love freely. I eat to make the world go away, and the little while stretches, and stretches, and stretches into a terrifying eternity, and the world doesn't go away and I eat more.

I eat when I am reminded of how unfair life is, of how regularly people are hurt and hurt each other, of how mundane evil has become, of how easy it would be for someone to push the button and exterminate us all as though we were vermin. I eat when I am reminded of how isolated I am, how terribly lonely, how scared. I eat when I hear hateful epithets thrown around, when I read about racism in our justice system, violence against women, homophobia disguised as religious righteousness. I eat when people look at me and immediately write me off, when people do not take my intelligence seriously because I am a woman, when people instantly and easily label me uncool. I eat when I remember that people will resort to utter irrationality rather than open their minds to the pain of growth and healing, and I eat when I see myself doing the same thing. I eat because I do not cry about AIDS deaths or crack babies or drive-by shootings or the S&L scandal or the million other daily outrages. And I eat because I am afraid the world will go merrily on its way to hell in a handbasket without my being able to make a difference or turn the tide.

I eat when I am reminded of how unspeakably wonderful the world is, of how miraculous people are for going about their lives and caring for one another and creating beauty along the way. I eat because I want to care with people and about people, and am afraid I can't. I eat because I want to create beauty and live my life in appreciation of beauty, and am afraid I can't. I eat because I am afraid that all the caring and all the beauty is not enough to keep the world from going merrily on its way to hell in a handbasket.

Food is my most passionate lover, my oldest friend, my solitary vengeful and loving God. I have lusted after Oreo milkshakes, been consoled by bologna and cheese sandwiches, tasted of the dark chocolate candy bar of life and drunk deeply of the egg cream in remembrance of holiness. Eating is sensual, every flavor, every texture a delight, a moment in paradise which I would freeze to stay there forever if I could. I once spent half an hour eating an Egg McMuffin, willing the exquisite taste to linger on my tongue, wondering whether a sexual partner would ever excite me in quite the same way. (None has, though some have come close.) The smell of chocolate at the Hershey's factory in Pennsylvania, the feel of an apple or banana, the sound of bacon frying; the photos of fudge cake and barbecue sauce in the Sunday paper coupon section; all send a light shiver down my back.

Food and I go back a long way, back to the first moments of loneliness, the first betrayals, the first anger. I trust food as I trust no person: to be there, to understand me, never to make demands. When I have had a long day, I get on the phone and invite food over for a visit. Food shares my victories and helps me get through my defeats. Food and I have had a lot of fun times together; when I want to remember those times now, I recreate them with the Ring Dings or American cheese I used to eat. Food is dependable; should the world crumble, should everyone I know walk away, there will still be coffee yogurt and chocolate chip cookie dough.

In my weakest moments, I turn to food for help and comfort; in my celebration of life I turn joyously and gratefully to food. Anguished and alone, I eat and pray and cannot tell one activity from the other, aching to be nearer my Kraft Macaroni and Cheese to Thee. On warm bright summer days, with songs I love running through my head, I walk through the Boston Common, offering my thanks with the hot dog or Peace Pop in my hand. And though evil shall tempt me, I am not afraid, for food is my guide as I walk through the world, the cans of Spaghettios and cups of pudding my signposts and markers. Here is familiar territory, whatever else may be foreign and threatening. Thy well-stocked aisles and Drake Foods display racks comfort me.

Food is also my prison, my pain incarnated, my deserved torture for not being stronger, not being kinder, not being thinner, not being perfect. Food is weakness, giving in, giving up. Food marks me as a loser, a loner, a deviant. While I did not establish the laws that I use to judge myself, I am the strictest of judges, as though I could save myself by destroying myself before anyone else does. I judge myself with food, deliver the verdict with food, carry out the punishment with food. Food is my life sentence, and possibly my death sentence. Food is poison. I eat it in silence, in fear, in repentance, and it is sawdust and stone in my mouth.

Food is my danger, the danger I have agreed to face in return for getting to bypass the other dangers—anger, sadness. Food made me a bargain I couldn't refuse at age seven when the pain got too great. Now, when I could perhaps refuse the bargain, I am afraid. Visions of uncontrolled howling rage and destruction, of endless agonies of loss, grief, emptiness tearing me apart, these visions haunt my dreams; if I can ransom a night's peace with sweet Gherkins and tortellini Alfredo, it is worth the numbness, the extra flesh, the fear of bodily illness. Most of the time, at least. And sometimes it is even worth the loneliness, the casual judgment in the eyes of strangers, the difficulty fitting into seats and through turnstiles designed for thinner people. For I am afraid that, confronted with the truth of my pain, I simply would not be able to live. I am afraid I am just not strong enough. And the food confirms this fear and increases it daily.

I know the literature on women and eating disorders. I understand the ways in which women are rarely free in this society to relate comfortably to food. I have seen the movies, have read the books and articles. I can offer an academic account of the economy of food, of the structure of the diet industry, of the prejudice and discrimination against fat women, of the overconformity of the anorexic. I eat anyway. The more I know, the more I eat. I eat, in part, because I know—and because, knowing, I am angry and afraid.

Once, I lost a third of my body weight on a food plan. I exulted in the discipline, in my self-control. While I was at it, I passed up sex, music and all the other things I love too. I spent months gleeful that nothing got to me: no pain, no beauty, no jagged edges, no sunlight. Finally my body and mind revolted, and I embraced food and sex and music and life again. I was not technically anorexic during the weight loss; I would have had to lose much more weight to endanger my health. Nonetheless, I experienced utter delight in my ability to deny myself and my passions. To this most private and self-directed of holocausts, I now say: never again. I will eat the food I desire and work toward the day when I desire food for better reasons.

Every day, I see people treat food as a tasty, nourishing part of life. It is not magic for them, not dangerous, not mythical, not a ritual to torture or ease their souls. It has meaning for them, but meaning in its proper place; it is not an idol, neither a god to worship nor a demon to fear. This is my hope: that I will reclaim from food all the wishes and pains and gladness and frustrations with which I have burdened it, and take them on myself; that I will dare to laugh, cry, rage, love and struggle with the world in simple honesty; that I will confront the bleak morning head-on and walk with grace into the light, stomach gently full, hands in the hands of those I love, body and mind at peace.

The Unanswered Echo

by
Sima Rabinowitz

1

Lust keeps me thin. Lust for language. Lust for bodies. Women's bodies. Fantasy feeds off the homeless energy that inhabits a body fueled by hunger and denial. Fueled by the appetite that only abstinence can nourish.

Every hour without food brings me closer to the moment when anguish is energy, when energy is production, creation, completion, and finally, sustenance. Sustenance, a humble and compelling reward.

To enjoy sustenance, to deserve it, I must earn it, wait for it, have a right to it, make it a part of me. I have to believe both that I need it to survive—that it is biology and beyond the scope of my power, that I am driven to it by an earthly will outside my own—and that to eat, finally, is my choice. I can refuse it, reject it when satisfaction might become saturation. When I might become complacent because I am comfortable.

2

I was always more than myself. I was one of two. My twin was tiny, frail. Always the shortest and smallest, her physical aspect presented a drastic contradiction to her psychological/intellectual presence. She was cautious, but clever, articulate and persuasive from the moment she could talk. In school she was always the smartest and the best. People were impressed by her, marveled at the little girl who used big words.

She was the champion of superlatives. Since she was always both the least (in size) and the most (in everything else), I could never be either.

The two things I wanted most, the two things I thought were more important than anything else in the world, were to be small (smaller, smallest) and smart (smarter, smartest). Often I was confused, believing that small and smart were part of each other; if not one in the same, then a necessary part of a whole.

3

In my round, awkward adolescence I grew pudgy from the coffee cake and chocolate bars I ate in mid-morning and in the lean hours between classes and dinner at home. I ate the wrong foods at the wrong times certain I would be hindered by the routine of meals, the fact of lunch. (I never learned to enjoy lunch, and even now, when my routine of two jobs sometimes requires that I eat lunch or not eat at all that day, I am often ill and sluggish after the mid-day meal.) I was waiting for dinner, for the large reward at the end of the day, compensation for a job well done, an "A" on a French test or an original idea for a Social Studies project. I did not believe that coffee cake and candy bars were food. I did not believe that being puffy around the edges really had anything to do with this habit of denial and indulgence. And even though I knew that the extra helping of meatloaf at dinner was solace for the "B+" (instead of the "A"), I thought that the extra food wouldn't count when it was replacing something else.

I grew full and thick. But I was a waif. What I lacked, what I desired (affection, attention, affirmation) I could not make up for in bulk. And eventually being pudgy made me feel weak and undisciplined. I discovered that, while brownies and hot fudge, Hostess cupcakes and Heath bars provided a moment or two of comfort and delight, the pleasure of will-power, of feeling in control, of overcoming the most basic of needs, and finally the pleasure of tracing my palm over the deflated plane of my belly, was more lasting and more satisfying. Every small success offered me greater incentive, another opportunity not to eat. The events and sensations that had motivated me to consume were the same ones that incited me to go hungry.

Feeling thin was its own reward. Food, fat meant failure. Discovering and rediscovering the flat, smooth line of the flesh over my hips, pelvic bone, ribs, thighs became an obsessive ritual, the first thing I did on waking, the last before I slept. Wanting, lusting, desiring, and not having kept me hungry, kept me needing, kept me going. I began to equate not having what I needed (what my body craved) with success and consequently with survival.

4

Away from home, in college, I ate to quell anxiety. I ate because I was bored. I ate because I didn't really know how to be the kind of fun-loving, party-going roommate, dorm-mate, classmate the others seemed to understand instinctively and act out. I ate because I didn't care for men, they were boorish and uninteresting, and because I didn't know yet that loving women was an option, even though I knew I loved them. I ate because, after all, I was a thinker and the corporeal didn't really matter, and because if you didn't "watch your weight" and fret about your looks and fuss over your clothes and hair, it proved you cared more about the things that really did matter: poetry, philosophy, politics. I ate because I was lonely.

I ate because I didn't have the money to go to the movies, or to travel on spring break, or to take the bus into the city. I ate because I was distraught about how much time, effort, energy, it would take to lose the weight I had gained. I ate because I missed my twin sister. I ate because sometimes I knew I didn't miss her at all. I ate because a moment at the vending machines was a break from the books. I ate because the verse I was writing seemed sophomoric and insipid. I ate because every slice of chocolate cream pie, every Hershey bar with almonds, every bag of potato chips was the last one anyway.

5

From college I went immediately to graduate school with its seminars and extensive oral presentations, lengthy written examinations, talk of careers and tenure, publications and professional personalities. I wouldn't eat because I was anxious. I wouldn't eat because when I wasn't in the classroom (studying or teaching), I was bored. I wouldn't eat because I didn't really know how to be the kind of know-what-I-think-about-everything, know-what-I-want-from-the-world kind of professional the others seemed to know instinctively and to act out. I wouldn't eat because I understood one morning, during a discussion of the history of the Spanish language, that the reason I adored this course was because I was in love with the woman who taught it, and that during the long hours I spent in her office, discussing philology, what I really wanted was to open her blouse in a room of perfume and candles. I wouldn't eat because I was lonely. I wouldn't eat because not eating made me numb, sense-less, and, after all, I was a thinker, a professional thinker, and the corporeal didn't really matter, and because if I didn't let myself get too involved with food it proved I cared about the things that really did matter: having a profession, getting that Ph.D. I wouldn't eat because I was worried about money, about paying the rent. I wouldn't eat because there was nobody to miss. I wouldn't eat because I was distraught about how much time, effort, energy it would take to lose weight if somehow I lapsed and started overeating again. I wouldn't eat because time away from the kitchen, restaurants, the grocery store was more time for my studies. I wouldn't eat because every ice cream cone that tempted me, every piece of lasagna, every bag of donuts might be the first of many.

6

I would rather link my arms around a woman's fleshy waist than feel them scrape and press against the hard, slender edge of bone. I want a woman whose body is strong and full. I desire a woman who is muscles and magnitude. I lust after a woman who has thick hands, legs like tree trunks, who is solid and even against me. A slender woman, a skinny woman does not interest me, does not move me, does not make me want.

I want to be thin. Slight. Slender. Sleek. Weightless.

7

Not having what I need (what my body craves, what my spirit desires) is what I have grown used to, how I have taught myself to survive. In much the same way that small and smart were part of a whole for me as a child, mediocrity and moderation have meant the same for me as an adult. Nervous and suspicious that I might choose my pleasures in excess, I am motivated by the opposite extreme of exaggeration. Especially when it's about food. Mostly, but not only, when it's about food. Sometimes about work, sometimes about companionship, sometimes about relaxation, sometimes about sex, sometimes even about love. Almost always about food.

Lust keeps me hungry. Being hungry keeps me thin. Lust is the unanswered echo. Hunger is the river between exhaustion and exhilaration. As long as I am hungry I am not comfortable. As long as I am uncomfortable, I am not complacent. As long as I am not complacent, I can count on myself to keep going. As long as I keep going, I will live for that lust.

8

Appetite is more appealing than what happens after. Appetite is being in the middle of the essay instead of at the end. It is expectation, anticipation, fantasy and promise. The meal is the last paragraph: the end of a process for which the plan has been more satisfying than the conclusion. Looking forward to the feast is always more pleasurable for me than actually consuming it. Finding myself on any page between the first and the last is safer and more pleasing than finding myself in the blank space between texts.

Writing is teaching me finally, slowly, very slowly, to eat. Food is not the end of hunger, of wanting, of energy. Feeling satisfied, full (with food, love, work, passion) will not curtail, will not eliminate the lust. The end of every text does not mean the end of any text. Satisfying the hunger, the need, the empty spaces does not have to stifle or still every lustful impulse, does not have to quiet every aspect of the energy that keeps me hungry, keeps me needing, keeps me going. Satisfying the hunger, the need, the empty spaces does not mean I will consume (food, words, affection) until I am sick, weary, numb. I will know when to stop. I will learn how to judge when something is finished, ready, over, ended, complete. I will know how to begin.

The Dieter's Daughter

by
Anita Endrezze

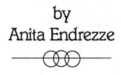

Mom's got this taco guy's poem
taped to the fridge, some ode to celery,
which she is always eating.
The celery I mean, not the poem
which talks about green angels
and fragile corsets. I don't get it,
but Mom says by the time she reads it
she forgets she's hungry. One stalk
for breakfast, along with half a grapefruit,
or a glass of aloe vera juice,
you know that stuff that comes from cactus.
And one stalk for lunch
with some protein drink
that tastes like dried placenta,
did you know that they put cow placenta
in make-up, face cream, stuff like that?
Yuck. Well, Mom says it's never too early
to wish you looked different,
which means I got to eat that crap, too.
Mom says: your body is a temple,
not the place all good Twinkies go to.
Mom says: boys remember
girls that are slender.
Mom says that underneath all this fat
there's a whole new me,
one I'd really like if only I gave myself
the chance. Mom says: you are
what you eat, which is why she eats celery,

because she wants to be thin,
not green or stringy of course,
am I talking too fast?
but thin as paper,
like the hearts we cut out
and send to ourselves,
don't tell anyone,
like the hearts of gold
melons we eat down
to the bitter rind.

Hunger

by
Rhoda Carroll

"Well," said Ruth's mother, who could peel cucumbers and interrogate her daughter with the same smooth slices, "Are you just going to stand there? What did you eat today?"

"Nothing," said Ruth. For her mother she would barely open her jaw and the word came out compressed.

"What's that?" said her mother, her hands flying. "I didn't hear you." She worked fast and green slivers piled up on the newspaper spread out over the counter.

"I said, nothing."

"Are you going to give me a hand here, or what?"

Before Ruth could move she finished the last cucumber and gathered the newspaper full of salad peelings into a neat packet. Into the garbage, one, two, three. "Tell your father supper's ready," she said. "You can at least do that."

At dinner Ruth's mother promoted the salad. "Hardly any calories" she said, forking the vegetables onto Ruth's plate. "And you're allowed a slice of this nice pot roast."

Ruth watched lettuce, tomato, onion slices and imitation bacon bits fall onto her plate. The slice of meat was insignificant. Of course she had stopped at a bakery on her way home from high school and bought a dozen chocolate chip cookies. She took them into an alley she knew about and ate half of them at once. Some of the chocolate chips had already begun to go soft in the desert heat, but if anything that made the cookies easier and faster to chew. She stood chewing behind the big garbage dumpster and knew that no one was likely to surprise her here. If they did, she could always pretend she was throwing the cookies away. She refused to think about the smell coming from the dumpster. She felt safe there, and full, and it was worth it.

Ruth took some lettuce on her fork and began to chew. She had the remaining six cookies hidden up in her room, and she pretended that the lettuce was chocolate.

"You like the salad?" said Ruth's mother.

Ruth nodded her head yes, pointing and gesturing that she couldn't speak with a full mouth. She stuffed another torn piece of lettuce into her mouth. The cookies upstairs gave her some consolation but there was always the risk of having the hiding place discovered. Once her mother had whooped all through the house yelling "I found a brownie in her shoe, her goddam shoe," and Ruth had heard her mother calling her a sneak and a pig.

Chewing, Ruth thought about whether or not she should try hiding stuff in the cellar, a place her mother might never think to look because the cellar was her father's territory. He went down there almost every night to store canned goods. He would watch the papers for sales and buy cases of grapefruit juice, green beans, sliced potatoes, Boston brown bread, beets, corn niblets, loganberries. "In case of nuclear war," he told Ruth. Ruth knew from science class that fallout would go right through cans but she didn't feel like getting into an argument with her father. She felt heavy and jealous when she went down to the cellar and examined his rows of canned foods stacked three and four deep along the cool walls. He was lucky. He could store his food outside his body.

"Don't put so much lettuce into your mouth," said Ruth's mother. She broke her potato into bits and speared the bits, one at a time. She enjoyed giving demonstrations of graceful chewing and she enjoyed being thin. She never gained weight in any real way. "I can feel it," she would say, "an ounce at a time. I can feel an ounce of weight on me. Then I take it right off." She could go for a couple of days drinking coffee and saying she wasn't hungry. She got tremendous pleasure out of not eating. "I never indulge past a certain point," Ruth's mother would say. When she felt good and light she would wear her bikini around the house as if she were getting ready to swim in the pool or had just come out.

"You don't have to eat those onions," said Ruth's mother. "Who knows, maybe a boy will come over to see you tonight."

"Nobody comes over to see me," said Ruth.

"Well they might," said Ruth's mother, "if you'd lose some weight. The way you are now, who can blame them?"

Ruth looked down at the plate of vegetables and said to herself, Okay, I didn't hear that. I'll just go on with this salad like I didn't hear that. Ruth played with a hunk of tomato on her plate, pushed it into a little pool of Diet-Rite Bleu Cheese Dressing.

Even though she was not looking at her mother she could feel her, the lean body in a bikini the color pink that would show off a tan. Ruth put the tomato into her mouth and chewed slowly, working her jaws until the tomato began to decompose in her mouth.

"Christ," said her mother. "You even make eating a tomato look disgusting."

Ruth sucked in the tomato flesh. "You're the one," she said, "who always makes such a big deal about chewing slowly."

Her mother leaned back. "You don't act like you're hungry. I asked you before, you eat anything after school?"

Ruth felt color move up her neck but she didn't worry. She knew how things would go.

"I'm talking to you."

Ruth selected a cucumber circle and cut it into fourths. She began to eat them one at a time.

"Look at me when I'm talking to you."

Ruth lifted her face and allowed some diet dressing to ooze from the corner of her mouth. Her heart beat a little faster. She was counting on her mother's reaction. Usually when Ruth did something disgusting, her mother would lose her concentration and forget the main point of her argument. Somewhere along the line she would draw Ruth's father into the discussion.

"Morris," said Ruth's mother. "Look at your daughter. Just look at her." She chipped at a piece of loose polish on her thumbnail and then began to inspect her other nails.

Morris looked at his daughter, smiled, and looked away. "I'm about finished," he said. "Guess I'll drive into town. There's a sale on water-pack tuna at Safeway."

"Christ," said Ruth's mother. "Are you going to drag more canned crap into the house? You sure don't look like you need anything to eat."

Morris gathered up his plate and glass and silverware and put them on the counter next to the sink.

He left the kitchen without looking at his wife or his daughter. They heard him go out to the carport and start up the station wagon and drive away.

"Tuna," said Ruth's mother. "Christ." She looked around for a cigarette. "He hates tuna." She got a cigarette and lit it and began trying for smoke rings. Her breathing was all wrong for smoke rings so she stopped.

"I like it," said Ruth.

"Like what?"

"Tuna."

"Oh, you'd eat anything."

"No I wouldn't."

"Sure you would." Ruth's mother ground out the half-smoked cigarette in her plate and pushed her chair away from the table. She eyed her daughter. "Think you can manage to stack the dishes?"

Since they'd had the dishwasher installed Ruth's mother felt justified in leaving the entire clean-up of the evening meal to her daughter.

"Sure," said Ruth, pretending that she didn't want to but that she was making an effort to be cooperative. Actually Ruth enjoyed cleaning up. Sometimes there were tasty drippings left in the crock pot or the roasting pan and Ruth could always get at them with the crusts her father left. Those crusts were a story in themselves. Usually Ruth's mother wrapped up anything good in foil and put it in the freezer so her daughter wouldn't get any but she seemed blind to the crusts, and every night Morris would leave them. Nobody who knew anything about food could miss the importance of the crusts. They could sop up gravy, they could carry spaghetti sauce into the mouth, they could absorb salad dressing, and they could be used on ketchup or mustard or margarine or green pea juice or anything liquid left on a plate. Ruth's mother always froze or spoiled good stuff; she would put potatoes into cigarette ashes and pork chop bones into used coffee grounds, but she acted like the crusts didn't exist. There were a couple of hundred calories of bread crust and drippings abandoned after every meal and Ruth couldn't figure it. If anybody knew the calorie count of bread, her mother did.

"Need any help?" her mother asked. She clicked her nails on the back of the vinyl chair.

"No," said Ruth. "Are you going to watch your show?"

Ruth's mother noticed the half-loaf of Italian bread and wrapped it in foil. "Wouldn't want this to go stale," she said, tossing it into the freezer. "If you want me I'll be in the den."

Ruth's mother walked down the long hall toward the den touching the white walls but not leaving any mark. Most of the furniture in the house was large and white because Ruth's mother liked things solid but light or invisible. The living room was full of large pieces of white furniture and the thick carpet was a deep forest green "to give the feeling of grass," she said, "to offset the desert." There was a huge glass coffee table in front of the couch. It was bare: no art book, no cactus in a Mexican ceramic bowl, no onyx ashtray. The living room was all green and white and glass and it looked like it was under water. Ruth never went in there and neither did her father. Both of them had cracked their shins at one time or another on the invisible coffee table and neither had any desire to sit on one of the white chairs. Even Ruth's mother hardly went in there. When she had company they entertained out by the pool.

Ruth got up from the table to survey the kitchen. Not much. The crusts, and the thin coating of gravy left on the pot roast pan. It would have to be enough. She rubbed the crusts on the bottom of the pan and stuffed them into her mouth. Dry and hard to chew. She liked her crusts heavy, dripping with gravy. She noticed the bits of potato stuck to her mother's plate near the ashes from where she had ground out her cigarette. Hardly enough to bother with.

Ruth turned her head to check for the sound of the game show in the den. Ruth's mother got a big kick out of guessing what one hundred people would say if you asked them to name something that you would wear on a hot day or something that tastes better raw than cooked. She liked to see the host kiss various women contestants, some pretty, some old, some even fat. He would kiss anyone. Ruth could hear the louder volume of a commercial and began to run water in the sink. When the show came back on she flicked the cigarette stub and most of the ash off her mother's plate and licked up the bits of potato. She worked her tongue fast and got as much as she could. When she got so close she could smell the ash she stopped.

The rest of the cleanup went smoothly. Scrape up the pieces of potato stuck to the fry pan. Check the salad bowl for vegetables or dressing. The salad bowl was the size of a Jacuzzi but Ruth's mother insisted on using it even for just the three of them; she liked the grain of the wood, she said, it reminded her of forests.

There was always a lot of dressing stuck to the big bowl and Ruth had to put her whole head into the bowl to get at the sides and bottom. Wouldn't it be great if she caught me like this, Ruth thought to herself, but the bowl was smooth and she licked fast so she never got caught.

By the time the game show ended Ruth was sponging the table. Her mother came in.

"What takes you so long?" she said. "I could finish in half the time." She clicked her nails on the table edge.

Ruth got out the Windex and sprayed the formica counters and swabbed them with a paper towel, knowing her mother liked this last step to get rid of the soap film. "See," she said, "I remembered the Windex."

Her mother looked at the Windex and the paper towel.

"Congratulations. I'm going outside while it's still light. I may swim a couple laps."

"So soon after dinner? Aren't you afraid you'll get a cramp?"

"Don't be ridiculous," said Ruth's mother. "I hardly ate anything. Besides, it's been a half hour."

She checked to see if Ruth had been sarcastic. "What are you going to do now?"

"Nothing," said Ruth. "My homework, I guess." It would be better if her mother were out in the pool splashing around where Ruth could hear her.

"Fine," said Ruth's mother. She flipped at the elastic of her bikini bottom like a teenager.

Once Ruth had tried to imitate her mother. When she was younger but already heavy she had stuffed herself into one of her mother's stretch bikinis and marched out to the pool where her mother was entertaining friends. Ruth pranced all around the pool perimeter wiggling her hips, believing that everyone would understand that she was doing an imitation of her mother. Brown ripe droppings from the date palm littered the corner of the yard but Ruth took careful mincing steps around the fruit. The smell of the dates decomposing in the sun bewildered her but she heard her mother say clearly, "Poor Ruth. She has so much trouble keeping to her diet. I do everything I can to help her, but just look at her. I try so hard not to pick on her."

There was no breeze falling down from the mountains that day and her mother's words hung in the heavy air. Without looking at her mother or her mother's friends Ruth grabbed a towel and turned toward the house. Walking fast made her hips jiggle, unintentionally now, and when she reached her room she was overwhelmed by a need to eat.

The memory of it could still make her hungry. Ruth switched off the light over the kitchen sink and moved quickly down the long corridor to her room. She opened the door and saw that there was a faint footprint in the dusting of talcum powder she had placed on the floor.

She knew that her mother had been in her room but she liked to have this kind of proof. Here was the imprint of a foot, a smallish foot with a good arch, bare and just to one side of the center of the powder. Ruth brushed the powder away and went to her desk and reached behind the books for the bag of cookies.

It was there with all six cookies intact. Sometimes Ruth would be sure she had hidden six cookies or two brownies or whatever, and when she went to the hiding place she would find five cookies or one brownie and she would feel crazy. This time she was pleased that all six cookies were there and she began to eat immediately. "Poor Ruth" kept echoing in her mind just as if her mother were still saying it.

Finishing the first cookie she reached for another and devoured it. Chewing rapidly, fighting against an urge to hiccup, Ruth began to feel a little better. By the fourth cookie, Ruth began to notice the soft slap-slap of her mother's arms hitting the water at regular intervals. Backstroke, her mother's favorite, her face-out-of-the-water-stroke, her watching-Ruth stroke.

Ruth went over to the window and looked down at the pool. Her mother was on her back and looking at Ruth's window. Ruth sensed that her mother could see her but in the changing light she didn't know how it was possible. Still Ruth could feel those eyes. She checked again. Yes, her mother was looking straight into the room.

Ruth waved. Her mother didn't wave back, or yell anything. Nothing. Couldn't her mother see her? Ruth waved again. Nothing. She stuck two fingers up and watched for a response. Nothing. She felt her heart begin to pound. She stuck her middle finger up.

Still nothing. She raised both arms and stuck up the middle finger of both hands. Nothing. The sun hung on the edge of the sky, a glittering ball shedding gold light on Ruth's skin, on her teeth. Ruth reached for another cookie and held it in her mouth and put her face in her window. Nothing. She began to chew the cookie and let crumbs fall all over. Now the sun was slicing in through the branches of the date palm but Ruth kept chewing and held her middle finger high in the air. She ate that cookie at her mother and then she ate the last cookie at her mother.

Slap, slap, slap. Her mother's backstroke flapped steadily up one side of the pool and down the other. Ruth stared. Without changing the position of her head she reached around and felt far back in her desk drawer for her emergency Junior Mints and bit open the box. She poured all the mints into her mouth and let her bulging face hang in the window. Slap, slap, slap. Ruth reached farther back in the drawer for the emergency licorice. Still there. She peeled a black strand off the main clump and balled it up into a mass and shoved it into her mouth. She let part of the strand hang out and she put her face right up to the glass. She reached back for another piece and stuffed that in too. She waved her arms with her middle fingers raised and leaned into the window. Slap, slap, slap.

The sun blanked out behind one of the mountains and the light in her room turned translucent and watery as it bounced up off the pool. She kept chewing the mass in her mouth and forced herself to try to swallow. Saliva mixed with licorice and mint and tasted like some kind of chemical, it tasted like chlorine. Gagging, Ruth reached for another rope of licorice and stuffed it into her mouth. Slap, slap, slap. She could feel the black stickiness spread over her mouth and chin. She chewed and chewed and chewed, growing invisible and more powerful every minute.

Like Mother, Like Daughter

by
Nicole Annesi

———— ⬤⬤⬤ ————

When I first decided to share my story I wanted to tell the tale of the great confusion and pain I endured for so many years during so many crucial points in a young girl's life. But, as I typed the words across the screen of my computer, I thought to myself, another sob story of a female blaming her family for the voids in her life. Then I realized my story was different. My family was not dysfunctional due to alcohol, my father did not beat us, no one was on drugs or unwed and pregnant. My family suffered from a problem that was health threatening, yes, but also common to over sixty percent of America today: We were a family with an eating disorder.

I grew up like any other normal (if I may use the abnormal term normal)— girl who patterned herself after her mother. I vacuumed alongside her Hoover with my Fisher Price Bubble Vac. I applied my Barbie make-up on her dressing table while she artistically streamed the vibrant colors across her eyelid in front of the bathroom vanity. I wanted to be like mom, in every sense.

Mom was a woman that was in demand. She worked as an office manager, kept a house that contained a husband, three boys and an impressionable young girl in control, and was constantly volunteering for any cause she thought was worthy (which was usually all of them). Mom was definitely a woman I wanted to be. I remember constantly following my mother around, like a little shadow. My Dad would always comment, "It figures I would have to have a backwards family, instead of Daddy's little girl and Mama's boys I got Mom's little clone and Daddy's boys." He was right though. I guess in a way I was obsessed with my mom, not in a crazy sense, but I admired my mother, I watched my mother, I copied my mother, and on occasions, I watched her even when she didn't know it.

I was seven years old the first time I was exposed to my mother's bulimia. It was after dinner one evening. I can recall her complaining because she ate too much that night. The meal is still quite vivid in my mind. We had a huge spread of Italian food, like we usually did on Sundays. After Mom and I cleared the table, our usual Sunday ritual, she quickly disappeared into the bathroom. I found nothing unusual about this, after all going to the bathroom was not an unusual act. What was unusual about these visits was that they became consistent. After each meal Mom would visit the bathroom and come out a few minutes later looking pale, yet refreshed. Once I tried following her in; it wasn't strange for me to go to the bathroom with Mom, after all we'd take baths together, dress together, and do the usual, intimate girl things. When I attempted to follow her, she'd stop me saying that she wanted to be alone. Alone. Mom wanted to be without me. At first I was offended. Then I got curious. She must be doing something that she didn't want me to see, or anyone for that matter. Dad sometimes would visit her in the bathroom too, but even he was rejected. Then I finally figured it out. She was doing something that I wasn't old enough to do yet, like wear real make-up or drink coffee. Yeah, that was it. Well like any curious little girl, I set myself out on a mission, a full-fledged sneak attack on Mom. Actually looking back on my plan, it was kind of funny. I can somewhat chuckle to myself about it because I remember the feeling inside. My stomach was knotted, butterflies were in there, but I wasn't nervous, I was determined, determined to see what it was that I couldn't do yet, determined to see what she didn't want me or anyone else to see. So after the dishes were cleared away that evening, I disappeared into the bathroom. I hid in the tub, behind the navy blue, opaque curtain. My only fear was that my intuition was wrong. What if Mom took sponge baths after dinner, or soaked her feet or something? What if I breathed too hard or had to sneeze, what if I coughed? While I was worrying, in came Mom. At first I didn't notice because of all the "what ifs," but like clockwork, in she came. I peered between the curtains to find my mother bent over the toilet, like she was going to get sick or something. And then I watched her do the most unusual thing. She placed a popsicle stick down her throat and made herself sick. How weird, I thought to myself. Mom comes in the bathroom every night to stick one of those doctor sticks down her throat! I wondered where she got those things. Maybe she stole them each time she took us kids to the doctors, or perhaps she saved the sticks from all the fudge ice cream bars we consumed.

Whatever it was, and however she confiscated these articles, that wasn't the question. The inquiry was why she did this. Why would my mother want to get rid of the wonderful dinners she so carefully prepared for us each night? The questions were continuously going through my mind that night after Mom had put me to bed. I remember looking up at her as she tucked me in. I wanted so much to ask her why she did that weird thing in the bathroom earlier, but I didn't want her to know that I was watching her. So it stayed with me, all the next day, the following night and so forth. I didn't dare discuss this with any of my friends. Besides, I wasn't going to tell them my mom makes herself sick every night; they might think I was weird or something.

Again, like any kid who was the least bit curious, I began to do some thinking myself. Maybe what my mother did was what all girls do. I knew when I got sick, afterwards my stomach would flatten out. I felt lighter. So one day after school I ate a bag of Pecan Sandies. I stuffed myself until I couldn't swallow. Afterwards I made my way to the upstairs bathroom and locked the door behind me. I turned on the faucet so that nothing could be heard. I lifted the toilet seat and crouched over the same way mom did. I had everything exactly the same, my position, the toilet, but I had no stick. How was I going to do this without a stick? Quickly I looked around me; shampoo bottles, razors, toothbrushes, nail files. Nail files, that was it. I'd use a nail file. And that was the beginning of my newfound project...

I wanted to see how flat I could get my stomach. Maybe I could get it as flat as Mom's was. That day I became a seven-year-old bulimic.

As a child I was never overweight, I was average, so my weight loss wasn't too noticeable, besides I played every sport there was imaginable. If my parents thought I was losing any weight, they probably attributed it to my constant activity.

Growing up with my habit wasn't too difficult for me, after all, this was like any other addiction, I thought, like smoking. I didn't do that, so making myself sick cancelled out any other habit that was common at my age. Actually, as a teenager I thought I was pretty good. I didn't smoke, do drugs or swear; I was a saint compared to the other girls I knew. So I didn't digest my food. I was skinny, the guys liked it, that was all that mattered at the time anyhow, guys. So I continued on with my instant "tummy-flattener" sometimes I thought of marketing my instant weight loss plan. I would watch the girls at school struggle with their weight, eating morsels of food at lunch, never participating in that taboo ritual, dessert. I would giggle to myself because I had the best of both worlds. I could have my cake and eat it too, literally.

Looking back now, I am amazed at the human body. The system really can take a lot of abuse. Anytime I felt a little full, I forced my body to do the most abusive thing, I reversed the digestion process. I thank my body for sticking in there with me. I had read articles about bulimics who have had their esophagus explode because of all the damage. I recall thinking those were extreme cases, someone who must get sick constantly, all day long, at every meal. One day it happened to me.

I had just returned from my last class of the college semester. I celebrated by gorging down an entire box of Ho-Ho's. I quickly ran to the bathroom to withdraw any of my body's festivities. When I began my usual ritual, it felt different. It did not feel familiar, it felt foreign. I started to experience a burning from the bottom of my throat. When I looked down at the toilet, to my surprise I found blood instead of the Ho-Ho's. The amount was the frightening part. I had brought up blood before, but not in the amount that was here before me. Suddenly, my mouth was bringing up more blood; the amount was beginning to scare me. I started to panic. I knew I couldn't call anyone or show anybody, they'd want an explanation. I was getting very anxious, I knew something major was wrong and I knew I needed some help. I ran to my mother who was in the living room watching television and I showed her my hands that were covered in a bright color of red. She looked at me horrified and asked me what I had done. I actually didn't know until I spoke with my doctor at the hospital. My mother called an ambulance for me and cleaned off my hands and mouth to the best of her nervous ability. The ambulance was quite efficient I thought and quick too. I had made a mental note to tell one of the higher-ups at the hospital after I found out what exactly was wrong with me.

The people that were around me were amazing, it was like they were all trying to save me from some horrible trauma. I still didn't know exactly what I had done to myself; my mind was telling me it was a blood vessel or vein that I had popped. What I didn't realize then was that people were trying to save me from a serious trauma. I had brought severe damage to my esophagus. Later the doctor had informed me of what I was doing to my body. The constant loss of food was causing a strain on my body. The acids that I was bringing up were literally tearing away at the tubes in my throat, causing them to weaken. What had happened to me was the conclusion to the story. It was inevitable, the doctor told me. At the rate I was going, it was going to happen sooner or later.

My secret was out, I thought. All those people who thought I was naturally thin are now going to know my secret. That was my initial thought. Then I worried about not going to the Genesis concert that Friday. My thought process was absurd, the things that were bothersome to me were really kind of sick. My doctor must have thought that when I got sick I lost some brain cells too. The real problem, he said, was my not admitting that I had a disease. I felt like an alcoholic. Everyone watched me constantly; instead of making sure an alcoholic didn't drink, they did just the opposite, they made sure I ate. My family was on constant surveillance with me, my friends as well. It got to the point where I was stared at by anyone who thought they knew me. I began to get ashamed. I wasn't allowed to transfer to another college because my family was afraid I would start up again. I began to gain weight…

All this time my mother remained silent. Sometimes I wanted to shake her because I knew she still got sick every once in a while. You'd think after what happened to me she'd stop, she didn't. I know this because she still did her "after dinner routine." I also knew the look that she carried on herself afterwards. It was the same look she had fifteen years before, the same look I had each time I visited the bathroom. The feeling of satisfaction, like you beat your own body to digestion. It's a sick way. I wanted to talk to my mom about the entire thing, I wanted her to know I watched her. I wanted her to know how impressionable little girls are, and how she was my hero. I even wanted to ask her how she started. Did she get it from her mom too?

It never happened. I was never scolded for my bulimia, just misunderstood.

Everyone thought I was missing a couple screws so they were really gentle on me. I never minded it. I got away with more, so it was to my advantage.

I now live on my own. I'm graduating from college and my bulimia is behind me, everyday, stalking me. I'm like everyone else, all those people that I snickered at in high school. I'm sitting next to them everyday, eating my morsel of food and skipping that taboo ritual that we call dessert. I look at the skinny girls who eat junk food, cheeseburgers and such at lunch. I can always tell which ones are really, truly skinny and which ones aren't. Those are the ones who disappear shortly after eating. I wonder if they watched their moms too. I wonder if they are in a group of some sort. I wonder if I'll ever reign again physically. Until I do, I remain content with watching what I eat, counting calories and fat grams. I never blame my mom though; I realize now that she is suffering far more than I ever had to. In a sense, the rupture of my esophagus was a gift; it allowed me to have a second chance. Actually, I'm learning that there is no easy way out. I hope for one thing though, in my next life if there really is one, I want only one thing: a fast metabolism.

Letter to My Mother from the Volcano

by
Karen Erlichman

———— ⬡⬡⬡ ————

16 August 1990, Day One:

Dear Mom:

I am twenty-eight years old. Yesterday the doctor I work for molested me. He grabbed me and touched me and warned me that he's after me. "You better watch out," he said, his scratchy beard against my cheek, "because I'm a single man now." He wiped himself with my body and walked out. I feel so dirty and damaged. My heart is pounding in my palms like a cat's soft, frantic heartbeat. Weak hands and legs, I sit with my nausea and terror in the empty office, waiting for the rage to kick in. One day later, it hasn't. The rage is still simmering in my belly, in the depths of my forgotten wounds.

I wanted to call you and tell you, Mom, but I didn't know what to say. I can't face your silence. If you can't get back what he took from me, there's no point in my calling you. I imagine calling you, recounting "the incident," only to hear your birdlike voice at the end of the phone. "Oh, honey, he didn't mean anything by it! He was just complimenting you. He probably feels comfortable with you." Is that how *you* felt when your doctor touched your nine-year-old body with his cold, hairless hands? Is that how you felt when your mother shamed you for telling her what he did to you? I don't get it; why am I angrier at you than I am at the doctor?

For twenty-eight years I have learned to "Be strong, act like nothing's wrong. Shake it off. Get back in there!" I tried to go back to work today. It's only been twenty-four hours; I feel as though my heart and body are responding to every act of human violation I have ever witnessed in my life. Each act is like a pinch, a touch, a grab, a slap. Each memory is a hissing, nasty word: stupid bimbo bitch bossy know-it-all. Each memory flashes in my thoughts like a dirty photograph smudged with fingerprints and dust. Each voice echoes in a whisper inside my head. My stomach is burning; my hands are shaking and my head is tight. It's been twenty-four hours and I'm waiting to feel better. I'm still waiting.

After twenty-eight years I've found my body. So has somebody else, and

96

they're trying to take it away from me. I found it buried under the trash. I buried it there myself with years of food and hatred. This morning when I got dressed for work, I tried to bury it again under my baggiest clothes. Maybe he won't notice I have a body if I hide it. Maybe my breasts will be hidden underneath the folds of my blue cotton sweater. Maybe I'll cut them off.

I know this is not only the grown-up Karen talking. Baby Karen is here too. She's sucking her thumb and holding her ear, tracing the edge of her ear with her little finger. She's looking for a hiding place too, but somehow knows that the era of hiding is over. I feel like the woman in the pantyhose ad, you know the one where there is a trail of mirror images behind her like an acid trail. Except, in my case, each successive image is a younger and younger Karen.

College Karen: the hippie child with long hair and Central American print skirts with bells on the belts and multiple beaded earrings. High school Karen: eyes red and glassy from a recently smoked joint in the school parking lot, wavy black hair falling around her face and shoulders, clothes too tight, fingernails painted brick red. Twelve-year-old Karen: loud and talkative, head down, legs crossed, arms folded, too much make-up, too much hair spray, too much noise talks too much wants too much eats too much. I can't get much younger than twelve. Where is Baby Karen? Where is eleven-year-old Karen on the day of her first period, sitting on the toilet staring at her bare thighs and the bloody tissue? The bathroom is dark, and I am calling out for my mother who every day for the last few months has asked, "Didja get it yet?" I got it Mom; I guess I'm a woman now.

After all this, I still haven't brought up the food. Oy vey, the food. Dios mio, oy gottinyu, god help me, the food. Remember when we would go to Gino's in Wayne on Lancaster Avenue? We'd buy a barrel of chicken (finger lickin' good!) and eat nearly half the barrel in the car on the way home. I remember your bananas and skim milk diet. I remember Dr. Atkins, Weight Watchers, behavior modification, liquid protein; I remember your hidden stashes of cookies over the oven, in the dining room bureau; I remember being too short to reach the lock on the kitchen closet, so I'd find a broom or stick to poke it open. Six packs of Fritos, bags of Chips Ahoy, Oreos, raisins, Mallomars, Pop Tarts, frozen Sara Lee cakes (why defrost it? Just eat it frozen; scrape off the icing and put it back. Nobody will know you did it.)

In high school, I'd come home from school, smoke a joint and make myself a toasted peanut butter sandwich on whole wheat bread. I'd spread that peanut butter on *really thick*; so that when it toasted, the peanut butter would ooze out over the edges of the bread. Then I'd make a big tall glass of coffee with lots of milk and Sweet 'n Low (of course), sit in front of the TV and munch out. The hot gooey peanut butter, the coarse toast, the creamy coffee; it's all about texture. And the show's not over yet, so let's make another sandwich! There's still a couple of hours 'til dinner.

I have to eat in front of my co-workers every day, because we have lunch during case conferences. The sound of unwrapping foil or plastic wrap is enough to send me into a silent Pavlovian frenzy. My eyes dart around the table to inspect and covet each person's meal. I watch the nurse dive into her burrito. She adds a spoonful of guacamole and sour cream to the top of the burrito after each bite. I have dutifully and gratefully heated my chicken and vegetables in the microwave, and I pierce a zucchini slice with my fork. "That looks too healthy!" they usually remark as I eat. The doctor always brings some kind of sandwich with yellow mustard; the nutritionist bring gourmet leftovers from the night before, Jambalaya or curried chicken or marinated pasta salad. I've got everyone's number.

Every morning I stand naked in front of the full-length mirror and touch my body to remind myself it's mine. Today I am smaller than I've been in years, but I still wake up and feel like I'm the size of New Jersey. I think shame is the cornerstone of our family. "It doesn't matter if you're comfortable; it only matters if you look good," says Grandma, urging me desperately to buy a girdle. "Honey, that hair on your upper lip, it's showing." "I think if you lost some weight you'd feel a whole lot better." Mom, remember when you and Dad offered to give me a dollar for every pound, if I'd only stick to a diet? Now there's a good middle class solution for obesity!

If only I knew how all these things were connected.

Day Two:

I tried to go back to work yesterday, I really tried. But after being there for nearly an hour, I began to weep. Pains moved across my chest like thunder and lightning; I could barely breathe. The spit in my mouth felt slimy and warm. I talked to my supervisor. She said, "Go home, take care of yourself, rest. I'll see you on Monday." I wanted to crawl into a corner of her office and cry. I scooped up my things and bolted for the bus. What is happening to my body today? I ate my usual breakfast and still wasn't full. Maybe it's because my girlfriend ate waffles for breakfast as I nibbled at the green food. But later I ate my usual lunch and felt quite full. I don't get it. Today I made a list of things I can do to take care of myself:

> Take a hot bath.
> Read a book.
> Make a phone call.
> Get a massage.
> Take a nap.
> Write.
> Paint my toenails.
> Go for a walk.
> Do nothing.

Too bad I never learned how to make myself throw up, I think. A good puke would hit the spot right now. Even at times when I've had the flu and felt god awful, that sense of relief after throwing up was worth it all. Especially at times like this when I feel "bar mitzvah full." There's a sign of a true food addict: I've got little phrases which refer to the different levels of fullness after eating. God help me.

Fortunately, I don't have to deal with the doctor for at least three days. The thought of looking him in the eye terrifies me. I want to spit in his face, slam my hand into his glasses, scream at him, throw Betadine all over his starched white jacket. Rachel suggests we graffiti the hospital, perform guerilla theatre, warn every woman we know that he's armed with a pulse, and dangerous.

Anyway, Mom, the weather's here. Wish we were beautiful.

Love,

Karen

Sisters

by
Dorothy Stone

————— ⦻ —————

Seeking first-person nonfiction narratives about women and food.
—*Classified ad in* The Women's Review of Books

Just what I've been looking for—a chance to write about myself and food. How hard can it be? I'm a woman, I eat food, and all I need to write nonfiction is to describe a slice of my lifelong relationship with food.

But wait—the narrative is supposed to be in the "first person." How can I tell this story without telling about my sister? Would it be OK to write about her in the third person? Or maybe we can tell our story together—after all, the ad doesn't specify "first person *singular.*"

So here's our first-person plural narrative: about Doll, Dot, and food.

Doll: I've always had a healthy appetite. My mother told me I was so eager for milk in the hospital that a nurse called me a "little snapping turtle." I enjoy eating all kinds of food—Vietnamese, Ethiopian, Italian, you name it. I love going to new restaurants, especially if they serve cuisine of a nationality I've never tried before. I pride myself on not being a picky eater.

Dot: Food scares me. I'm less and less able to force myself even to enter a supermarket. And when I do get inside, I feel overwhelmed by a sense of boredom and futility. Not carrots again! Not prepackaged burritos again!

When I cook for company, I find it hard to notice what I'm eating, to really taste it. I haven't invited anyone over for dinner in years. And the thought of cooking for myself somehow manages to panic me and seem dull at the same time.

Doll: I enjoy cooking for company. I'm pretty careful, so I can follow most recipes, as long as they don't involve any tricky techniques like deep-fat frying.

Dot: I don't actually know how to make the most basic things—roast beef or a Thanksgiving turkey. My problem is partly time—finding the time to cook is a chore. Any time spent preparing food feels wasted.

Doll: I got a crock pot and a microwave oven to help save time.

Dot: That crock pot stuff is usually pretty desiccated. And sometimes even putting a Lean Cuisine in the microwave seems too hard—I want it *now*.

I often feel overwhelmed by the desire for a particular food. For chocolate mousse, for peanut butter on an apple, for lamb chops.

Doll: I usually eat what I want, assuming it's available. If I have a craving, I usually give in to it.

Dot: When I do that, I tend to binge. I go through the stage of enjoyment, on to the point where I can't eat any more. To avoid that, I sometimes try what I think of as "preventive eating": I eat more than I really want of something like broccoli, especially at a meal, in hopes that it will protect me from craving a snack later. Sometimes that works, but sometimes it's as if I've got two different stomachs: the broccoli goes into one and even fills it up, but that doesn't keep the other one from craving Reese's Pieces two minutes later.

Doll: I know a lot about nutrition, and I mostly eat foods that are good for me—I eat a lot of chicken and seafood, I almost never eat chocolate, I eat whole-grain bread.

Dot: I don't eat chocolate either, but that's because I'm such a chocoholic that I had to go cold turkey. I allow myself to eat it only at Christmas and Easter, but lately I've been interpreting those holidays pretty loosely. Every time I have some, I lust after it for days afterward. Let's change the subject.

Doll: My weight has had long periods of stability. It was stable through most of my thirties: just going up five pounds in the winter and down again in the summer.

Dot: I've gained fifty pounds in the last twenty-five years. And that wasn't even gradual; it involved some big swings. Several times I've gained twenty pounds in a year. I was bulimic and anorexic in high school.

Doll: I just about reached my full height when I was twelve, and I weighed only six pounds more by the time I was sixteen. I was a Homecoming Princess my senior year in high school. At my twentieth reunion, I weighed only two pounds more than when I was nineteen.

Dot: I gained twenty pounds my freshman year in high school and twenty-five my freshman year in college.

I worry constantly about my weight and how my body looks.

Doll: I believe it's more important to be physically fit than to worry about your weight. Three times a week I do aerobics and work out on weight machines.

Dot: I have a desk job and do very little walking. Walking feels like a waste of time, even though I know it's good for me. It's boring: I don't like being alone with my thoughts. And that aerobic and Nautilus stuff is just a displaced diet—just another way to force your body into what other people want.

Doll: But I like doing aerobics. I get absorbed by the music, the movement. And lifting heavier and heavier weights really gives me a sense of progress.

Dot: Haven't you made enough progress? You've got a graduate degree, a professional job where everybody admires you. My job is a constant source of stress. I feel I'm usually struggling in vain to balance what other people want against what I need—and I still have a lot of trouble even figuring out what I need or have a right to.

Doll: I've gotten more assertive. A lot of times it turns out that if you stand up to people they back off.

Dot: You know, we've gotten away from the topic of food.

Doll: But aren't stress and self-confidence tied in with it? So is body image. I know this sounds strange, but I feel affection for a lot of my clothes. I've got a good sense of color and line—a bit unconventional, but so what? I've got my own style.

Dot: I've got a closet full of clothes, but most of them are too small. Yet I feel that, if I give them away, I'll never lose weight. Or, if I do lose weight, I'll have to spend money on replacements.

It's been a long time since anybody's looked at me twice anyway. I've been in only one romantic relationship in my whole life that was mutually committed. Otherwise either the guy didn't care, or I didn't care, or we both didn't care. Devastating or embarrassing or wistful.

Doll: I've been married to the same man for over twenty years, someone who really cares about me and respects me.

Dot: Good for you. You know, the ad said this was supposed to be a *narrative*. What I can't stand about my life is that it feels as if nothing ever changes—I'm stuck in the same old traps. This isn't a film; it's a still photograph. What if this isn't what the editor wants? I feel guilty.

Doll: I wish I could help you.

Both: Let's go eat together.

The Scream

by
Rochelle Natt

I feel as if I'm standing on a bridge, eyes bulging, mouth wide open. All I can do is watch. No one will listen to me. I'm only ten. My big sister, Heidi, is eighteen, and Tina, my middle sister, is seventeen. They're so grown up that they hardly speak to each other. Mom's so busy talking that she never listens to me or anyone. And what if, for a moment, someone did stop to hear me? What would I say?

Should I tell them that Heidi locks herself in her room so she can eat candy bars? I know because she stuffs the wrappers in her pockets, stops up the toilet with them or burns them in her metal waste paper basket. You can smell chocolate on her, but Mom never seems to notice.

Tina is the opposite. At meals, she cuts her food into slivers and pushes it around her plate. To keep herself from eating, she chews gum all the time. When she thinks no one's looking, she hides food in her napkin. Afterwards, she goes out to the yard and buries it or something. Stray cats hang around crying and clawing at the screen door.

Tina used to eat the right amount until she saw Heidi putting on all that weight. Tina says, "What if I suddenly can't stop eating? I'd die before I let myself get like Heidi." I get scared Tina's really dying. She's so weak that sometimes she faints. On weekends, she sleeps the whole day. I saw Mom put a mirror to Tina's mouth to check that she's still breathing.

Like Tina, I'll get as fat as Heidi. Sometimes I don't eat for a whole day. My stomach growls like a mean dog. Then I get scared that I'll get pencil-thin and weak like Tina, and I eat and eat till I have to wear my skirt unbuttoned. But when I see Heidi, her face red, huffing while she walks, her thick legs apart as if she's going to pee standing the way we do behind bushes on long car trips, I can't eat at all.

Mom used to be plump. She says after having me so late in life, she never

103

was able to take the weight off. She's always telling me, "I never looked a day over twenty until you came along."

"So who asked you to have me?" I say.

She doesn't answer. She only talks about what *she* wants to. She shows me pictures of her and my sisters from before I was born. They all wore the same dresses. "Everyone thought we were sisters. You should have heard the 'ohs' and 'ahs.'" Mom sighs. "Now we've broken apart like poppy beads. Nobody ever notices me."

"You could sew a dress for you and me."

"It wouldn't be the same," she says.

That was before Mom went on her diet to make herself look young again. The refrigerator is almost empty except for stuff like low-fat cottage cheese and marinated artichoke hearts. She eats so many carrots that she turns orange. "Buy some real food," I tell her, but she never listens to me. My sisters scream their heads off. Finally, she gives in. Once the food's back in the house, she can't resist it. Every morning she's on the scale crying.

Now she gets the idea that smoking will make her thin. With the cigarettes, she can drink coffee all day and just eat a little dinner. She smells like smoke, even from far away. She wears my sisters' pedal pushers, cinch belts, cardigans buttoned down the back, dickie collars...My sisters won't walk down the street with her anymore.

Even though the cigarettes make Mom cough and her voice sounds gravelly, her friends say, "You look so well." If Heidi's around, they add, "You could pass for sisters." Mom giggles and thanks them, but Heidi's face turns red and her hands tighten into fists.

Then Heidi gained so much weight. Mom said she wouldn't buy her clothes unless she lost it. Now she has to wear Mom's old clothes. Mom doesn't mind buying new clothes for Tina. "Tina could be a model," Mom says.

But Heidi keeps getting fatter. Her belly is so big she has to stand back from the sink to wash her hands. Now she can only wear mumus. Her boyfriend broke up with her. Mom kept yelling at her, "He's left a loaf in the oven," and Heidi banged the door in her face and wouldn't come out of her room.

Today Mom takes Heidi to the doctor. She drags me along, but makes me stay in the waiting room while Heidi gets examined. I wish Tina was here. Maybe the doctor could see she's sick. What'll he say about Heidi?

After a long time, Mom and Heidi go into the front room where the doctor tells you what's the matter. I hear Mom's booming voice. "At least I don't have to worry about becoming a grandmother. I'm too young for that." Why does she have to talk so loud? The people in the waiting room eye the door. "It's the strangest thing," Mom goes on. "My middle daughter chews all day, but can't keep weight on. The big one barely puts a crumb in her mouth and look at the size of her."

When Heidi comes out, she keeps her head down and walks as fast as she can. Just as she reaches the outer door, Mom announces to everyone, "He said to take her to a gland man."

Instead, when we get home Mom gives Heidi a pack of cigarettes. "I'm at the end of my wits. Try a cigarette. Smoking will take the weight right off you."

It's 3:00 a.m. I smell smoke. Heidi screams. I rush to her bedroom. Her curtains are on fire. Mom runs in, throws water on them and starts hollering, "What's wrong with you? You're old enough to know how to smoke a cigarette!"

Is Mom nuts? Can't she see the unopened pack of cigarettes on Heidi's dresser? There are matches all around the waste basket. And candy wrappers half-burned. Heidi stands there trembling. With every tremble, the rolls of fat on her jiggle. I smell the smoke. Tina looks as if she's about to laugh. Instead she passes out. My mother yells, "Get the rubbing alcohol."

All I can do is stand here, my mouth open while Heidi sobs and Mom keeps slapping at Tina's wrists, her face. "Wake up! Wake up!" Mom shrieks. Even when it's all over and I go downstairs to my room, I smell the smoke. It's late, but I can't go to bed. I'm afraid to close my eyes. I feel a scream rising up my throat.

In Father's House

by
Eileen Kostiner

Marilyn balanced several plastic containers, a milk bottle and a large plate of cheesecake on her way upstairs to her sister's bedroom. She didn't like fetching and carrying for Joan. They were too close in age, only a year apart. Joan was the dancer, the smart one, and she looked like their father, so, naturally, Joan was his favorite. When he spoke he always looked at Joan. He said someday Joan would write his biography because she inherited his gift for words.

Marilyn was born lean and hard. She was the athlete, but no one in the family put any value on athletics. At least she would never have a weight problem like Joan. Joan was getting heavy, but Marilyn wouldn't tell her. She had purposely chosen the most caloric leftovers to bring to her sister. Now, because she was so much thinner, Marilyn was sure she was the prettier of the two with her large, dark eyes and the dimple on her chin. Her new hairstyle, long and wavy, was like Lily Marlowe's.

"Hurry. I don't want anyone to see you." Joan yanked Marilyn into her room and locked the door.

"If you're so hungry, why did you leave the table?" Marilyn asked, arranging the plastic containers on her sister's bureau.

"Why? Because I was choking. How can you sit at that table with what's going on? It's disgusting!" Joan mimed being sick to her stomach.

This postprandial gorge on her bed was becoming a Saturday night ritual. It was the night Lily and John Marlowe came for dinner. Lily was beautiful. Even Joan liked looking at her. She dressed to ravish men. Tonight she had worn a white, diaphanous blouse and tight, black velvet pants. Slender as her name, Lily had no appetite for food. Without kitchen help, her mother was too busy with platters in the pantry to witness a typical meal with the Marlowes. Joan saw. Her father was in love with Lily, had been for three years. Her husband loved her too, enough to put up with the triangle because he liked to see Lily happy. He played his part by acting oblivious, or he would retreat into one of his headaches.

106

"Did you see what Lily did tonight?" Joan asked Marilyn as she pushed a hunk of garlic bread into her mouth.

"She was looking straight at Daddy. Then she stuck that long, red Lily tongue out of her red, Lily mouth, and slowly licked her lips. That's when he put his hand on her lap underneath her napkin."

"Oh, he was just being friendly. I didn't know what happened. All of a sudden, you started choking." Marilyn watched her sister eat, oblivious to the wreckage of her room, clothes inside-out, empty bags of snack food scattered about. "How can you live in this mess?" she asked.

"That's the question. 'How can I live in this mess?' " I don't know who I hate more, Mom for being such a simp and putting up with it or Dad who dares act it out right under her nose. When I tell Mom she gets angry with me! She won't believe it."

Joan finished eating a greasy piece of beef Wellington and went to her camp trunk, bringing up from its depths a kitchen carving knife. She carried it to her bed as if she held in her hands the only possible way out. Sensuously, she ran her finger along its newly-sharpened edge, gleaming malevolently.

Wide-eyed, Marilyn watched the rebellion moving across her sister's features. "You aren't planning to kill him?"

"I've thought of it. Again and again, I've plotted it all out, how I would plunge this knife right between his shoulder blades while he is sitting at his desk. I can hear the thud of his head as he slumps forward. I've even thought of how to bury his body. But right now, it would be an ugly botch. I'm not strong enough yet. Probably when I'm fifteen." Joan shoved in a piece of cheesecake.

"I'm not helping you." Marilyn stated flatly. "Mom says Daddy just has a complex about friendship. That's why he has to see the Marlowes every week."

"Three times a week," Joan broke in. "And dinner on Saturday."

"Besides," Marilyn continued, "I like Lily. She listens to me when I talk. No one else does. And she's so beautiful. When I'm grown up, I'd like to be just like her and have two men in love with me."

"The trouble with you is you're a simp just like Mom is. Sometimes, I think Mom really knows what's going on, that she hates Daddy as much as I do. I saw her pouring oil on his food when he was on his diet. That's why he never lost any weight. Anyway, she's afraid of divorce, so we are all stuck." Joan finished the cheesecake with her second glass of milk.

"Have you had enough, or do you want me to smuggle in something else?" Marilyn offered.

"I never have enough. It quiets the beast. Unless I keep it well fed, it gnaws and gnaws at my insides. Someday, even if I don't use the knife, I'll find a way to kill him." Joan lapsed into the solitary comfort of her vengeful dream.

Accustomed to her sister's sudden withdrawals, Marilyn let herself out of the bedroom, closing the door to what more and more seemed a cage.

My Sister's Problem with Bulimia and Me

by
Margaret McMullan

———— ⟨⟨⟨⟩ ————

Christmas Eve two years ago, my sister Catherine was lying in her bed in the next room. The doors were open between our rooms and she was telling me all about this guy she had just broken up with. Hours before, she had eaten a plate of Christmas cookies, an entire sheet of homemade toffee our neighbors had brought over, and most of the leftover cornbread our father used for his oyster stuffing. She said she felt sick and I thought, well of course you feel sick. She wondered out loud whether there would be any other men in her life. She wondered if she would ever be able to feel anything for anybody again. Then she got up, went into the bathroom, and I listened as she made herself throw up.

It is one of the saddest, loneliest sounds—the sound of someone retching late at night—and it was even sadder that night, a night when Catherine and I usually sat up listening to my mother wrapping presents downstairs.

I heard the toilet flush and then I heard her start all over again. She has done this before, I thought. A real pro. I lay in my bed just then thinking of what I could do to help. She'll be cold. I'll bring her a robe. And I got her robe and quietly opened the door.

"Cat?" I whispered. The room smelled bad.

She was at the sink washing her hands. She was wearing a t-shirt from the Museum of Contemporary Art that said *What will it do to you?* on the back.

"Don't come in. Leave me alone. Leave me *alone!*" As she screamed at me, I saw the flash of her well-manicured red fingernails. Her hands were laced with vomit.

When she came out, she said she was sorry. She said she hadn't known that would happen. Did that mean that sometimes she had it planned? I listened as she got back into her bed. She asked me how long I was going to be at home this time, why did I have to leave the day after Christmas? And when was I planning on coming home again?

I wanted to yell at her. For crying out loud, I wanted to say, there are a zillion holes in the ozone layer. People are starving in New York and other third world nations. AIDS is wiping out a population equivalent to the size of a good-sized country, and you—my own flesh and blood sister—are spitting up everything you eat. But I didn't tell her any of this. Her voice that night was tired and sad and desperate.

"Just go to bed," I said. I remember hoping the sounds of reason and common sense in my voice would make their way across our rooms. In my mind I made commands: Don't think about it anymore. Try not to think about food. I knew this was hard. I knew that to Catherine everything was food.

"Think of Christmas," I said.

I have known about my sister's eating disorder for six years. She says it started when we were kids. We would come home and eat saltines and dry cereal because my mother didn't believe in buying junk food. It was 1965 in Jackson, Mississippi, and we were the only children with a mother who had such beliefs. Catherine figured out a way around her. She started a game called Visiting. We would walk up and down Northover Drive, knock on somebody's door, introduce ourselves and say, "We're visiting you." They in turn would invite us in and feed us in exchange for our small talk. Our goal: junk food. The people who let us in were mostly the old and lonely widows in wheelchairs—the maids and the younger wives tended to ignore us unless they knew our mother. We got peppermint stick ice cream, vanilla wafers, and once the old lady in the wheelchair at the corner—the one with the big black lab tied out front—served us chocolate-covered cherries.

When we moved to Chicago my sister and I attended a Catholic all girls school. After a year or two of bake sales, mother/daughter lunches, spring fashion shows, and dances at the neighboring all boys school, Catherine and her group of friends developed a pattern. Starving themselves for that month's event, they lived on Tab, pressed turkey and carrots for a week, skipping the Eucharist bread at mass. (Later Catherine would tell me that it wasn't because she worried about the extra calories the "body of Christ" would cost her, but because the sweet bread that the nuns made was so good, she would crave more.)

Catherine and her friends would inevitably get hungry and they would reward their weight loss with their own bake sale. Those sales always came right after a week of starving for a spring fashion show or a dance. Hungry, my sister and her friends would buy up all the cookies and brownies they had brought for the sale. They would sit on the steps leading up to the nuns' quarters, near the chapel outside the cafeteria, and with relief and ceremony, they would finally eat.

She started throwing up later. In graduate school, maybe. She's shy about the details. After she received her MBA, she got a job at a good brokerage firm in New York. She was very thin then, but not "anorexic thin." She looked good, maybe a little tired and tense, but wasn't that how most women with MBAs from the University of Chicago looked in 1986?

She jogged a lot. Eight to ten miles a day. Then she fell and hurt her knee and she says that's when things really got bad. She worried that since she couldn't run, her weight wouldn't "even out." She was scared to eat because she couldn't run it off, but then she would get anxious and restless and depressed over her condition—her leg was in a cast and she hobbled around for six months on crutches—and she would sit alone in her apartment, pouring over investment reports and Wall Street printouts and eat whole bags of cookies and brownies. I often imagine my sister when she was alone in her room that year, feeling full and nauseated and guilty afterwards. When she called me back then, her voice was always quick. Hyper. Later, she told me she didn't tell me about her eating problems then because she was embarrassed and she figured I wouldn't understand. I wonder if I would have understood. I probably would have told her to chill out, order a pizza, and read a book. Only now do I realize that she had no one to talk to that year she was living alone in New York.

When she called me in Chicago she would ask me what I was doing. And then, before I could start, she would tell me everything she had been doing, as though she were trying to figure something out. She would say, laughing, that she had eaten a lot that day. "God, I'm such a pig." But there was nothing unusual about her saying that. This is what Catherine always told me. It was almost a game: she would always be disgusted with herself and I would contradict her.

I often thought what my sister needed was a man. Someone to compliment her, take her out and feed her. But she kept going on these disastrous dates and I got to wondering: is it them or her? She described men in terms of desserts: He's just like a big piece of chocolate cake. That meant she wanted him, but he was to be avoided. But I also knew that if he persisted, if he took her to dinner, told her that she was beautiful, kissed her a certain way, there would be one night of "bingeing." But, like the food my sister consumed, these guys were just a temporary fix.

I often thought my sister overate because she was lonely. The puzzle suddenly made sense—she was trying to fill the void in her life, and then, realizing what she had done, she got rid of it all, ran twelve miles the following day, and started starving all over again. It was not fair of me to be angry with my sister because of a problem she had with food. But I couldn't help getting mad when I put the pieces together: moderation was not in her vocabulary during those years, nor was responsibility.

I have met other women like my sister, and I often wonder why *I* didn't have an eating disorder. Don't I care enough about the way I look? Having "problems with food" has become a mark for women—a badge. At parties these women refuse desserts and announce to everyone in hearing distance, "I'm bulimic. My system just can't handle sweets." They never blame themselves. Their *systems* are at fault—not them. For a long time, I was angry and a little jealous of my sister. She was just like all those other women. She was skinny, but she would not accept the horrible consequences of *how* she had gotten to be that skinny.

Everything changed when Catherine moved to Chicago and started having problems with her teeth. She went to a dentist. The hygienist took one look at her, closed the door, and as she flossed my sister's teeth, she told my sister in a near whisper all about her own food disorder and the havoc it had wreaked in her mouth—the acid from her own vomit had decayed the enamel on her teeth and they all needed recapping.

"It looks as though you might have the same problem," she told my sister, throwing away the bloody string of floss.

"I don't know if I'll ever have a normal relationship with food," Catherine told me later that night on the phone. I remember thinking she sounded dazed, as though she were coming out of a dream.

Then her eyes started getting bad. They would turn red and puffy without warning. An eye doctor said it was a common problem among anorexic women. Her problem was caused by a severe vitamin B12 deficiency that could cause blindness. In other words, malnutrition.

"Malnutrition?" I yelled into the phone when she told me the diagnosis. I could no longer be the faithful sister who just sat and listened. "Look Catherine, you are not a four-year-old in Indonesia. You're a thirty-two-year-old stockbroker in Chicago, Illinois, USA. You shouldn't have these problems."

I listened to her breathing. I knew I had said the wrong thing.

"I'm sorry Cat, but I just don't get it."

"Never mind," she said. I could barely hear her voice. She seemed a long way off that night.

Catherine bought herself a new $90 electric toothbrush and an armful of self-help books. She had a complete physical and the doctor confirmed that she was anemic. She bought cookbooks and a subscription to *Eating Well*. She watched "The Karen Carpenter Story" on TV, and she talked to me because I stopped yelling.

I sent her hotline numbers for people with eating disorders, pamphlets I picked up from booths at health fairs, and articles I cut out of women's magazines.

At lunch or dinner, I found myself staring at a piece of chicken or a heap of potatoes, wondering how my sister faced her food. What did she think? Will this be enough? No. It *won't* be enough. I will want more. It will be so hard to stop once I get started so I'll make it easy on myself. I won't get started. I won't eat any of it. Was this the scenario my sister had to confront three times daily?

I sent her recipes that would improve her red blood cell count. I told her she shouldn't call her binges binges, because her body simply craved food.

"If you eat right you won't want to eat all at once," I said. "You're just not eating enough regularly." I always worried if what I told her was the right thing to say and if it was true.

The psychiatrist was Catherine's idea. After the first session, she called me and I could tell by the sound of her voice that she was trying hard not to cry.

"I asked her about self-help books." She sniffed. "She said they only help one person—the person who wrote them."

"I like this woman," I said, laughing. "Did she help any?"

"I don't know," she said. "This whole shrink thing just seems so self-indulgent."

"Look," I said. "It's not like you're running off to Mexico to have a mud bath."

She took a deep sigh.

"Yeah, but I feel like I'm in AAA."

"That's AA," I said.

I could hear her smile and I wished more than anything that I was with her.

"I don't want to see someone for help," she said all of a sudden. "I don't want her to tell me how it all goes back to Mom or Dad or my childhood or bed-wetting or whatever. This is *my* problem. I just don't know what to do about it."

I suddenly had a flash of all the food that my sister had consumed over the years—the Sara Lee cheesecakes and brownies half thawed, the chocolate chip cookies and the fudge from school bake sales, the fruit pastries and the dinner rolls left over from my mother's luncheons, the turkey stuffing that she would pick at while we did the Thanksgiving or Christmas dishes. It was as though I was finally watching my sister digest all this food. She wasn't spitting it up anymore. And she was going to feel full and uncomfortable for a while, but she would know now not to do this again. She was making herself responsible for what she had eaten, and that seemed like everything to me right then.

"You're going to be all right, you know," I told her. I had said this before, but this time I believed it. "You are."

Now it's as though she has been through a drug re-hab. She will call to tell me she's in trouble again, and most times I just listen because I don't know what to say. But we both have our sensors up—we know the warning signs—fatigue, bad blind dates, drinking too much. We have gotten to where we can predict an "episode."

Next week marks a big moment for the two of us—we are planning our first dinner party together. We don't live in the same town—she's in Chicago and I'm in Evansville, Indiana—but I'm flying up for the weekend. She calls every other day regarding the menu.

"Mom is saying jambalaya, but I'm thinking lasagna with scallops, what do you think?" She calls from her office.

"Make what you want to eat," I say. We go over various food combinations, and when we hang up, I stare at the phone, wondering what it will be like to cook with my sister again.

She has a new job, working for my father. She bought herself a new apartment with a view of Lake Michigan and she had her walls painted Pepto

Bismol pink because, she says, the color makes her happy. She has a maid so she has time to cook. She has figured out how important it is to eat regularly. Healthily. Her closets are filled with new clothes in normal sizes and for the first time she is making a home for herself. Sometimes, I admit, I worry that she will come home late one night, tired from work, maybe a little depressed. She won't bother turning on a light and maybe then she'll notice movement in the next building across the way and she will see a family sitting down to dinner. She will go into her kitchen, open her refrigerator, close it, open a cabinet then close that. Then she will go back into her living room and she will stand there in the dark, hungry and alone, watching this family of strangers eat.

Hearts

by
Tricia Bauer

We knew them long before we knew
their names: anorexics, bulimics.
They were the ones with eyes set
in deeper and deeper wells of face,
the ones who tried to wipe their food
clean before ever presenting it to their lips,
the ones who toyed with knives and forks
and spoons as if those utensils were clues
to some trick question, some pop quiz.

They were the ones who could take nothing
into themselves without questions
of their own. And, in turn, nothing adhered.
Not flesh to their fingers thin
as number-two pencils,
not quick legs without a pinch of excess,
not hips, not breasts. Even their hair
thinned as they grew smaller,
as if every part and extension of them
was a conspiracy of retreat.

We were all girls then, but they
chose to stay in one place
perfecting their girlhood, their doll-sized
arms better to hold dolls,
their miniature legs
never to outrun their dolls.

Holding their bodies back,
fulfilling themselves in another time,
abbreviating now to no,

while the others of us spent our new bodies
on lavender and musk, midnight blues and pink passions,
silky dreams of saying YES without consequence.
The thick boy-lips wet with promises, legs
strong as young silver birches we could only try to bend,
bristled chins brushing ours in a whisper of pain.
We welcomed our bodies thickening
for the size we somehow already knew
we would have to be
just to support our hearts.

My Heart Licked Perfectly Clean

Feather, 1948

by
Denise Duhamel

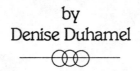

My mother prepared me
for the party. I was coming out
in a long-waisted silk dress,
real pearls. Real flowers in my room.
Three powders, each of a different fragrance,
on my vanity. I had everything—
although my mother did not make me
feel guilty or remind me of this.
Instead, she told me, her favorite daughter,
"Here darling, put this feather
in your purse." The plume was a purple
of royalty and courage. I stroked it
trying to imagine the bird
from which it was plucked.
"Dance and flirt. Drink
and eat as much as you want,"
my mother said, her gaiety strained.
"But remember, we don't want you getting fat.
Remember that you have your feather.
Mid-evening, go to the bathroom,
and use it."

Finger, 1988

by
Denise Duhamel

This morning the talk show host
said people like me
don't usually live this long.
Heart attacks over the toilet bowl.
Heart attacks right in the streets.
Finally in 1979, there became a name
for me, for what I do. Bulimic, bulimia,
like Adam and Eve uttering tree,
sky, bird, flower. Like Adam
and Eve using verbs: uproot, bang
your head against a wall. My teeth
have been capped three times—
my dentist's confrontations
as tentative as a small child's tap
on his busy mother's shoulder
when he's afraid of her wrath.
The glands in my throat bulge
like beads on a necklace,
like two extra breaths, two extra
breasts, like elbows pushing to the front
of a crowd. For forty years now,
everything has come to me
in groups: a cookie means bags
of cookies, ice cream, potato chips,
jars of mayonnaise. "No thanks" means
you hate me, I did something wrong,
I'm a terrible person, I hate myself, I hate you.

The Key to Happiness
—a monologue—

by
Michelle Blair

———— ◯◯◯ ————

The big change—puberty that is—should not be underestimated: really, it's the start of it all. It's traumatic enough for boys I suppose—squeaking voices, constant boners, morning puddles, etc. But for girls it's the upheaval of everything that has been known and traversed before, and the onset of something mysterious indeed. Once I was asked "At what age is a woman most powerful?" I imagined it must be sometime after menopause, after so much of the nitty gritty has been conquered. But no: my friend said a girl is strongest at eight or nine. It is then that she is invincible: body like a boy's, tough as wood and attitude to follow suit. As the flower blooms, conversely her heyday ends and she is left to spend the next decades trying to create, not even from the rubble, but from scratch, some kind of moving, of thinking, of being that is remotely comfortable, that is hers.

It was no different for me. I have a picture—faded color, early '70s—in which I stand in a psychedelic one-piece bathing suit. My thighs are slight, smooth, no hips, no chest, no butt, just a belly protruding in eight-year-old defiance. I was thin, I guess, but I never thought about it. I was whatever I was, you know, a kid, lithe and blithe and free. A couple of years later, however, at summer camp, a flat-chested girl of twelve told me that she always wore a bra and, as she said so, her eyes wandered incriminatingly down to glance at my rapidly-ceasing-to-be-flat chest.

Thus, my mom took me to Bloomingdale's for bra-and-undy sets. I felt so mature, so grown-up, but I also felt bizarre, alienated from those sticking-out things on my front and from the cloth thing which strapped across my back to hold them, and I only wore the bras on days when I was wearing a huge sweatshirt. Nonetheless, the boys always found out. I suppose, looking to be in cahoots, I'd whispered to another developed acquaintance, "I'm wearing a bra today," and the next thing I knew, otherwise shy and silent David Bahn was running toward me in the cafeteria, perfectly plucking through the thick fabric with a snap, and sing-songing to one and all, "Michelle's wearing a bra. Michelle's wearing a bra."

Eventually, I wore bras with ease, and not just under large clothing.

Eventually this was natural, certainly more so at thirteen than at eleven. But when the hips came soon after, when the thighs came, when all the female parts of me started boinging out in all directions, out of my control. I felt like a cartoon, like a caricature of a woman, and I was thoroughly unprepared.

It was then I began to eat. Oh, and I ate a lot. I loved food like a friend. I loved food like a lover, spending with me such sweeping, languorous hours. When I'd arrive home from school where, beyond freak, I was such an outsider that I did not fit into even the lowliest of categories; and right before dinner, when I was soooo bored; and even after dinner when everyone was sleeping and I should have been too, or studying math, or down at the bar those my age and much cooler drank Southern Comfort or at least in the arms of some lanky fool boy. But no, bare feet tacky on the linoleum, I opted for the kitchen.

I was my own sort of connoisseur, mixing the Bumble Bee with loads of mayonnaise, catching the frosted Pop Tarts as they leapt from the toaster, microwaving the coffee bun so the margarine could seep in just right. And I was an expert, too, of disavowal; somehow, I managed to believe that I was not eating what I was eating. I *ate* fruit and vegetables and salads and plain chicken; what I did with the other crap was off the record. Something would turn off in me. I was barely conscious. I was content, euphoric. Until my stomach would press against itself from the inside, taut and just about bursting like the gut of a goat roasting on the spit, and queasiness would overtake me, causing me to remember, and then stare, naked and hateful, at my body in the full-length mirror.

By fifteen, I was overweight; by fifteen, I was miserable. There were all the signs any school advisor, any compassionate peer—of which, alas, there were few—could have pinpointed. The all-black clothing, for example. "You think," my mother would say, "that wearing dark baggy clothing makes you look slim but it doesn't, it just makes you look like you don't care about yourself." My hair, lank and unbarretted, growing painfully slowly out of a passé Dorothy Hamill. My complexion oily and blotched, tiny pimples like goosebumps rimming my face. And my body—"Fat," I would bark, although my friends would politely concede, "Well, maybe just a little bit chunky," everything all over the place, everything out of my control. Really, I did care about how I looked, it's just that I looked so bad, it seemed that there was nothing that could be done.

Except for one thing, well, two things actually, but the first thing had thus far proved impossible, the first being finding a boy to love me and cherish me until death do us part, and thereby eliminate all of my pubescent *tsuris*. But ultimately I opted for the second, which wasn't really so bad, which was, in its way, quite brilliant after all. I could lose weight, ten, twenty, even thirty pounds. I wanted to be below 110. I could change my body, and with it, my mind, why, my entire life could be reimagined. And all it would take, all it would take, would be never to digest my food.

I don't remember quite how I came about it. I was not yet familiar with Mary's long-term habit, which I later found out even had a clinical name. Had I ever even heard of the infinitive, "to induce?" I just knew somehow, I just knew, that what went down should be able to come up, that I should be able to eat as much as I wanted and then rid myself of it all.

The task, however, was proving more difficult than I had imagined. Much later of course, I came to realize the gravity of such counter-gravity, such an unnatural process. At the time, however, when I first began trying, I was perseverant as Columbus, again and again sticking my fingers down my throat, pushing pushing pushing, come on you can do it, as though coaching myself for Lamaze. But there'd be nothing but gags, nothing but heaves. I'd rise dejected, rinsing my pink-knuckled fingers, staring at my uneven face, my eyes bulging, red vein in my forehead pumping. I was disgusting. I *was* the failure my parents thought I might become. I knew that once I succeeded, however, I would be alright, everything would be alright. My stomach would be empty and hollow and very soon—I cold hardly wait, the want alone superseded the frightening sounds and shifts in my uncooperative stomach—very very soon, all those parts of me which had so recklessly been fleshing out without my consent over the past few years would flesh in, shrink in, deflate, and I would be as petite and happy as Twiggy.

I sat in Mary's kitchen. I was a high school senior, she was a freshman. It was a grey February Friday. We ate. And we ate. Cookies and ice cream and dim sum still frozen from the freezer. Pieces of bread with jelly, with peanut butter, with honey, with cream cheese, with liverwurst, in myriad combination. Yodels and cereal and chocolate and chips.

After some time Mary excused herself. I could hear the throaty thrusts from the bathroom. I could hear the plopping sound of the bowl receiving her offering. I could hear a flush, then another, a cough, then another, finally, the faucet. She came out, her eyes teary and vague, her face rosy.

"Your turn," she said.

"I told you," I whined. "I can't do it. I've tried and tried, but I just can't do it."

"And I told you. Pull back your hair, roll up your sleeves, drink as much water as you can, and lean over. Persevere. Stick your finger as far back as it can go."

"Which finger?

"Oh, it doesn't matter. I use three, these, but it doesn't matter, you've got to find your own way. The key is, relax. And it will work, I promise." She squeezed my shoulder warmly, encouragingly. I walked into her bathroom. I was going to do it, no matter what.

And so I did, and when it finally gushed forth, what a wonder it was, what a release, like orgasm, the expulsion of all that was bad. And it was all my own, my secret, my best friend, the key to happiness.

An Image of Myself

by
Hendle Rumbaut

It is strange, looking at the image projected on my living room wall. A fourteen-year-old girl smiles at the camera, surrounded by her mother, father, younger brother Max and older brother Steve, standing in front of a blue Ford Fairlane station wagon. Dressed in Easter outfits, they are ready to go to St. Ignatius Catholic Church a few blocks away. She wears a pink shirtdress with shiny white buttons, and gold, pointed flats. But what is strange is that she is undeniably thin.

She is me, twenty-eight years ago, and I see now that I have always been thin. It took this dusty slide to provide the evidence. I look at her as a mother might, wanting to protect this emerging adolescent from the self-image she would soon adopt. It was then the mid-sixties, the time of toothpick-thin Twiggy, and other icons of a culture suddenly insisting that a woman could never be too thin. Even my best friend Denise, a petite, voluptuous beauty, wanted the figure of a tall, skinny boy. Now it seems insane.

And, of course, peer pressure was at its height. We read calorie charts with the same seriousness and intensity as our beloved movie magazines. "Look," said Wendy, as we walked from Algebra to P.E. She squinted down at a small, dog-eared booklet, "A potato—without butter, of course—has fewer calories than a slice of watermelon!" So we joyfully added potatoes to the short list of "allowable foods"—boring, bland things like celery sticks, raw carrots and zucchini, and grapefruit. Water, too, was required, in impossible quantities. What we craved were hamburgers, french fries and milkshakes, but we pledged to one another not to succumb.

So, secretly, away from my girlfriends, I followed the diet. At home, however, I wolfed down my mother's fried chicken, ice cream, and fudge brownies, competing with Steve for seconds and thirds.

And I knew, even as I swallowed these satisfying morsels, that they would not be with me for long. After a brief attempt at conversation with my family members, I was the first one to excuse myself from the table. No one suspected a thing. After all, teenagers were supposed to pull away from their family, and tie up the bathroom for hours. "Primping again?" they teased. So I would emerge from the bathroom with my hair freshly teased and sprayed, and sporting the scent of fresh cologne.

To them, it all seemed to fit. But for me, almost nothing did, for, much to my dismay, I found myself doubled over the toilet silently retching my guts out. I would first lay some toilet paper on the water to keep the vomit from splashing in my face, which revolted me, or making too much noise, which worried me. Then I would watch sadly but with relief as I identified the various components of the last meal hitting the water—the Neapolitan ice cream, the lemon pie, the cheddar cheese, the fried chicken, all in reverse order from the way they had entered me.

At the point where I saw carrot sticks and celery, I would stop and flush. Of course, the longer the food had been affected by stomach acids, the more vile it tasted and smelled. Hence my use of cologne, applied before facing my family. I checked and double-checked to see that all evidence had disappeared. Only once did my mother notice something suspicious in the toilet bowl. She came running after me as I walked down the sidewalk to go to Denise's house, and asked if I had just thrown up.

"Just a little, Mom," I said, rubbing my stomach lightly. "Must've been something I ate."

She seemed more worried by my nonchalance than at anything else. Before I turned fourteen, vomiting was always a big deal, something broadcast loudly to the household, and taken seriously by all. Mom would call the doctor, take my temperature, and let me stay home from school. Now I only prayed to be spared detection.

It was a miserable time, and all the more so because I thought I had invented this horrible habit, one which threatened to overtake my life. I was Catholic, and saw it as a sin, a dark deed without a name.

Finally I had to confess it. My bulimia came one Sunday morning right after Mass. Those familiar with Catholicism know the seriousness of the Holy Eucharist. Everything revolves around the concept of transubstantiation, in which Jesus literally becomes the body and blood for us to eat and drink.

So I had confessed the Friday before, and fasted as required before going to Mass. But as soon as I arrived back home after Communion, I automatically went to the bathroom. To my horror, I watched the grape juice and what I imagined to be tiny bits of communion wafer land in the nasty toilet water. I cried inconsolably.

"What's the matter with you?" said Steve, as I went into the living room, where Aunt Harriet was showing slides of her trip to the Holy Land. Even in the dimness of the room, Steve could see the redness in my eyes.

"Oh," I mumbled, as Mom looked up from the couch. "I think Bobby and I are about to break up."

"Oh, honey," Mom sighed. "Don't blow it out of proportion. There are plenty of fish in the sea."

Steve snickered. "Did you dump him or did he dump you?" I shot him daggers with my eyes.

Aunt Harriet came over and patted my knee. She was fat, and though she was my favorite aunt, I was always embarrassed to be seen in public with her, pretending to trail along behind her distractedly.

"Puppy love is so hard, isn't it?" she said. She went back to her place behind the projector and pointed to the blur on the wall. "This is where Our Lord was buried," she said solemnly. "I was really there, where they laid Him after the crucifixion!" Mom gasped and made the sign of the cross.

The next Friday I was back in the confessional, as we all were every Friday afternoon. This time, however, I didn't apologize for the usual transgressions of hitting my brother, or yelling at my mother. When the priest asked me to make my confession, I steeled myself and took a deep breath. This surely would not be just another venial sin, but rather a mortal sin capable of excommunicating me and sending me to burn in hell forever.

"Yes?" said the priest.

"Well, Father," I whispered slowly, "I threw up Our Lord and Savior, Jesus Christ." I held my breath as Father Moriarty tried to make sense of my remark. I repeated myself and explained how I simply had not waited long enough after Communion to make myself puke.

"Make yourself—?" he said.

"Well," I said, stretching the truth for his benefit (how could I expect this old man to understand my bizarre habit when I didn't understand it myself?), "Well, I needed to throw up, see, and it wasn't very long after Communion. So I just thought that, since Jesus transforms into the body and—"

He mumbled something, and I imagined him flipping through a nearby theology book looking for the answer. Catholicism has an answer for everything, after all. To my amazement, he told me to recite the usual number of Hail Marys.

Back in my pew, I looked up at the statue of the Blessed Virgin Mary and asked forgiveness again. Her smooth marbled face looked down with humility and compassion. Perhaps I wasn't going to go to hell after all. The resplendent stained glass reflected glorious purples and reds on my clasped hands, and my heart eased a bit.

I decided that it was better to be fat than to have to go through that again. I would prefer to risk the taunts of my peers as I ballooned into the shape of Aunt Harriet. I would eat only "allowable foods," and gradually, gingerly, introduce some that I really wanted. I told myself that what went into my mouth would not come out again. The next six months were hard. The gag response was so strong that I had to invoke the image of the Blessed Virgin Mary to keep the food from boiling up from below.

But the saddest part was having no one to support me, the feeling of being unable to talk about it with a family member or a school nurse or even my best friend. Mama never knew the triumph I felt in my heart as I realized I had turned it all around. Any positive change in my attitude was usually attributed to me and some pimple-faced guy getting back together. I didn't protest; I was just happy in my victory. The terms "bulimia" and "anorexia" were unknown then. Only much later did I hear that many of us suffered the same private torments.

I look down now in this dim light at my middle-aged, veined hands, and then up at this other version of myself, soon to be wandering in the dark. Fortunately, she found her way into the light.

"Dear one," I say to her. "You were never ugly, not even for a moment." I smile and blow her a kiss.

Always

by
Maria Bruno

———⊙⊙⊙———

It wasn't easy growing up with the last name of Bruno. It seemed like all the Brunos back then were either sitcom Nazi generals, mafioso from Palermo, sleek Dobermans owned by security companies; once even, Larry Pinnazo joked my father kidnapped the Lindbergh baby. Worst of all, there was Bruno the Magnificent, on Detroit's Midnight Wrestling, a pre-anabolic steroid hunk, his neck as thick as a thigh, his large body filling our small thirteen-inch black and white screen like a Saturday matinee monster. I'd stay up at night to watch, eating mayonnaise on soft Wonder Bread, knowing full well the kids at school would torment me on Monday morning. "Hey Bruno," they'd say, "How's your half-nelson?" or Popeye variations on the name, such as "Hey Bluto!" and a Shakespearean "Et-tu Brutus?" on account of we were almost through *Julius Caesar* in fifth hour Honors English. They all thought I was big. I thought I was big too, until I look back now at the yearbook pictures and wonder what all the fuss was about. Whenever I'd hear a remark at school, I'd rush home and challenge at least three bowls of Frosted Flakes, several glasses of Welch's grape juice, and then I'd sneak off to the A&P and buy a ten-cent pack of Hostess cupcakes, breaking each one in half and slurping enthusiastically on the sugary white filling, as if it was some kind of nectar from the Gods. Only one day, old Mrs. Harrison, a neighbor straight out of a Grant Wood painting, told my mother I was slurping on the sidewalk, and since I had "Such a pretty face," shouldn't she be watching what I was eating? After that, food became a real issue in our household. We had just left the Fifties and my mother still really cared a lot about what people thought, so she started checking my pocket for paper wrappers, and my mohair sweaters for Twinkie crumbs, and wanted an itemized account of what I did with my weekly fifty-cent allowance. "I saw *The Tingler*," I'd say, again and again, alternating it with *The Blob* when necessary, "and I didn't buy any Jujubes." I'm not sure she believed me; and old Mrs. "Ding Dong The Witch Should Be Dead" Harrison still peaked out her window every time I walked from the bus stop. I could see her grey hair springing from a Kresge hair net, her yam nose separating the turquoise fiberglass drapes, her skinny teeth wearing little yellow cardigans; some days I'd buy a fudge bar and stand in front of her house, licking it slowly, as if there was no tomorrow. Or I'd stand there, look old Yam Nose straight in the eye and unwrap a Scooter Pie, tossing the cellophane wrapper ever so lightly on her newly sodden lawn. Lawns were really big back then, and this act of insubordination was tantamount to Bruno the Doberman squatting and leaving a little gift himself.

"So, you were eating a Scooter Pie," my mother said to me as she hung up the phone. My brother Anthony was eating crusts of Italian bread from Lombardy's, dipping them into a thick red sauce. I wondered why he was allowed to eat and nobody cared. He could have been on Midnight Wrestling for real. He played Varsity football and was a growing boy. He would fill a big noodle pot with Wheaties and a quart of milk, and pour it into his mouth instead of using a spoon. He'd do the same with the Welch's, letting his runbacks trickle back into the jar.

The next day my mother took me to a diet doctor, and he gave me a six-month supply of Dexemyl, an amphetamine. I flew through those six months on one apple at lunch and a small steak in the evening. By the time President Kennedy died, I was thin, raw, angular, thinner than the grieving Jackie. I began passing out in the Junior Petite section of J.C. Penney's, at the Battle of the Bands during the Shing-a-ling Competition, and during morning field hockey exercises in Miss Jean's gym class. No one even bothered to ask anymore how my half-nelson was at school; Old Yam Nose no longer leaped from her chair to the window; my mother started saying, "Eat, eat, you look so thin!"

My brother, Anthony, the linebacker, made City All Stars, and I, on a steady diet of Dexemyl, didn't have time to pause and reflect on whether I was happy or not. I did have some strange recurring dreams, though. I'd be on my way home from the A&P, wearing Bruno the Magnificent's loincloth, my bare breasts looming large, as if they could nurse the universe. I'd have a Scooter Pie in one hand, and a Hostess Cupcake in the other, and I'd be juggling the two high into the air, right in front of Mrs. Harrison's, and I let them fall into my mouth, gulping them each in one breath. I kept growing like Alice in *Through the Looking Glass*, bigger than any all-star linebacker, ready to take on the Tingler, the Blob, Bruno Hauptmann, any Mafia don. As I remember it now, I always woke up smiling after those dreams. Always.

Being One With Mrs. Blinder

by
Bonney Goldstein

I grew up in the Jewish section of Brooklyn called Flatbush. Cities were still safe in the early 1950s and I could go anywhere I wanted, anywhere in the neighborhood as long as I didn't cross any big streets. I felt free to wander in and out of my neighbors' homes, helping myself to cold drinks from their refrigerators, taking naps in their bedrooms, sitting down to dinner with them. Anything was okay as long as I was home by six o'clock for dinner.

There were many kids on our block and we all spent our afternoons playing together. Most of the time we played at Mrs. Blinder's house, a small cramped two-story brick house that was at the far end of the block. She always had a fresh baked cake or cookies waiting, and candy: chocolate-covered marshmallow twists, Hershey kisses, Mary Janes, Tootsie Rolls, amply stashed in cut glass bowls that you could help yourself to without asking permission. This was food for eating and it was just there for the taking.

This was a unique concept to me; in our house we had the eating food and the buying food and they were different, and you were born with the sixth sense of knowing which was which. The eating food was the food you ate on an everyday basis: milk, bread, cheese, etc. The buying food was carefully chosen and put into the pantry and saved. It was the good stuff: candy, cookies, foods that tasted good, forbidden foods, foods that made you fat. For some unknown reason, just having them in the house was important: just in case, you could never tell, some kind of emergency, you just might need it someday.

We also had only one night a week when you could eat candy. My mother kept a pantry, a small closet, 14" x 14" x 14", with a lock that only got opened on Thursday nights.

My father was never home for dinner on Thursdays and for dessert my mother would unlock the cabinet and my sister and I would pick out one thing. I always chose M&M's. I would take the bag to my bedroom, open a good book, and systematically eat the candies: first the red and green ones—they were my least favorite—then the orange and finally the favored brown. People still tell me they all taste the same, but I know different.

My mother hated Mrs. Blinder, and hated that I went there. The Blinders were not accepted by the rest of the families on the block. My mother and her friends said they were too poor to be living there, on that block, with them; but even though I was young, I knew it was really because Mrs. Blinder was fat. She wasn't just fat—she was enormous. When I was six my mother began to threaten me by saying that if I didn't watch out I'd grow up to be just like Mrs. Blinder. "If you keep eating like that," she'd yell.

And so at six and seven I began to think of myself as weighing over three-hundred pounds and I still see myself as that. My mother never meant to be mean, she just wanted what was best for me. A husband. Everyday I awoke to hear her saying, "Get up, get dressed, get married." And it was common knowledge that men only married skinny girls. I think that rule was written in the bible somewhere, or maybe just passed down from generation to generation, but my mother had a lot of evidence to prove her point. The fat women who we knew were old maids, and obviously very unhappy. I don't know how she knew that, but I believed her.

Mrs. Blinder was the exception; the only fat lady my mother knew to be married, and she often said that one only had to look at Mr. Blinder to realize just what a fat woman gets to choose. Mr. Blinder was not a great catch. He was fat, and he didn't make a lot of money. He was not a professional man. And that was what she had in mind for me, a dentist.

It didn't take long for my mother to insist that I stop going to the Blinders after school, and so I learned trick number one: to sneak what I wanted. I became a pro at sneaking food without anyone noticing it was missing or anyone seeing me eat it. I ate on the way to places, as I cleaned up my room, as I washed the dishes, on the way to the kitchen table, in the bathroom. I never ate much at mealtime.

Living like this I developed a very strange belief system about food. I still believe that anything eaten while standing or lying down doesn't count. When I began counting calories, I never had to figure these in. They were considered tasting foods, a free bite you were allowed.

"You're getting just like Mrs. Blinder," I heard my mother scream at me everyday. But at eight, I liked Mrs. Blinder and didn't mind being like her. Then one day my mother went over there and had a talk with Mrs. Blinder. Then she put a sign on my back that said *Please Don't Feed*, and Mrs. Blinder stopped feeding me and soon I stopped going there. I don't know what my mother said to her, but I don't think she was comfortable having me there after that. I missed the family terribly. There was always something going on there: games, a new toy, paint to get into; once she even let all the kids help paint a wall. The Blinder's was a fun place to go to.

The more my mother yelled, the more like Mrs. Blinder I was becoming. I remember standing in front of a mirror in my parents' bathroom dressed in my mother's clothes, staring in the mirror looking for Mrs. Blinder. I couldn't see her in there but I knew she was there someplace, so I kept on looking.

I had all the lights on and was looking at my reflection and seeing the layers of fat my mother was always talking about. I was wearing her long red dress and had on black high-heeled shoes. I remember my mother coming in and laughing as she pointed to me in the mirror. She lifted the dress off the floor and I danced around in circles. She held my hair off my face and tied it up with a red bow. My mother cinched my waist with one of her belts and told me to suck in my stomach so I could see how wonderful I'd look if I was just skinny.

But I couldn't see any difference. All I could see was myself in Mrs. Blinder's body, and I couldn't figure out what was wrong with that.

When I told my mother this, she became determined to show me once and for all how bad being fat was. She pulled on my waist, tighter and tighter with the wide red belt until I began to see the layer of fat falling over the leather of the belt. Hanging out for all the world to see, leaping straight out of the mirror, and eventually overpowering the little girl I thought I was.

"Tomorrow you better start a diet," my mother told me that day and although I didn't know what diet meant, I didn't like the sound of the word; and by nightfall the next day I had learned how bad being on a diet was. It meant being hungry and getting yelled at and being told that I didn't need something I wanted.

"Suffer a little today and tomorrow you'll be glad you did," my mother said.

But I wasn't sure I would live till tomorrow. And anyway I knew she wouldn't let up if tomorrow ever came because she'd been going on about this since I was four and I didn't think she'd just suddenly stop.

"Mrs. Blinder seems to be feeding you again. We'll put that sign back on you. Didn't I tell you not to go there anymore?"

"I don't go there anymore," I remember telling her.

"Well, someone's giving you too much to eat and it's not anyone in this house."

And then it was six o'clock and the family dinner time, and you were expected to sit down with everyone and eat everything on your plate. Many nights I was yelled at for leaving something over; being hungry had nothing to do with eating. See that was the problem: I got yelled at for eating, but I also got yelled at for not eating. My mother told me it was important to eat what she gave me, it was healthy and good for me and people were starving in Europe.

And then of course, there were Thursday nights. It was always okay to eat on Thursday, although I never could quite understand why. It was just another of those strange rules and it had something to do with Thursday being "a girls' night" and since my father was not coming home we didn't have to eat a "real" meal. You can see how easy it was for a child to get very bewildered about what to eat, when to eat, and when to leave stuff over.

By the time I was nine it was all too confusing for me to handle and one day after I forced myself to finish everything on my plate I went into the bathroom and threw up all over the floor.

And the next day my mother told me how skinny I looked, and I think that's when I learned my second trick.

Nine years later it was 1963 and I was in college and I was a pro at throwing up. Long before anyone heard of the word Bulimia I was a practicing bulimic.

Twenty years later, in 1983, I was living in Dallas, Texas, and Mrs. Blinder was still there. Every time I looked in the mirror she was there; she had followed me all the way from Brooklyn.

By 1984 I had enough food stored to feed all of the starving children in the world.

In 1985 I finally decided it was better to be fat than dead and so I finally stopped throwing up or starving myself, or doing a number of other tricks I had learned over the years. Bulimia, anorexia, all the little games I learned to play around food were tough to give up, they were games I had become so good at.

It is now 1992, and I live in a small college town where the average age is twenty-six, average height 5'8", average weight 120 pounds. Since I'm neither twenty-six, tall, nor 120 pounds, Mrs. Blinder is still with me.

Forty years have gone by and I am finally tired of diet programs, obsessing with numbers, and having my mood be dictated by an instrument I was insane enough to purchase in the first place. Last year, to keep my sanity intact I did the only thing I could think of—a final act of desperation. I took my scales (all three of them) and placed them in my driveway. Then I ran my large Jeep tires over each one, one at a time, slowly, enjoying the pleasure. I threw them in the woods where they still sit covered with twigs and animal feces and irreparably broken.

Now if I could only bury Mrs. Blinder. Not the nurturing Mrs. Blinder of my youth, but the Mrs. Blinder of my fears—that ugly, unacceptable lady that still haunts my imagination and often sneaks inside my mirror: the Mrs. Blinder that I am afraid of still lives inside me, waiting—just waiting.

Literary Weight Loss

by
Sibyl James

Stout Mama doesn't understand the science of weight loss. Gaining is easy. The food comes to visit and, like poor relations, stays. Doritos in her thighs, the round blush of chocolate-covered cherries in her cheeks. Maintenance is also clear. The population stabilizes like a small town in Nebraska, and everybody else just drives through on the Interstate. But once the food attaches to her bones, how does it leave?

One day after lunch, Stout Mama wanders over to the college library, to the home ec. section, which she thinks will be more scientific than the shelves on medicine or self-help. She looks up weight loss. This, she reads, means "eating fewer calories than you burn." Stout Mama imagines tiny brushfires breaking out beneath her skin. Perhaps the book is right, for weight loss seems as uncontrollable to her as brushfires. Like an arsonist, she carefully selects her target, but the flames keep taking hold just up the block. To start a conflagration in her thighs, she has to starve her face and breasts to ashes.

Still, Stout Mama finds it hard to understand the logic of such science. She wishes nature were more literary, more Shakespearean, direct and clear as Shylock's pound of flesh. She knows exactly where she'd carve.

Happy Losers

by
Lois Fine

———⟨◯◯◯⟩———

"Hello, everybody. My name is Myra Koplodsky and in the past eighteen years I've lost forty-seven pounds. But, more importantly I've kept it off. What's my secret? Stay here this evening and you'll find out."

From the time I was twelve until I was fifteen, I was a "Happy Loser." Week after week I'd pay my money, take my place in line, take off my ring, my necklace and my socks, let out all my breath and step up on the scale.

"Very good, dear. You've lost a quarter of a pound."

Thank god. That makes seven-and-three-quarters pounds altogether. To celebrate I'd buy a bag of Happy Losers chocolate candies laced with Saccharine, some Happy Losers hot chocolate mix and the latest edition of *Myra's Secrets*, a magazine of low-cal recipes. Then I'd take my seat in anticipation of the evening lecture. But first, the cards. One by one our names were called out. If we lost, Myra would say how many pounds or fractions thereof we had faithfully shed. Everyone would applaud. If we gained however, it would just be our name, no one would ever hear if it was half pound or five, just, "Having trouble dear?" or "Was it someone's birthday again?"

All around us were the slogans on the wall. "It's in to be thin, it's out to be stout, it's square to be round." "A minute on the lips is an inch on the hips." "If it's spreadable, it's inedible." I guess that means cream cheese. But of course, I knew exactly what it meant. I knew how many calories were in a slice of bread, how much protein was in a can of tuna and how many grams of fat in a potato chip. I brought my dieter's scale to parties and dances and, when everyone was eating pizza and drinking coke, I was eating tuna, oil drained, on whole wheat with a glass of skim milk.

Eventually I left Happy Losers and tried my own method: I starved myself, jogged five miles a day and managed to wear my body down to 115 pounds. I loved what I looked like. Here I was, the kid my uncle had called "fat stuff" and I was fitting into a size 26 waist jeans and my hip bones were sticking out. But soon enough the dream died. Bit by bit I gained my weight back. Bit by bit I gained more than my weight back.

There were days when I wouldn't let myself go out. Convinced that I'd gained too much weight to look presentable, terrified that anyone should see what a failure I was, I stayed home totally depressed and often alone. Then once I was home and depressed anyway, what better thing to do than eat. So I'd eat. And eat. I went through whole containers of ice cream; I invented sandwiches of unheard of combinations; I sat in front of the television swallowing spoonful after spoonful of it mattered not what, anesthetizing myself with food, numbing out of my life. I would be awake when everyone else was asleep and then I'd be exhausted in the day. Too exhausted to think, too exhausted to connect with people. The only thing I could manage to do was more of the same kind of feeding of my body and starving of my heart and soul. Eventually I gained over forty pounds.

I tried the Scarsdale diet. Sounded perfect, all you could eat of whatever they were allowing, you just had to follow the proper food combinations. I followed it to the letter. When my family was sitting down to a Friday night meal of chicken soup, meatballs and roast chicken, I was wolfing down spinach by the bunches and choking on cottage cheese, which I hate.

It worked. I lost eight pounds in the first week. Even though you're only supposed to stay on it for two weeks at a time, I was hooked. I stayed on for eight consecutive weeks and lost forty-five pounds. People noticed. Aunts, uncles, friends. "You've gotten so thin," they would say. "No, not really, just a few pounds." I'd feign indifference but inside I was screaming with joy. They made my day. They called me *thin*. But, I wondered, how long could I keep it up? I couldn't stay on Scarsdale forever. Terrified of gaining back even an ounce, I devised a new way for staying skinny. Laxatives.

Ex-Lax is a good trick. You can eat all you want, as long as you keep taking Ex-Lax. I experimented with other brands of laxatives, settling on little red pills that I took with every meal. I became more weight obsessed and neurotic than ever. Any meal that I had not expelled within an hour had me worried, almost frantic. I took more little red pills. I sat in the bathroom and waited. I spent half of my waking hours in those days on the toilet.

I became so obsessed that I was aware of the minutest bite of food lingering in my system longer than I deemed necessary. Once I took my starving, skinny little body to Burger King, ordered a Whopper, managed to take a whole bite and spent the rest of the day swimming, jogging and doing sit-ups, focusing on the Bite of the Whopper, where it was in my body and how much work needed to be done before I could relax and know that no real damage had been done.

I devised my own fat tests. I would look at my wrist and see if the bone on my wrist was as prominent today as it had been yesterday. I mean people would actually be thinking that I was in a conversation with them and there I'd be measuring my fat.

Writing this now almost feels like true confession. Here I am, a self-loving, woman-loving, strong and smart woman and I have spent years, hours, days of my life completely distracted from my life, concerned only with what I looked like and how fat I was, how fat I would be, what I was eating, what I would be eating. It has taken me a longer time to heal from my self-inflicted damage and also to understand where the desire to do this damage comes from.

It's no mystery. Turn on the TV on Saturday morning and watch corporate North America sell rocket launchers to the boys and aerobic centers to the girls. Need I say more? The messages are all around us. We inhale them from a very young age. In my family as well, a huge emphasis was put on our bodies and how fat we were. My parents were constantly dieting and all of us would learn to be "up" when our parents' weight was down and "down" when it went up.

One of the saddest parts for me, because there are lots of sad parts to this story, is when I think of all the time I lost. Lost years. Lost years spent staring at a particular bone on my wrist, lost years spent waiting for me to get really thin so that my life could finally get better. Lost years spent listening to meaningless lectures, reciting meaningless slogans from signs on the wall.

I can still recite them now, for kicks, for laughs with my friends. But every so often, Myra Koplodsky's words come back to haunt me. There are days when I look in the mirror and all I can see is a fat body staring back at me, days when I feel ugly and unlovable because I'm too fat. Even now when I'm supposed to know better, it takes all that I've got to remember to love myself, to practice self-acceptance. I like to think I'm a very different person from my Happy Loser self but I know there's still a ways to go before I can free myself from the "dieter within," the woman who looks at the piece of chocolate cake and says with all the conviction she can muster:

> The diet is within me I shall not cheat
> It leadeth me to choose the legal food whenever I have the urge to eat
> Yea though I may wish to eat sweets or cake
> I shall eat them never
> For the diet is with me
> And I shall reach my goal
> And remain slim forever
> Amen

Amen, Myra. Maybe someday we'll be able to teach our children that their value need not be measured by their waists but rather by their hearts.

I've Always Been Afraid of Getting Burned

by
Becky Bradway

———∞∞———

My husband is a nurturer. He cooks wonderful, elaborate food. It usually involves meat: steak, when we can afford it; a rare roast; often chicken, roasted, fried, baked with lemon and dill. We have salads with egg, sweet red pepper, cukes and carrots; we feast on potatoes with gravy like sauce.

I go home for lunch, for supper. Mealtime is a gathering. My little daughter picks at her food and we give her choices. I never nag. I frown at my husband if he nags—because he is the cook, her dislike of the artichoke is sometimes, to him, like rejection. We watch the weather and read magazines while we eat; sometimes we talk. My daughter squirms and sings.

I always leave some of each thing, one lettuce leaf, a bit of beef, milk in the bottom of the glass. "Little dabs," my husband says, shaking his head, resigned.

I am the cook for breakfast. My daughter stirs the eggs and pours them into the frying pan. She lays the bacon in careful strips and listens as it pops. We eat sweet cereal and toast each other with bright plastic glasses.

She also helps my husband in the kitchen. At three, she carefully uses a knife to slice tomatoes. She tears the lettuce and laughs as it falls into the bowl. She doesn't like to eat salad, but delights in its making.

My daughter will do anything she can to cook.

I watch, because I am afraid of making a mistake. I was told that knives cut, stoves burn, matches can catch clothes on fire. Before I was an adult, the only thing I made on the stove was canned soup. Once, in my twenties, I made bacon for the first time and poured cooking oil into the pan, unaware that bacon makes plenty of grease on its own. Naturally, I was greeted with hoots.

Growing up, I was not allowed in the kitchen. "Get out of here!" my mother would yell. She was afraid—afraid I would be burned. "Remember what happened

137

to Dorothy?" Dorothy, our neighbor with a six-inch-high beehive hairdo, had scars from a flaming pan of grease.

Mom was afraid I would drop a glass lid. Afraid I would track in. Afraid I would spill and she would have to slap my face.

I stayed out of the kitchen.

Mealtime gave me a stomach ache. We only had "big meals" on the evenings when Dad was home—he worked swing shift at Firestone—and on Sundays. Mom would work hard and produce a charred roast, some Shake-and-Bake pork chops in greasy white gravy. We sat at the rectangular table—me, my brother and my parents. Grace was said, by my brother: "God is great, God is good, and we thank Him for our food, A-men." Once he said it in jazz beat and my father hit him across the room. Once he laughed and was beaten with a belt.

We bowed to our plates and attacked our food with quiet seriousness. We had to eat every bite. Had to, or we were hit. Yelled at until our faces turned red with humiliation. We didn't talk. There was nothing to talk about. My dad worked, my mom stayed home, we stayed home—we lived in the country—my parents had no friends, no one visited other than relatives, my friends were miles away.

Mealtime forced us to be together. None of us wanted to be there.

On days when Dad wasn't around, we ate at the counter in the kitchen. Our delicacies were canned soup, bologna sandwiches, Kraft macaroni and cheese. We scarfed and then watched TV in separate rooms, scattering like spilled beans.

What do I like to eat? Candy. Sweettarts, Sprees, lollipops, Double Bubble. Reese's Peanut Butter Cups.

Once every two weeks, my mother, my aunt and us kids would drive into town for food. I would get candy, then hoard it as long as I could, savoring it, never, ever sharing. In college, I lived on Cokes. Six, eight Cokes a day, sometimes a Coke mixed with Sprite for a little variation. Lunched on Almond Joys. Drank Kahlua and Cream at night.

Now, in my desk drawer, I have a bag of Blow Pops, some stale peanut brittle, a half-eaten bag of microwave popcorn, and half of a Reese's Peanut Butter cup. I don't share with the office.

At home I take vitamins. I make sure I have eaten. Low blood sugar and bad nutrition added to my early-adult depression. "I've never seen such watery blood," a nurse once said. I'm even now. I am in balance.

I look at my daughter who begs to beat the eggs and knead the bread dough.

Who loves candy but always offers some to me, and never throws a fit when I say, no, you can't have more. Who also loves apples and oranges and pears, snatching them from the big bowl, taking one bite from each when she can get by with it. The natural sweetness is good enough for her.

I hope food will always bring her joy, and not guilt; that it will always be her nurturance, and she will never grow thin from lack of love. I find there are practical things I can teach her, and many more I can learn. I make a mean bowl of chili, and even a decent cheese sauce. In my home, nobody criticizes the food. I try to remember that.

The Flavor of My Existence

by
Dorothy Ryan

I'm going to give it to you straight. I eat my heart out frequently. I'm the mother of a nine-year-old girl who is neurologically impaired, hyperactive and mentally ill. And I'm in therapy for incest survivors. Frankly, the reality of living with my daughter and dealing with my past is sometimes so difficult I eat to escape.

I don't stuff myself with junk. I'm not plagued by carbohydrate cravings. But neither do I always fill my aching soul with apples, oranges, pears. Or yogurt and tofu.

When I feel overwhelmed by my child's needs I satisfy the child in me with candy. Gumdrops and chewy chocolate candy are my favorites—Snickers, Milky Ways and Barton's Almond Kisses. Some of my candy cravings are seasonal. Give me a holiday and I'll match it with a candy:

Halloween	*Candy corn*
Thanksgiving	*Chocolate turkeys*
Christmas	*Candy canes*
Valentine's	*Caramel hearts*
St. Patrick's	*Chocolate shamrocks*
Easter	*Jelly beans (spice)*

But I don't need a holiday to munch. My favorite all-time stress releaser is a bag of gumdrops. When I'm on a gumdrop roll I hide a bag in the laundry room and a bag in my home office.

For instance, the other night I staggered into the kitchen sagging under the weight of a laundry bag filled with my daughter's clothes. She was parked at her favorite spot—the kitchen table—listening to the radio. I shuffled into the laundry room and started stuffing clothes into the washer.

I was feeling angry, sad and stressed out. Our mid-winter vacation had been filled with appointments. Most were for my daughter—psychologist, psychia-

140

trist, optometrist, optician, horseback riding lesson. My first day back to work as a nursery school teacher had been more demanding than usual—it was conference time. It was already 9:00 p.m. and my husband was asleep, recuperating from a hectic business trip.

As I crammed the dirty clothes into the washer my resentment mounted. One more thing to do for my child when my inner child wanted to play. The water was rushing into the machine, making it impossible for me to hear the radio. A little switch clicked on in my brain. If I couldn't hear the radio then my daughter couldn't hear me.

I eased open the overhead cabinet and carefully felt for my bag of gumdrops. I reached in and grabbed a fistful. Chewed fast. Chewed hard. Swallowed. So good. Reached for more...

"Mom?"

I froze. Turned an angelic face to my child. Had she heard me? Had she seen me sneaking forbidden goodies?

No. Just a child's ESP. Could she have something to eat? I reminded her that she already had dessert and offered her some fruit. Then I went back to the wash. And my gumdrops. And my guilt.

I don't indulge my sweet tooth on a regular Monday through Friday basis or weekends only. My daughter is not impossible to live with every moment of every twenty-four hours. Sometimes it's mornings that are toughest, sometimes afternoons. Always evenings. She has never had a consistent sleep pattern.

But it's not just my daughter's behavior that provokes my candy or gumdrop raids. Give me a rough session with my therapist and a flooding of memories of sexual abuse by my parents when I was a child, and when I get home I may grab a handful of the rainbow-colored treats.

When I was a child my daughter's age I liked to take my time selecting gumdrops. You remember. A green one or a white one? The purple or the orange? Three red and one yellow?

Then I had the time and the desire to choose. Now I cram fistfuls when I'm sure I won't be observed.

Since indulging my sweet tooth is my only vice I guess I shouldn't lay too big a guilt trip on myself. I just wish that the urge to stuff my face stemmed from feeling joyful and not from feeling trapped.

But most of all, I wish I didn't get the urge.

Scavenger to Angel

by
Gayle Brandeis

———— ⬤⬤⬤ ————

I am cupping frozen veggies in my hands, thawing them under warm running water for my son's lunch. They are such bright creatures—orange cube of carrot, green sphere of pea and cylinder of bean, yellow teardrop of corn. Next to them, the lima looks subtle, elegant. Arin bypasses this proud plump of protein, however, plucking cube after orange cube from his highchair tray, his mouth soon dense with carrot. He chews little and swallows less; great bright vegetable masses fall from his tongue to his shirt, the chair, the floor. I eat what he does not—the fallen mash of pea, ignored gleam of corn, choked-on skin of bean. I hope my husband doesn't notice as I furtively pick up the carrots from the floor and pop them into my mouth. It is bad enough that I lick my plate and eat all the leftover pizza crusts. Such a scrounger I am—coaxing the last smear of yogurt from the carton with my finger, filling the nearly-empty jelly jar with milk, shaking the last globs free and drinking them down. I am, I suppose, like a human composter—I take in what is normally left on the plate (scraps of spaghetti, mince of onion) and turn it over in the dark mystery of my organs, composting food not for a garden, but for my sprout, my son. These sandwich crusts, these shreds of cheese, become milk, pure and white. As I nurse Arin, I am transformed from scavenger to angel, and I am fed—my heart licked perfectly clean.

I'm Really Beginning
To Hate Lettuce

Before

by
Carol Sue Muth

Before I go on this diet I will eat
everything in the house except
the dried parsley flakes.

This last molasses cookie,
the leftover lemon meringue pie,
every sweet and perishable will be

consumed until I am full and weak
as ceremonial tea. I will prepare
the house for its losses.

Some Days I Even Eat Breakfast

by
Gladys M. Furphy

———◯◯◯———

I was not born fat. But I spent most of my life fat. Fat consumed me. Fat made me hide. Fat made me lie. My entire life was ruled by fat with but one desire—to be thin.

Fat must have attacked somewhere in grammar school. I have very few memories of ever being not fat. My Girl Scout uniform was a "Chubbette"—I looked like a green wave in my camp shorts. During my teenage years my bedroom became my Maginot Line. After my clandestine visits to the bakery shop, I would stash the empty boxes in a drawer, waiting for a chance to discard the evidence of my eating, my shame. Upon reaching my haven one day, I was stunned by an overwhelming sight. These "binge boxes" were piled on the floor in the middle of the room. My mother did this and never said a word to me about my sin of sins. If shame could kill, I died.

Mother was thin; mother's daughter had to be thin. Mother was still at it even after I was a wife and mother. Mother was an excellent cook. We often went to Grandma's house for holidays. The extremely caloric and delicious-looking dessert was always presented with a flourish. Mother would pause, look at her only daughter and proclaim, "You, of course, don't want any." Shame on you, daughter dear, you are fat—you cannot share my offering, was, of course, the message I received. Engulfed in shame, I would eat everything in *my* house when I got home.

Innumerable diets were spawned over the ensuing years. At times I was almost "normal" in weight. But never quite. This was elusive. Many times I nearly grasped it, only to have it slip away with the tide.

Unfortunately, my shame gave birth to guilt. Guilt is impalpable. It does not have form; you cannot touch it. But it pervades the mind like pain does a tooth. Guilt is a woman-attacker; quite probably since we are extremely sensitive beings. The seeds of shame and guilt are insidious. They grow like weeds in an untended garden. Their roots grow deep into the earth. I never weeded my garden. The weeds covered me like chocolate sauce on ice cream.

As is the case with many fat girl-children, I grew into a submissive woman. Submissiveness so often leads to a lack of esteem and power. After all, I didn't want anybody to see my fat, so I had to be agreeable and placid. To express anger would be akin to having a spotlight shining on my fat. I learned to present a smile to the world. I would be unflappable. I would be safe. My thoughts were kept inside my mouth. And always accompanied by food.

One day I tried a new diet. That diet worked. I lost eighty-five pounds. I delighted in myself. Oh, if only mother was alive to pat me on the head for my thin body. But how could I hold on to that size eight body? Such an obvious solution— I would buy a Diet Center.

And so I did. But I was surrounded by food. Food and fat-people-wanting-to-be-thin pervaded my waking hours. It permeated my dreams. It drove me to eat. It drove me away from the scale. It haunted me. It nearly destroyed me. I was becoming fat again—I had gained twenty pounds. But a weight-loss counselor may not be fat.

What to do? I could not diet. It didn't work anymore. Hypnotism hadn't worked. Nothing worked. My only option seemed to be a psychiatrist. Give it a few weeks and I'd be that thin person again—so I thought.

I realized early on that I was not there to embark on yet another diet. I had to determine why I ate and ate and ate. My defense against the world was my fat. It insulated me from my inner anger, shame and guilt. My mouth rarely opened to communicate—it more often than not opened only to accept food.

I accepted the fact that I had to learn to express rather than repress. But, oh, this was so difficult. To vent my anger, to erase my guilt and shame could only make the people in my life aware of me. They would look and see fat. My mouth could still not speak, only eat.

But one day my hand picked up a pen and wrote instead of putting food in my mouth to eat. Page after page filled with words. Although I was not communicating with the world, I was at least communicating with myself and the doctor. My words, though, were bleak and morose. Sunshine never flowed through my pen, only the shadows of midnight appeared. My anger, shame and guilt found a new bedfellow—depression.

Months later I still considered myself fat. But then at a group session I found yet another idol. Sue. She was the psychotherapist at this meeting. Sue told me that I was not fat. Those words inspired me. I would prove to Sue that I was fat by becoming thin. So easy. So I entered my anorexic stage. My "diet" consisted of cauliflower, mushrooms, tomatoes and an occasional peach. Very occasional since fruit equals sugar! Eating was confined to dinner. Copious amounts of coffee filled my stomach throughout the day. My counseling to my dieters however was never compromised and right on target. If only I could listen to my own good advice.

Over the next couple of months I was again wearing my size eights as well as a few size sixes. The world was a glorious place to visit. My depression lifted. I soared with the birds. The doctor threatened hospitalization. I promised to eat. But nothing was able to pass my lips beyond my cauliflower, mushrooms and tomatoes.

But now a war waged in my head. Fat vs. Thin. I visualized myself as a Vulture—the Fat Me, and as a Snake—the Thin Me. The only resolution I could see was the Snake slaying the Vulture. But the Vulture refused to die, she kept picking away at me as though I was but carrion on the road. My no-eating was in danger. Everything became black or white. Don't eat or else binge.

Life became one big scale. One day at the office I weighed myself seven times. I would rush home at night and try on all of my smaller-size clothes and peer in the mirror looking for bulges. My dieters loved seeing my thinness. What a role model! And, of course, I was always so cheerful. The smile never left my face. My counseling skills were honed to a finer edge. Each lost pound improved these skills, each pound put back softened these skills.

The Snake was winning the battle with the Vulture. Until disaster struck. Sue left the group. I was being rejected. It seems not for the first time. I was now equating Sue with my mother. To get Sue's attention I had to stop eating. This made her sit up and pay me heed. In my sick state of mind, Sue had become my mother. They had now both rejected me.

Then something happened which triggered my bulimia. My son's house burned down one bright summer day. So, Allan, his wife Kathy and my grandson Daniel moved in with us. Utter chaos existed. My house was no longer my own. I reverted back to using my mouth only to eat and not to speak. But I was much too bright to vomit after bingeing. After all, I was an expert on nutrition. So I swam every possible moment available. Just laps, back and forth, back and forth. When the summer ended and the pool was no longer usable, I would just stop eating for days on end. My system of purging. Nothing so nasty as vomiting for me!

My eat-all or eat-nothing phase lasted for seven months—until Allan and his family moved back to their house. Within a week I was at Silver Hill, a psychiatric-care hospital. I was to remain there for seven weeks. But I still had not learned my lesson. I was much too literal a person. I expected the doctor, nurses and dietician to do as they said. We each gave a little in regard to my diet. I agreed to eat many of the foods on the dietician's list, but there were a few I choked on. So we struck a deal. I would even eat three meals a day. Unfortunately, the hospital treated me strictly as a bulimic. I could go nowhere alone the first few weeks. I had to sit at the table for an hour after each meal even though I swore to them that I was not into vomiting. When the doctor realized how long I was swimming each day, he forbade me full use of the pool. So I would show him, I stopped using it completely. But, oh, did I ever get in a lot of walking—rapidly at that.

And then one day I realized that they were not living up to their end of the bargain. I rebelled. They were only interested in seeing that I did not binge. That left the door wide open. For my last three weeks there I ate nothing but yogurt, small cubes of cheese and breadsticks. I'd show them! When would I learn? But I still have to say that theirs was also a strange mindset. I was weighed every day and not much was said about my loss of weight. I guess all hell would have broken loose had I gained. The day I left the hospital I was much thinner than when I entered. I was even wearing my jeans again. But the only thing I learned after seven weeks was how to beat the system.

Eleven days after checking out of one hospital, I was checked into another hospital. I was suffering from severe diarrhea and attendant weakness. After many horrible tests, they concluded I was suffering from ulcerative colitis, but they did not know what caused it. On the eighth day, they discovered my problem. My system was just about out of beta-carotene. I was allowed to go home. They told me to drink carrot juice. Oh yes, I lost quite a few pounds in those eight days—I almost never ate the meals they sent me!

While at Silver Hill I was strongly advised, rather told, to sell my business. After all, they reasoned, you wouldn't expect an alcoholic to work in a bar. A person with an eating disorder should not work at a Diet Center. Sound reasoning. But I could not agree with them and so I returned to the life of a weight-loss professional. My dieters were thrilled to have me back. They had been told I was in Florida taking care of my sick father. I was also quite thin at this time. Eight weeks in two hospitals had seen to that.

It is now four years later. For many reasons, I opted to hold on to my Diet Center. But I also opted to fight my eating disorder. It has been a very weighty four years. It is particularly onerous to spew forth information on nutrition and dieting when you are a fat person. I learned a great lesson regarding shame. It led to honesty. Honesty in dealing with my dieters. They helped me learn how to handle shame. It no longer resides deep inside me, sat upon, waiting to pounce back at me. I can now laugh when I find it extremely difficult to get out of the back seat of a two-door compact car. Such happenings no longer ruin my day and lead to bingeing at night.

My mouth now speaks words when I am aggravated over other people's actions. It no longer must be stuffed with food for relief. It is still difficult at times to get the words out, but, after all, recovery is a slow process ending the repression of my feelings for so many years is like finally using a door with rusted hinges. It takes a lot of oil to get it going.

And now the frosting on the cake (we just can't escape food!)—my eating habits have taken a change for the best. I haven't had a binge in many weeks now. The wonderful thing is that I don't miss them! Some days I even remember to eat breakfast. I don't just remember; I get hungry. Really hungry. It's a unique feeling. Now that I am no longer using food to escape my feelings, it is just a pleasurable occurrence when I eat. I am not dieting. I do know that "dieting" is a thing of the past.

And the best thing is that I shan't retain my present weight. It is weight added by my eating disorder. Now that food is pleasurable and not a crutch to assuage my feelings, it no longer consumes me. I consume it, but in a normal manner, no longer bizarre. Give it few months or so and my body will weigh what it should—neither too fat nor too thin.

The Big Decisions

by
Mar Preston

Walking to the vending machine
Casual as a thief
Like it didn't matter

I see myself reflected in its glass
Definitely too wide for
   not so tall
And having *no business* eyeing the Snickers

A skinny young girl
Twenty years
Twenty pounds
younger fairer

Steps up beside me
clinkclink
punches up E10
Brisk
and kerwhap and chunka chunka
down the chute my Snickers bar

I'm still standing here
Long after
My quarters hot in my hand
Arguing

(Since when was it fair?)

In the Belly of the Beast

by
Susan Ito

——— ∞ ———

Most people get postcards from their relatives who are away on vacation; I got menus.Those paper placemats with the menus printed right on them were my mother's favorite, otherwise she would ask the restaurant for a "souvenir" and photocopy one to send to me. That way she could mark them up right as they sat at the table. "Stuffed Flounder" would be circled with a felt tip pen, with an arrow pointing to it that said, *Daddy had this, very good!* Then a circle around the spaghetti, that was for Nana, and another around Crab Legs, with an editorial comment: *Not worth all the work.* In the margins, scribbled notes about the bread (*by the time they brought it, it wasn't even hot*) and the salad dressing (*bleu cheese had plenty of nice chunks*). Sitting on my living room sofa three thousand miles away, I could compose their entire meal, from the appetizers to the inevitable dessert (*we ordered just one, with three forks*). So is it any wonder that I have an obsession with food?

When I was seven, I decided that Mallomars were my favorite food, and that stale ones were better than fresh. When they were nice and old, the cookie's chocolate-covered shell grew hard, the marshmallow underneath was deliciously chewy, while the cookie base dissolved into soft old crumbs. My family paid attention to this, and they aged the cookies like wine, carrying the yellow boxes down into the cool cellar. They marked the date with a ball point pen and six months, nine months later they would emerge, triumphant, and crack one open for me like it was an oyster. "Like this? Is this the way you like it?"

If food was the language of love in our family, it was the language of pain, as well. It was food that absorbed all discussion of topics too difficult or embarrassing to speak out loud. Instead of telling me about menstruation, my mother spent extra time on the slow simmering of her tomato sauce. Instead of discussing the cold tension between my uncle and our family, we went out for icy slush at Dairy Queen, a lime-flavored "Mister Misty" that passed through us with a freezing ache. Instead of politics, it was potato chips, eaten by the bag in front of the glowing blue television lights.

Food could be offered in one hand like a gift, and then quickly, without warning, it changed to a weapon. This was a hard lesson in adolescence, sitting at the kitchen table after school with my mother. She wouldn't look at me, I wouldn't look at her. We didn't speak, but shared in the silent afternoon ritual called Snack. A handful of Oreos, a slice of Sara Lee pound cake warmed in the toaster oven. No conversation, until I got up to put my plate in the sink. And then her words at my back: "Aren't those slacks getting tight around the hips?"

When I discovered that my husband-to-be couldn't cook, and worse, that he had absolutely no interest in learning, I panicked, and nearly called off the wedding. All my previous boyfriends had wooed me with food. Denis, with his grandmother's recipe for buttery rice and almond pilaf; Paul's mile-high grilled cheese and tomato sandwiches. They fed me chocolate truffles and garlic olives with their fingertips, and I swooned, following them into misbegotten relationships.

This last one was different though, he fed me with words, real words, and real talk that left me hungry for more. He stood next to me in bookstores, offering up poetry by Rilke, speeches by Martin Luther King, delicious little stories by Gary Soto. It's not that John didn't eat, or that he didn't enjoy it; it's just that food wasn't the center of his universe, his reason for existing. His relationship with food seemed cold, empty, purely utilitarian, and I wondered if I would really be able to spend my life with someone who didn't know how to make pancakes on Sunday mornings.

It took me a long time to figure out that I was the one with the problem and not him. I tried to make it a political thing, to say that society oppresses people who are fat, that it's the corporations who are making money off women's paranoia, and that my goal was to like myself the way I was. It's a good goal, but *the way I was* increased twenty-five pounds in a year. I couldn't keep up with myself. All that about society's discrimination against fat is still true, and I still believe it. But it didn't help me enjoy being fat. I wanted to like it, to accept it, to feel good about it. But it *didn't feel good* when I couldn't make it up the stairs without wheezing, when I had to give away all my clothes because they made me too depressed to look at them, let alone try them on. It wasn't a cause for celebration when I realized that I now qualified to shop in a "Large 'N Lovely" clothing store.

It took having a child and finding myself a year later, with a body that wouldn't quit…growing. And a mouth that said "feed me" when I felt bored. When I felt angry. When I was anxious, or afraid. I found myself cooking up boxes of neon-orange macaroni and cheese, and eating from the pot with a big spoon. Every night, I inhaled half a roll of Pillsbury sugar cookies. I went back to wearing maternity pants a year and a half after my pregnancy.

It was painful, this cringing each time I got close to a mirror, averting my eyes so I wouldn't have to see. I hated myself for being unhappy at this weight. I berated myself cruelly for bending to the pressure of fashion magazines and billion dollar diet industries. Each time I saw a "before-and-after" ad for some weight loss program, I sneered at the skinny "after" picture: *sellout*. Every time I went out with a friend who ordered a salad or mineral water, I would roll my eyes in disgust, and then defiantly order milkshakes, onion rings, fettucine. I couldn't see that I was cutting off my nose or rather, adding extra chins, to spite my face. My growing face.

This was an obsession that led me around on a chain, a thick heavy one that yanked on my neck, yanked me in a thousand confusing directions at once. It pulled me into bookstores, seeking out Dining Guides to every city, every country on earth: there I would sit, crosslegged on the floor, reading desperately the descriptions of Chinese food in New York, bistros in Paris, New Orleans cajun. It had me flipping through the Sunday paper, throwing out the sports pages, the business section, searching for the food critic's column. It had me curled on the sofa with a pile of cookbooks, organizing fantastic dinners.

I realized that the old, confusing, distressing message from my parents, "Here, eat—but don't get fat" is pervasive throughout our entire culture. There is a simultaneous obsession with slenderness, and with vast, obscene quantities and types of food. Here, in this culture, we are in the belly of the beast, deluged with contradictions at every turn. If it's here, I thought, if it's available, then it must be all right to eat it. I couldn't imagine turning down an ad that beckoned me with full-color photos. Eat, they told me. And I ate.

It never occurred to me that the liquor ads that said "Here, drink me…" or the cigarette ads urging me to smoke, didn't have the slightest effect on my behavior. Alcohol and tobacco were addictions, filthy habits. What I was doing, eating, was pure necessity, something people did every day. Incredible as it seems, there are people who can turn down Mrs. Fields or Kentucky Fried Chicken without a second thought, but I'm not one of them. It takes a lot of second thoughts, and third thoughts, and finally, threats and tricks.

I recently traveled to Central America and stayed with a family there. They fed me rice and beans, in small portions, three times a day, with a little fruit on the side. That was it. I wasn't hungry, I didn't think about food. I didn't feel paralyzed and overwhelmed when I went to the market. I just lived, and did what was there to do: enjoying being part of a family, part of a community, studying Spanish, working. What a relief it was, to have all that stimulation fall away, the ads, the cookbooks, the menus and recipes, the food itself, gone from sight. When I came back to the United States, I had lost several pounds without thinking.

Almost immediately upon my return, though, I started devouring everything in sight, everything I had been "deprived" of during those weeks away. But something, some shred of consciousness, allowed me to stop for a moment, to consider what I was doing. I remembered the simple plates of food that kept me satisfied in Nicaragua. I thought about what a relief it was to feel my clothes had been loosening around me, rather than tightening like a vise. Something clicked. I looked at the excess of food in the stores, in restaurants, in my own cupboard. I thought, would the Gutierrez family be eating all this? I measured the amounts of food I took in against my memory of meals in their home. I called it the Solidarity Diet.

Today, I feel a little lighter, both in spirit and in body. I'm not measuring myself against models in Vogue. I'm measuring myself against the prisoner that I can be, the prisoner of obsession and compulsion. This week, I'm able to drive past Kentucky Fried without screeching to a halt, without sitting in the parking lot with greasy fingers and a guilty conscience. It's a freedom that I never thought I would have again, and in a way it feels like I've been given my life back.

But I'm not naive enough to believe that this is it, that I'm home free. I know that it's a tenuous victory, that the beast is lurking underground, and I could slip into its grasp at any time. It *does* take a tremendous consciousness, and vigilance. I need to constantly be aware of what it is I put in my mouth, and to question myself: Do I *really* want this? It's a slippery slope, this having to eat every day. If I'm going to live in this land of overabundance and contradiction, it's not going to be easy. I've got to step carefully to find my own way, that narrow path in the wilderness.

Fourteen Days in the High Sierra... Excerpts from a Diary.

by
Jan Wienpahl

—⊙⊙⊙—

August 18, 7:00 p.m. Day #1. I'm sitting on a rock at the edge of a lake in a broad basin rimmed by barren jagged mountains. We hiked all day to get here, and Cathy and Peter and I are the only human beings on this lake. This is the wildness I constantly long for.

Why aren't my thoughts lost in the beauty? Why now, as well as all day and for the four weeks since C & P invited me to come, must I be tortured by thoughts of *food*?

I feel hopelessly out of control of the situation, as C & P planned and purchased everything, except as I'll mention in a minute. The supplies:

margarine
cracked wheat cereal
whole milk power (Nido,
which they get in Mexico)
cheese
granola
bread (for the first 4 days)
crackers (white and Wheat Thins)
prunes, raisins, dried apples,
    pineapple and papaya
gorp (peanuts, sunflower
    seeds, almonds, cashews,
    raisins, and M&M's),
Wyler's (lemonade powder)
trout (caught by Peter).

Lipton's Cup-a-Soup
Lipton's Noodles & Sauce—
    Alfredo, Creamy
Parmesan, and Butter; to all of which
    will be added Nido, cheese, and/or
    margarine
Kraft Macaroni-and-Cheese (add Nido
    and more cheese)
rice
bulgur
mashed potatoes
Carnation cocoa powder
Jell-o instant pudding mix (to add to Nido):
    vanilla, lemon, chocolate, custard

Why do I make such lists—just to obsess all the more?
Well, yes, but I think also they help control anxiety.

One source of anxiety is the fat. Irrational as this may be on a fourteen-day trek of 140+ miles up and down mountains and I despise myself for it—but I've asked Cathy to take out my share of noodles before she adds the Nido, etc.; and I've brought along nonfat dry milk to add instead. (I cannot, however, avoid the cheese, cream, butter, salt and other chemicals in the mix itself.)

I've also brought "healthy" granola bars and similar items to eat instead of cheese, and also "lite" cocoa and Instant Breakfast, which contain less sugar and no fat. They're still threatening, but not quite as bad.

Still a cloud of anxiety hangs over me. I will never be able to fill my stomach enough with this concentrated food. These sweet and too flavorful concoctions will tease my taste buds to a frenzy. I hate people who say that if you eat less sugar, salt, and fat you'll lose your taste for them—why, after twenty-three years of trying, haven't *I* lost my taste for them? I wish we had nothing but flour and water. I might obsess a little less and need a little less will power to stop eating.

Am I going to spend the next fourteen days obsessing about how many calories I'm consuming and burning, about whether I'll end up weighing 104 instead of 102, and about how much will power I'll need to stop eating at every meal? I *hope* that hiking along the crest of the Sierra with a thirty-five-pound pack on my back will bring me some relief.

But at this moment I've got to shift positions, as my pelvic bones are grating on this rock...

9:55 p.m. (Writing by flashlight.) As I expected, the Lipton's Noodles & Sauce Alfredo was *too* tasty. Far from satisfied, my dominant feeling was of wanting more.

Also for dinner were bread and cocoa, consumed most avidly, I'm sure, by me; and five small trout, cooked on the fire wrapped in tin foil with herbs. I enjoyed the latter thoroughly, and they make me less anxious about the other things, as they're not overly stimulating. Nature didn't do a lot of expensive taste tests on them to beat out competitors in the marketplace.

That was the official menu. It seemed to satisfy Cathy, who is six inches taller (than my 5', 3 3/4") and outweighs me by more than forty pounds, and Peter, who is a 6', 1" marathon-running muscle machine who ran for an hour this morning before we hit the trail.

But *I* wasn't full enough, so I finished with half a granola bar and some "fiber snacks." (These latter Cathy had tasted before the trip and pronounced "like sawdust." At least I don't have to worry about her wanting any.) Although I secreted myself in the shadows to devour them, I don't feel guilty, because I brought these extras for myself exactly because I figured I'd need more filling up. Still, it is embarrassing to admit.

August 19, 5:30 p.m. Well, I hate to say it, but food, my body and the next time I "get to" eat have been without question the topic most frequently on my mind all day, as much or more than in civilization.

I hope these thoughts aren't as obvious to C & P as they are to me, or they'll wish they hadn't invited me. I don't think I have been *that* verbal...

August 20, 5:00 p.m. I was happy to halt for the evening, since my neck and shoulders were killing me, but my nemesis would have had us keep hiking, to burn more calories.

I am as obsessed as ever. Rationally I believe that *I*, via will power, am the agent: I must let go of the obsessions or kill them, as I let go or could kill the mice I catch in the Havahart trap. I *feel*, however, as if I were a mouse, the helpless prey of some kind of malicious spirit.

But Jan, you *are* in control. Or must take control.

Anyway, I'm wondering what would happen if I lost control right now over Jan-the-Ravenous. I have never been in a situation where anyone had or tried to forcibly stop me from ravening, but out here with limited rations and two strong companions who undoubtedly want their share...

8:30 p.m. I wonder if C & P were as satiated as they acted after dinner with their groans and rolling eyeballs. It *was* a bucketful of bulgur, plus soup, fish, and cocoa. Even I was pretty full, but not up to my eyeballs. However, although there was enough left for at least a "mini-binge" (yes, on plain bulgur), I managed to repress the urge, knowing I'd loathe myself and feel physically horrible and thus the evening and tomorrow would be ruined. I was relieved when Cathy threw the remains into the fire so as not to attract bears...

August 23, 6:15 p.m. I'm sitting on a rock outcropping on a slope several hundred feet above Lake Martha, facing the fiery sun across the lake. The lake is cut by a swath of blinding glare with sparklets dancing along the edges.

One reason I climbed up here was "so that I can eat more tonight." The faithfulness with which I follow the public health gospel to look for every possible opportunity to burn extra calories infuriates me. Why don't I act according to the contempt I feel for such slavishness?

Maybe, however, on this trip I am relaxing a *bit*. I'm not counting calories down to the unit, and am enjoying the crunchy sweet granola, the Noodles Alfredo, et cetera, without *unbearable* anxiety. I am allowing myself to indulge in Wyler's lemonade powder (instead of Nido—more phobic about fat than about sugar) to enliven the soft, bland, cooked cracked wheat.

Today while Cathy nursed her blisters, Peter and I climbed Mt. Reinstein, a 12,604-foot peak above Lake Martha. We had brought lunch with us, but it wasn't noon yet and we had eaten breakfast late, and I suggested we not eat there.

Although he said he wasn't hungry, Peter thought that eating on the peak would be nice, so we ate.

Of course I really was hungry, as always, but, as always, was trying to delay eating as long as possible so I could have it to look forward to.

The other, even stronger motivation was that, given the choice, I *much* prefer eating alone. I hate sharing my primary pleasure with *anyone*. I feel as if my territorial imperative expands infinitely when it comes to food and eating. It's not just a question of physically sharing food (although Chinese restaurant style *is* the worst). Having to respond to other people, yak yak yak etc., not only inhibits my concentration on controlling my appetite but also invades the oblivious-to-the-world bliss I seek in my affair with food.

According to anthropologist Lionel Tiger, "eating alone represents a breakdown of man's fundamental humanism and something most people prefer not to do, given the choice." What do you think of that?

August 25, 9 p.m. I don't know how C & P could have been satisfied tonight, with only Cup-a-Soup (which Cathy bypassed), Creamy Parmesan Noodles, and cocoa. Cathy's appetite may be dampened by pain, although mine never is, here or anywhere. As usual I took out my noodles before Cathy added the Nido and margarine, and my cocoa isn't as calorific, but that couldn't make the whole difference between their seemingly complete satisfaction and my "hunger."

I added a granola bar and some raisins and prunes (plus nonfat milk powder in my noodles), and still wasn't full and could have eaten as much again without being overly stuffed. Of course one can stuff oneself with impunity only with celery, unless one doesn't mind being a blimp. Oh for the days of anorexia, when I was always starving but abhorred being stuffed!

August 26, 10 a.m. Am on the trail, waiting for C & P to catch up. As I've been hiking through the sun-dappled forest this morning, I have been as consumed by thoughts of food and body as ever. The second most prevalent sensation has been pain in my neck or foot.

I certainly notice my surroundings. My mind is never *lost* in thought about food and body. But neither is it ever lost in the beauty surrounding me.

Mind/body dualism? Yes, but I think I am at least two minds: the one at war with body and the one empathic with, closer to, body—the animal one. But both minds are always painfully aware of and engrossed with *body*, never detached and lost in the surroundings...

9 p.m. Well, sorry, but again: *How* can they be satisfied with a Cup-a-Soup

(Cathy excluded), Butter Noodles, half a candied pineapple slice (Peter excluded), and less than a cup of vanilla pudding?

(I positively lust for the pudding. All our shares were tiny tonight because most of it spilled when Peter tripped on his way from from the river in which it had been cooling.)

I had Instant Breakfast in addition, and remain unsatisfied.

August 27, 6:50 a.m. While a bumblebee occasionally drones by, off to the flowers, I'm lying in my sleeping bag thinking the usual tiresome thoughts.

Peter's running must be as much an obsession as my food/body obsession is, but I believe that, far from fighting it, he welcomes it. I'm sure he doesn't fear or hate running as I fear and hate food and eating.

Reason-and-will-power is the only thing that controls it. I cannot rely on satisfied taste buds or distended stomach or some other "satiety center" to curtail my eating. From anorexia at age fifteen to I-don't-know-what-eating-disorder-it-is-now at thirty-eight, I have totally deranged my body's natural functions. Fortunately, my will power is pretty well-developed by now. (It should be, it's had so much practice.)

(I wish it could bring back menstruation. Not that I liked menstruating, but its absence during all these years has not been a total plus.)

Independent of reason and will, I could and would eat pounds of granola, prunes, noodles, gorp, etc. C & P keep saying things like "You or "one" couldn't eat more than one piece of dried papaya, it's so concentrated (meaning densely sweet)". They think I'm joking if I say that I not only could, but want to.

August 28, 9:20 p.m. "I," that is my neck and shoulders and foot, am in considerable pain. Thus "I" spend most of the day wishing the hiking part were finished, simultaneously obsessing about expending more calories so that "I" can "afford" the granola, gorp, etc. I hate all these "I's."

August 29. From what I have been saying the next may seem impossible, but I *am* enjoying a relative freedom, on this trip, from obsession with calorie-counting, food avoidances, etc.

My stomach at the moment feels reasonably full of Liptons Cup-a-Soup, Kraft Macaroni-and-Cheese, Jell-o Lemon Pudding, and golden trout. "Reasonably full?" Hope on the horizon?

I am afraid, however, the same old rituals will re-establish themselves after the hike is finished. The freedom here is only relative. Further, "rationally" I can relax here because nothing "terrible" (e.g., gaining ten pounds?) can happen in two weeks of trekking ten miles a day up and down mountains.

God I wish I could always eat what I want to eat, let my body weigh what it wants to weigh (120, or, God forbid, 130?), and have fun—be one—with it. *Why* instead *must* I devote myself to miserable self-control, managing my body as a calorie-balance machine, counting calories in and calories out, simultaneously having to battle a mutinous beast inside?

I don't know. But I do know that only will power keeps me from eating endlessly and only will power makes me exercise (so I can eat as much as possible without turning into a tub), and if it weren't for will power I fear I'd be hopelessly bulimic.

Some psychotherapies would prohibit this analyzing, dredging up the past, dwelling on negative feelings, etc. (as I did with Dr. W. for eighteen months). Well, I *have tried* to stop dwelling on food and calories, *have tried* to lose myself in the beauty. Also I have tried to accept that this is the way I am, which hasn't given me any peace of mind either...

What about Cathy? Like the majority of American women, she is not happy with her weight, and she has mentioned the hope that this trek will work a few pounds off her. But she eats with spontaneity, not oppressed with a thousand mental calculations, and I don't see a huge will-power contest at the end. And I'm sure that while she hikes she is *mostly* absorbed in her surroundings: the views, the geology, and especially the plants (she's a botanist). Peter may be addicted to running, but I believe his preoccupations while hiking are like Cathy's (he's also a botanist).

I *know* they do not *mainly fixate on the next meal*. Maybe they begin to when they're physically hungry and their stomachs begin to contract, but not from the minute the current meal is finished *or even before*. (And I doubt they feel physically hungry the minute they finish, as I often do.)

Of course they talk about food, and sometimes it sounds like they're obsessing about it, but these times are centered around meals and packing up when we count and joke about the supplies. That's normal...

August 31. God I am tired of being so harassed by food thoughts. Of course this is not unique to this trip, but I was hoping it to be less so out here. How can a person be as hatefully possessed by food thoughts as I am?

One thing I thought when I decided not to bring a book was that I'd write myself a story, if bored. I haven't been bored—but look what I've been writing. What story does that tell?

If my "struggle" is, as Susie Orbach (*Hunger Strike: The Anorectic's Struggle as a Metaphor for Our Age*) would have it, a "metaphor for our age," all I can say is what a pathetic age...

Surrounded

by
Kathy Anderson

Even outdoors
she sees food everywhere

strips
of sycamore bark
crunch
like potato chips
underfoot

dog turds
on the grass
look just like
Tootsie Rolls

Belly tight
she tastes despair
rolling around
in her open mouth

Are You Hungry?

by

Helen Trubek Glenn

An old woman who is very fat lives in the forest in a little hut. Perhaps she is your grandmother. To get to her house you have to be very hungry but not want to be.

Sometimes you trick yourself. For six months you used very tiny plates but you piled on the slabs of roast beef which hung over the edges and the coleslaw left damp white circles on the table. Then you tried using large ceremonial dishes with gold borders on which you placed two julienned carrot sticks and three asparagus stalks in the center. You became very hungry but did not want to be.

One day you arrived at her house. Strangely, she seemed to be expecting you. Two places were set with blue plates and red bowls on a tablecloth embroidered with flowers and birds. There were five pots with lids bubbling on a big tiled stove in the corner. She lifted one lid at a time and sniffed the steam, then asked, "Are you hungry?"

First she served the soup, then brought brisket of beef with root vegetables and potato pancakes. She told you there were apple dumplings for dessert. And when you replied, "Thank you but I am too full to eat any more," she got nasty and set down a plate of dumplings in front of you and put a large spoonful of whipped cream on top, and watched carefully as you ate.

Then she brought a glass of milk, fresh from the cow, with a layer of yellow cream on top. Into a mustard-colored mixing bowl she poured two spoonfuls of sugar from a jar containing a vanilla bean pod, and cracked open a large brown egg which she beat into the sugar. She added this to the milk and told you to drink it. She watched your throat move up and down to make sure you swallowed every drop. Then she brought you nut meats and candied fruit, but you placed these in the side of your mouth and refused to chew.

She looked at you very hard, her slack lips turned down and her milky blue eyes glazed. Then she opened her mouth wide and said, "You are too thin. If you don't eat, how will you grow up? If you don't grow up how will you ever catch a husband? If you don't catch a husband, how will you ever have babies?"

When she said these words you found yourself back outside, by the white picket fence. And then the house, which you hadn't realized had been sitting down, stood up on its chicken feet, spun around three times and disappeared into your thickened waist hidden under a knitted sweater and rough-woven jacket. You wore these clothes to trick yourself into believing that your waist could still be circled by two hands.

Breakfast/Lunch/Dinner

by
Kara J. West

Breakfast

Okay, it's 8:00. If I eat a good breakfast, I shouldn't have to eat again until dinner. I'll have juice and fix a bowl of oatmeal, a soft-boiled egg and eat an orange on the bus. Oh, I already had two eggs this week. I really shouldn't eat another one. Okay, I'll have a light breakfast and get a nice healthy salad for lunch. I'll just have two pieces of wheat toast with a smattering of marmalade on one and the other plain. And a cup of coffee. Coffee always fills me up. Oh, but the caffeine. I really should give that up. I'll have tea instead. No, that has caffeine too. Maybe this kind doesn't. Does jasmine tea have caffeine? I can't remember. Well, I'll just drink a cup of hot water, same thing. Alright, now what was I going to eat? An egg? No, that's cholesterol. Salad? No, that's lunch. Toast! That was it. Bread, bread, where's the bread? I can't find the wheat bread. Don't tell me all we have is white. Oh well, I just won't think about the preservatives. In you go Mr. Bread, say hello to Mr. Toaster. Now, where is that marmalade? Mayonnaise, mustard, milk (skim, of course), marmalade. Marmalade? No marmalade. Oooo, what is this? Moldy yogurt—yuk! I don't know why I buy the stuff, it always goes bad before I get around to eating it. You buy it because it's good for you. Oh yeah, I buy it because it's good for me. What am I looking for anyway? What's that smell? What's burning? Oh no, my toast! Ow, ow, hot, hot, hot. Shit! Charbroiled bread—I don't think so.

Lunch

Thank God, 12:00. I am so hungry. Burning that stupid toast this morning made me miss my bus and I didn't even get anything to eat. What should I get? There's the deli downstairs. I could get a reuben with lots of sauerkraut. Mmmm, and mustard, on rye. Yeah, that's perfect...perfect except I'm cutting out red meat. Reuben, that's red meat right? What's it made with? Corn beef? Yeah, red meat. Well that's okay. Plenty of other choices. Let's see. I'd get chicken salad if it wasn't for all that salad dressing. Egg salad? No, cholesterol again. Pizza? No. Fast food? That's the worst. I guess I could get salad…again. I'm really beginning to hate lettuce. And besides it's not good unless you put croutons, bacon bits, eggs and all that stuff on it. And lots and lots of dressing which just defeats the purpose. God, what I wouldn't give for a nice big juicy—don't say it—burger! There I said it. And french fries, large. No, I'm not serious. I wouldn't, not really. Really, I wouldn't. You can trust me. I know—Chinese! That's it. I'll get Moo Goo Gai Pan, eat half now and have the rest for dinner. Two meals in one. But wait, I forgot I'm having dinner with David right after work. I really shouldn't fill up. Oh no, it's twenty after twelve. I don't have time to go anywhere now. I guess I'll just get a bag of pretzels from the machine and maybe some M&M's since I'm not having any lunch. That's okay, right? I'll get a diet soda to make up for the candy. That balances out, huh?

Dinner

Hello David. Kiss, kiss. Yes, this is a very charming place. How ever did you find it? What? Oh, I'm fine. Yes, you look good too. What? No, I haven't gained any weight. Bastard. What? Menu? Oh yes, thank you. Mmmm, pasta, steak, seafood. God, I could eat the whole damn thing. Lobster? No, that's too rich. Shrimp scampi? No, seafood is too expensive. Filet mignon! I haven't had that in ages. Red meat, it's red meat…no, no, no! Jeez, I'm going to pass out. What? Drink? Uh, uh, where are the beverages on this stupid thing? I'll just have water, thank you. I should drink more water anyway. What is it they recommend? Eight glasses a day? Or is it ten? What? The fettucine alfredo is wonderful, you say. Yeah, I bet. A moment on the lips, forever on the hips. God, I'm so light-headed. Where is that waiter? What? Oh, you come here at least three times a week for the all-you-can-eat lunch buffet? How nice! Bastard. Have another non-light beer. I wonder if I should try to make it to the restroom or just faint here? Curse that skinny little runt of a waiter! I could eat my napkin. I wonder how many calories it has. Thank God, here he comes. No, you go first David, I'm still deciding. Oh, he's having the filet mignon, rare. Bastard. Oh yes, make sure and bring extra butter and sour cream for the baked potato. What? Oh, me. I'll just have a salad. No really, I'm not that hungry.

One Evening

by
Joette Thomas

———⦿⦿⦿———

She arrives intending to eat salad. She selects turkey, provolone and sharp cheddar, tomatoes, garlic croutons and Italian dressing to decorate the lettuce. She is feeling very much in control, having passed up honey-cured ham and bleu cheese dressing, having resisted the temptation of a second handful of croutons.

She notices, while placing her plate in the dishwasher, an unopened package of chocolate chip-pecan cookies. She decides to allow herself two; they are exceptionally good and she eats four. She is starting to feel out of control, though she is not yet angry with herself, remembering the wise choices she made in selecting salad toppings.

She sits at the kitchen table to read a new book that her mother has given her. The book does not interest her much, but because her mother is in the next room she feels obliged to read at least a chapter or two. After seven pages she gets up and opens the refrigerator. It is a ritual, scanning the transparent plastic containers and labeled jars without really seeing them. She is drawn to a bag which contains the remains of last night's pizza. She selects the smallest piece and heats it, without a plate, in the microwave. Hearing the buzzer she grabs a napkin with which to hold the pizza and eats it, still standing, at the counter. She thinks that it is the worst pizza she has had in ages but continues to eat until it is gone; she is anxious.

She returns to the table and the book. Page fifteen marks the end of the first chapter, she decides to reward herself with another cookie. She knows, upon opening the bag, that one will not be sufficient and returns to the table with two. She finishes them and realizes that she is now angry with herself for losing control. Her mother asks her, from the blue chair in the next room, how she is liking the book. She answers that she has only finished the first chapter. She puts her hand on her belly; it is protruding and causes the elastic waistband of her skirt to pinch. There is no use in trying to control my food intake today, she thinks.

She reads to page twenty-three and gets up for a handful of mesquite-flavored chips. She does not generally like chips, but has decided to allow all of the things which she generally denies herself, as she has overindulged already.

By the end of chapter three she has eaten two more handfuls of chips and four large spoonfuls of tin roof ice cream. She tells her mother that she is tired and is going to bed. She closes the book and leaves it on the table, takes half of an apple fritter from a plastic bag on the counter and ascends the stairs. Being careful not to catch her reflection in the full-length mirror that hangs on the back of her door, she changes into a loose-fitting flannel nightgown. She brushes her teeth and turns back her covers. She descends the stairs, tells her mother that she thinks she will read a bit more before going to sleep. She goes into the kitchen and gets the book off the table and the half of apple fritter which she thought she would do without. She thinks, as she ascends the stairs, that it is better if she eats it tonight anyhow, that way she will not be tempted to eat it in the morning. She climbs into bed and turns out the light. She knows that in the morning her stomach will appear to bulge more than usual, and her hips will appear wider. She will wear the formless black dress that she purchased for just such days. She assures herself that tomorrow she will eat only fruit, and will run four miles; she promises herself that she will not lose control.

And So I Eat Again

by
Althea Rosenbloom

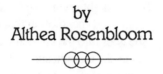

And so I eat again. Because I'm empty. Because I'm bored. Because it is the only way I know to be uncontrolled. Because eating is a rush, a thrill, a high. Because eating is love. And hate. And I seldom hate myself as much as when I've eaten—force-fed, crammed, consumed, devoured, obliterated every trace of what was, both the pain and the package. Two boxes of Girl Scout cookies gone in an instant, or seemingly so. Except the pain that stayed for hours. Sometimes sharp, sometimes dull, but always returning with a force that takes my breath away. And brings tears to my eyes. Or would if I could cry. But I can't and I don't and I won't. And eating is sedative (though far from sedate) and while I'm in it I don't think. The brain turns off and the voices recede. The eternal damned and damning chant fading away—crushed beneath the weight of one more cookie, one more slice of bread, as if I were carbo-loading in readiness for a marathon. But a marathon of the spirit requires a different sort of nourishment; sustenance of another form—and that I cannot digest. And don't know how to find, where to buy, and have not the currency to purchase.

The Space

by
Ann F. Price

potato chips
have a scrunchy sound
when you put four together
and bite down on them
they crumble and push each other
as they race
down your throat
filling ever so slightly
the lonely space

arms are lonely
bed is
days and nights are
and potato chips have a
scrunchy sound

frustration flails
at no one in particular
slamming doors
doesn't help
things aren't going right
the day started badly
ended and
middled badly
two chocolate chip cookies
gulped
slowly ease the tension

anger seethes
twisting the stomach
into a boiling pot
that begs for settling
french fries line up obediently
answering the call to duty
march with precision
into the pot
to simmer it down
and defuse the rage

one Snicker bar
chewed well
swallowed efficiently
hunts down the empty spot
and warmly melts around it

for an instant

I Wear My Stretchmarks
Like A Banner

Scenes From a Life, With Food

by
Anni Ackner

———⦿⦿⦿———

1. When I first thought about writing this, I was going to write something completely different, but today I have one of those awful, runny head colds *and* one of those awful, runny menstrual periods—the sort where you're afraid even to leave the house because you might have to change your tampon again before you get the front door locked—and it's pouring down rain and I feel as though my whole body had been caught in the path of a runaway Weed-Whacker and I want my mother. Or not *my* mother, precisely. My mother and I always had a lot of problems together and, anyway, she's been dead for six years. I want *somebody's* mother, the sort of mother who'd tuck you into a nice, warm bed with fresh, clean sheets (and wouldn't care if you accidentally got blood on them), and put a hot water bottle on your belly and a cool cloth on your forehead, and sit with you and tell you funny, very slightly risqué stories about how she was a virgin when she got married, and got her period on the first night of her honeymoon, making you laugh so hard you'd forget how miserable you felt. The sort of mother who maybe never really existed anywhere, except on television. Maybe not even there. Not the Beaver's mother, certainly—she wouldn't know how to cope with another female in the house and all that blood would appall her; somehow you got the feeling that she never menstruated herself, that Wally and the Beaver were born through some sort of antiseptic, otherworldly process that didn't involve sexual organs and tissues and tampons and never even *looking* at Ward's you-know. Not the Cosby kids' mother either—she was too smooth, too brittle, and she expected too much from her children; none of *them* ever blew their noses so hard that they tore the tissue and got snot all over their faces. Roseanne, maybe, although she might make too many jokes at your expense, or the mother on *Good Times*; someone large and soft and enfolding, but with enough sense of perspective to know where you began and she ended. I want that mother to come and take care of me.

Instead, I get up from the typewriter and make myself noodles-and-cheese, a huge pot of it. This was standard sick-in-bed food when I was a kid: thick white

172

egg noodles cooked to a firm pliantness ("How do you like your pasta?" Mark asked me one night, when he was cooking dinner for me. "Al dente or Al mushy?" "Halfway between," I said, and he didn't quite understand, but managed to get it just about right anyway), mixed with melted butter and cottage cheese—probably the worst thing in the world for you when you have a cold, with all those dairy products, but so wonderfully comforting and filling and satisfying. It conjures up images of being eight years old and too sick to go to school, but not sick enough not to enjoy the luxury of being the only one in the room I shared with my two sisters, with the television turned on for my special benefit, a pile of *Superman* comic books, St. Joseph's Aspirin for Children, with its gritty, orange flavor, and my mother bringing me noodles-and-cheese on the round, battered "silver" tray. These days, because I know about the benefits of low-fat diets in terms of breast cancer and other illnesses, and because I'm diabetic, I make noodles-and-cheese with soy bean margarine and low-fat cottage cheese, but it's still evocative, still comforting, still reminiscent of love in one of the few ways my mother knew how to show it.

My mother would have brought me Lipton's tea with a thimbleful of Manischewitz kosher wine in it, too, her standard cure-all for anything that didn't immediately require hospitalization, up to and including sprained ankles, chicken pox, and anything she couldn't identify but which she was always terrified would turn out to be polio (I'm young enough to have had both the Salk and Sabine vaccines against this disease, but she was old enough to remember being taken to "the country" during summer epidemics of polio, and friends dying, and friends in leg braces and iron lungs, and this fear never left her all through her life, although she had an implicit belief in the power of doctors). "It makes you sweat," she always said of this tea and wine combination. "Sweating is good for sickness." These days I don't drink alcohol, either, but I make myself hot, hot Bombay Spice tea, so hot it burns my mouth. It makes me sweat. Sweating is good for sickness. And never mind dairy products causing mucous and egg noodles giving you cholesterol, noodles-and-cheese is good for sickness, too.

2. My mother was a peculiar cook. She never was able to manage the simplest things—could never fry a hamburger without burning it, broiled lamb chops until they resembled old shoes with a bone stuck in them, hard boiled eggs until the yolks turned black with green tinges—but she could cook the most wonderful, elaborate Jewish dishes. *Gefilte* fish with a thin slice of carrot on top of each round ball, *chulupshes* (sweet and sour cabbage rolls stuffed with chopped meat and rice), breast of veal stuffed with potato *kugel*, *blintzes* full of potatoes and fried onions, and *sybleh kicklech* (onion cookies, which sound awful, but which are the most delicious things, especially after they've sat around for a couple of days, and they get hard, and you dip them in Maxwell House coffee). Chicken soup with *matzoh* balls, of course, and *kreplach* for festive occasions, and my favorite, salmon croquettes, made like I've never seen anyone else make them, with canned salmon and *matzoh* meal and an egg and Carnation evaporated milk, shaped into a patty that resembled a thick (unburned) hamburger, and fried to brownness in vegetable oil. I always looked forward to salmon croquette nights, not so much for the nights themselves—when we ate them warm, with mashed potatoes mixed with spin-ach—but because the next day I got to take one to school with me for lunch, on a Kaiser roll with sweet butter.

I haven't eaten any of these things since before my mother died, because the last few years of her life she was too ill to cook, and even when she was strong and well she was not the sort of Jewish mother who welcomed her daughters into the kitchen and taught them to cook. She was the sort of Jewish mother who said, "You're getting in my way in here. Go play, so I can get something accomplished." So I don't know how to make any of this food. My mother had a recipe book, though, a little, brown, three-ring binder with recipes written in her pretty, illegible handwriting, and pieces of paper stuck in any which way, covered with Grandma Miriam's copperplate and Grandma Bessie's spidery, foreign scrawl and Aunt Goldie's aggressive backhand. When my mother died, my sister Karen took this book as the thing she most wanted (Linda took my mother's wedding album and I took the gold chain my mother always wore around her neck). I speak to Karen infrequently, but when I do I always mean to ask her if she uses the recipe book. "Do you make *chulupshes*?" I want to ask her. "Do you make egg *farfel* and *matzoh brei* for *Pesach* and Grandma Miriam's plum cake that was so moist and heavy it just slid down your throat?" Somehow, though, I never remember to ask, and she never tells me.

3. But my mother was a great feeder of company, and this is one thing I did inherit from her. With my mother, even the most casual visits—from her best friend, Sydelle, who she'd known since high school and who lived a few blocks away from us, or my father's brothers, with their wives and children—called for egg salad sprinkled with paprika to make it look fancy, sliced tomato and onions, thick pieces of sour rye bread, sour cream chocolate chip cake from Dubin's or Ebinger's, or maybe, when we were really flush, *lox* and smoked sturgeon and cream cheese and bagels.

With my friends, I can't go to such elaborate extremes. For one thing, I haven't got the money, and even if I did, well, one friend is a vegan and one friend won't eat anything with wheat in it and one is lactose intolerant, and three are on reducing diets and I'm a diabetic and how do you reconcile all these things? Still, the urge to feed people is born in me. Company is here. Company means food. "Are you hungry?" is the first thing I'm liable to ask you. "Have you had lunch? Have you had dinner?" And I offer teas—I collect teas the way some people collect china and glass unicorns. People give me tea as gifts, Bengal Spice and Earl Grey and Ceylonese and Orange Blossom—and coffee, fruit, raw carrots, raisins and almonds, and pretzels, the great equalizer. Almost everybody eats pretzels. My mother used to eat the thin, brittle kind that came in a box unashamedly marked "Mr. Salty," and she dipped them in cream cheese. I like my pretzels thick and hard—I leave the bag open so they'll get even harder—and unsalted, and I eat them with coffee and (non-fat) milk. A mouthful of hard pretzel, well-chewed, and mixed with a swallow of warm, milky coffee—pure bliss after a long, dull day in an office, and the thing I most often offer company with varying and sometimes exotic food requirements. Even someone convinced that she needs to live on six-hundred calories a day in order to appear physically acceptable will eat a hard pretzel with coffee. Try it and see.

4. Thinking of six-hundred calorie a day diets reminds me of Debbie. For years—from the early part of high school until our mid-twenties, when we finally broke off what was, essentially, for a number of reasons, a very destructive relationship—Debbie and I were alternating dieting and bingeing buddies. In high school, we used to cut out after our first couple of classes—it was a huge, urban school and, as long as you showed up in home room and got marked as present, no one ever noticed that you were gone afterwards—and go to my house, which was only a couple of blocks away. Alone there—both my parents worked—we'd put the Grateful Dead and the Jefferson Airplane on my little stereo, open up two or three cans of tuna fish, add dollops of mayonnaise, and eat the mixture on Kaiser rolls, again thickly spread with sweet butter. (Did you know that there's a severe Kaiser roll shortage in this country these days? I haven't seen a really good one in years, not the sort that was mostly thin, crisp crust that broke off in pieces and got all over your clothes, with just a little bit of chewy, spongy white bread in the middle. A Kaiser roll, well made, was a perfect balance of hard and soft, and almost anything you put on one tasted good. All I see now are pallid imitations with no texture to them whatsoever, so absolutely uniform that it's difficult to tell crust from inside, not even fit to accompany a piece of cheap lunch meat, let alone some serious tuna salad or a salmon croquette.) Or sometimes Debbie would stay at my house on a Friday night and, long after everyone else had gone to sleep, we'd sneak into the kitchen— my room had originally been the dining room, and was connected to the kitchen by a pair of swinging doors, against which my bed rested. It was therefore possible, with stealth, guile and practice, to climb over my bed, push against these doors, and come out in the kitchen, bypassing the dangerous territory of my parents' bedroom—and come back with boxes of Screaming Yellow Zonkers—the name pulverized us—one for each of us, and eat them in the dark, while talking about

Music and Poetry and Art, and how miserable everything was on the East Coast, and how we couldn't wait to get to San Francisco, where things were Really Happening.

And we did get to San Francisco, too, sneaking away one day, selling everything we owned in order to raise the plane fare. I was seventeen and Debbie was eighteen and what was Really Happening in San Francisco, among other things, was that we both decided we were fat. Of course, we'd come to this conclusion at many other times in the past. It was almost avoidable. We were both tall and heavily built, with large breasts and hips, descendants of many generations of large, strong Jewish women, but this was the Age of Aquarius, not long after the Age of Twiggy, and girls were supposed to be mystical, ethereal, delicate creatures in lacy shawls and Indian print skirts that tied around the middle, bell-bottomed jeans and cut-off tee-shirts, wandering barefoot in the sand. Debbie and I just didn't fit the image, so on different occasions we'd foregone the tuna fish and Screaming Yellow Zonkers, the trips to the falafel shop during lunch hour on the days we stayed in school, our mothers' rich dinners and lived for several days on lean fish and Special-K and skim milk. It was in San Francisco, though, that surrounded by gentile hippies with long flowing hair and tiny breasts, and freed from our mothers' fears of starvation and consumption, that we decided to Really Do Something about The Problem.

First it was Weight Watchers. We didn't have enough money for both of us to attend the meetings, so we split one membership, and I went to the meetings—"You're more the group type," Debbie said—then came home and explained all the material and handouts and diet sheets to Debbie. What I remember most about this period was this thing called "Weight Watchers Spaghetti." I don't know if they use this recipe anymore, but it was very popular then. You took bean sprouts and boiled them to gumminess in tomato juice, and this was supposed to taste just like spaghetti. What it tasted like was bean sprouts boiled to gumminess in tomato juice, but if you were hungry enough—and Debbie and I were achingly hungry—you could close your eyes and pretend. Debbie and I pretended an awful lot during those Weight Watcher days.

And there was all that lettuce. Lettuce was a Weight Watchers' "free" vegetable—you could, theoretically, eat as much of it as you could cram into yourself—and Debbie and I used to sit on our porch steps on those warm nights—somehow it's always summer when I think back on Weight Watchers times. Maybe we only managed to last one summer. I don't know—and eat head after head of lettuce, sometimes two or three apiece, one leaf at a time, taking mincing, tiny bites to make them last longer, and talk about the lovers we'd have, the clothes we'd buy, and the food we'd once again be able to eat, when we were finally "thin."

After awhile, though, Weight Watchers just didn't cut it anymore. The meetings were boring and expensive, all that weighing and measuring was a drag and, most importantly, you didn't lose weight fast enough—you were lucky if you got off two pounds a week. Debbie and I felt that something more drastic was called for. We began devising our own diets, ultra-low calorie diets. six-hundred calories a day. four-hundred calories a day. No calories a day. It got to be a sort of contest—whoever could ingest the least won. "I had a slice of swiss cheese on a piece of diet bread and half a grapefruit today," Debbie would announce. "I had a hard boiled egg and a banana," I'd say, and we'd go paging through our various books of calorie charts, arguing about whether, even though I'd taken in a smaller amount of food, that food had more calories, so I'd actually eaten more.

Not that we could keep it up for very long. A week. Maybe two weeks, and Debbie would say one night, or I'd say, "Let's binge," and we'd look at each other, half in guilt and half in excitement, and quickly, before we could think about it too much, make a midnight run to the Seven-Eleven. Submarine sandwiches and huge bags of potato chips. Candy bars and that raw cookie dough that came in tubes. Tastee-Cakes and M&M's and Hostess Fruit Pies. We'd come home with our rattling paper bags, undress, wedge ourselves into the long, narrow single bed we shared—me at the head, Debbie at the foot, so we could face each other—and pig out, falling asleep with bursting, painful stomachs, covered with crumbs.

The next day, of course, we'd feel awful, both physically and mentally. Cramps, diarrhea, that dragged out, bad taste in the mouth feeling you get after a sustained sugar high, and the even worse feeling that we'd "sinned" again, we were "bad" again. And we'd swear we were never, ever doing to do *that* again. And we'd go back to starving ourselves again, until the next time.

Starve and binge. Starve and binge. It was the pattern of my life for so many years, with and without Debbie.

5. But, see, I didn't want to talk about the bitterness this time. There's been so much bitterness around food in my life, and I can't ignore or deny that—I don't even want to. It's all been part of me—those feelings of being too fat, too large to be loved, too gross to fit into the world, to deserve my piece of the world—and I've talked and written about it so much, and about my efforts to grow away from it, or grow through it. But just for once, just now, I wanted to talk about the joy, to reclaim the joy, to make it mine again.

Food as love. Food as giving. Food as warmth and comfort and happiness. It's weird, but when people say things like that, they often act as though it's negative. "Do you equate food with love?" the psychologists and weight loss specialists ask, and if you answer "yes" they say you have an addiction, that your emotions are mixed-up and misplaced, that you need to change your outlook, that food is fuel for the body and nothing more, and you must learn that, if you're ever to have a "normal" life.

Food is fuel for the body and nothing more...

My mother, sweat glistening on her forehead, presiding over the huge, special Passover *seder* meal she'd cooked in our tiny kitchen, chopped liver and onions, chicken soup with *matzoh* balls, brisket and potato *kugel*. My Grandma Miriam's plum cake. Thanksgiving at my friend Jo Anne's house, surrounded by her husband and five kids, and the huge extended family we've made for ourselves, Ed and Ricky and Paul and Nancy and all the others, eating turkey and stuffing, mashed potatoes and biscuits, and the sweet potatoes Gary always tries to make that never turn out exactly right, but always taste good anyway. Walking with Pat at Scenic River Days—our local equivalent of a county fair—stopping to sample fresh milk at the dairy farmers' exhibit, apple dumplings from the Ladies Auxiliary of the Hopewell Mennonite Church, Lebanon bologna from the Meat Packers Union. Irish cream coffee and chocolate turtle cheesecake with Mark at the Sixth Street Cafe. Egg salad with paprika on it to make it fancy. Hard pretzels and tea and noodles-and-cheese when you don't feel well. How can anything that carries with it the memories of so much love, how can anything that comes surrounded with friendship and sharing, how can anything that *nourishes* so, in all senses of the word, be an addiction, a detriment, the sigh of a warped and twisted personality? How did I ever let anyone convince me that this was true? How did I let myself believe that my big, heavy, enveloping, warm and human body was something to be hated and diminished in any way possible, something ugly and unhealthy? How can my passion for making and sharing and giving and taking food be anything other than joyful?

"Remember your joy," my friend Vijay always says, and every day I fight to do it.

6. When I learned I had diabetes, I cried. I wasn't sure why at the time. The diagnosis was no great surprise to me—virtually every woman in my family has developed adult onset diabetes, going all the way back to my great-grandmothers on both sides, and I was familiar with the signs and symptoms. So it was no shock and no surprise, but I cried anyway.

Later on I thought I had it figured out, and I told Mark. "It's because I'm going to have to start obsessing about food again. I've spent the past eight years trying to learn not to obsess about it, not to worry about every bite that went into my mouth, and now I have to start all that again." And Mark said—because Mark is sometimes a lot more honest than I'd like him to be—"But you never really stopped obsessing about food, did you? Has there ever been a time in your life when you didn't have some food restriction or another? When you were a kid you were kosher, so you had to follow those rules. Then there were all those dieting years, and, even after you stopped that, you were vegetarian for awhile, or you wouldn't drink a diet soda because it wasn't 'politically correct' in terms of Fat Liberation, or you didn't eat tuna because of the dolphins, or some damned thing or another. And if you weren't doing it, you were writing about it. So when did you stop obsessing?"

And he was right. I'm still obsessing, but now I try not to label it, but to live with it and love it, because now it keeps me healthy and off medication. Non-fat milk instead of whole milk. Whole wheat bread instead of cheesecake. No more apple dumplings, but a crisp, raw apple that fills my mouth with sweet water when I first bite it. Diabetes controlled by diet instead of medication. The numbers on a glucometer.

And in the Sixth Street Cafe—"Look, Anni. Here's something you can eat," Faerie, the owner, says, and presents me with a plate of the most wonderful pasta salad imaginable—olive oil instead of mayonnaise, succulent pieces of broccoli and spinach and carrots and tiny, tangy chick peas. Slices of orange and kiwi and whole, ripe strawberries on the side. Made for me. Made with love.

Remember your joy.

Fill 'er Up

by
Lou Ann Thomas

———— ⟨O⟩ ————

Food has been my friend, my therapist, my lover, my confidant, my medic and ultimately my greatest enemy. It has consumed more of my life than any one person, place or thing. You see, I'm a food junkie. I am almost constantly thinking about my next meal. Just as soon as one meal is over I begin planning, fantasizing, worrying about the next. I plan my days around eating and the food I want to eat. I plan social engagements around food. I turn down social engagements in order to stay at home and secretly eat. I have an addiction to food, but unlike most other addictions, my addiction to food is one I must learn to manage while still using. I cannot abstain completely from food and still live.

So much of our culture and society revolves around food. We gather around it for holidays, for dates, for social and business reasons. We see it advertised on television, on billboards, in our publications. We get coupons in the mail for it and can order it already prepared and brought to our door. Food is everywhere and encouragement to eat is everywhere.

My personal encouragement to overeat came from my family. When I was five my grandfather would have cheeseburger-eating contests where I was the only entry. He would announce to my cousins, "Let's see how many hamburgers Lou Ann can eat today." My brother, who was twelve years older than I, soon began doing the same thing. And so began my habit of gorging myself. It may have been negative attention I was getting from my grandfather and brother, but at least it was attention.

I often felt invisible as a child. My brother was the focus of my parents' attention and I was the next to youngest grandchild. Not the youngest, who often gets attention just because of their birth order, but the next to youngest. Nowheresville. Eating and the subsequent gaining of weight that naturally followed made me less invisible. People had to notice me as I got bigger, and bigger, and bigger. When I was ten and shopping for school clothes with my mother, she and the clerk began discussing my weight and size. My mother was talking about how worried she was about me. The clerk answered her concerns with "Don't worry. When she gets a little older and gets interested in boys she'll lose the weight." My mother nodded her head hopefully. I guess I showed them both. I never really got interested in boys. Their conversation clued me in that if I didn't lose weight boys wouldn't be interested in me. Perfect. I wasn't that interested in boys and I was afraid to have them interested in me, so I'd stay fat and keep insulated from them. As I grew older I did become interested in a few boys and even more women; unfortunately my weight kept me insulated from those I wanted to be close to.

As I began to feel more and more self-conscious about my weight and more and more unattractive and undesirable because of it, I used food as a way of filling my growing emptiness. I learned early not only to use eating and my appetite as a way to get attention, but also to use it as a band-aid and a balm. When I felt rejected, a peanut butter sandwich made me feel less so. Maybe it was the way it stuck to the roof of my mouth, making me feel a little less alone. And chocolate…chocolate was good for whatever ailed me. A broken heart called for pizza and ice cream. Pizza was always a good general anesthetic. Maybe it was the spiciness and that I would pick it up with my hands and with a primitive grunt tear off mouthfuls with my teeth. The ice cream was important for its numbing properties and in helping to remind me of the cold, unfeeling lover that I was now better off without.

One of the greatest challenges I face when it comes to my body image is a relationship to a lover. I feel such an intense longing for a lover, for someone to touch and hold me, for someone to make love to me. As strong as I feel this desire, this yearning, I also fear someone touching and seeing my body passionately and intimately. It has been difficult for me to allow someone to really make love to me, to my body. Did I feel I didn't deserve their love and attention? Yes. Was I ashamed of my body and believed that they would be repulsed and go screaming in horror from the bedroom? Most definitely. I think I have always closed down when my lovers were making love to me. I disconnected from my body. I became very uncomfortable and awkward when they would touch my body intimately and sexually. I would hurry myself as close to orgasm as I could, as fast as I could, just to have it done with so that we could just hold each other again.

I have never lost myself in orgasm in the presence of anyone else. I used to think that I just hadn't found anyone who loved me enough to make me feel loved and relaxed enough. But as I have learned to love myself more I realize it has been because I haven't been able to love and accept myself enough to relax with my body and allow it to be loved and appreciated by someone else. The answer has not been in finding a lover who loves me "enough," but in being a loving person to myself and that being enough. I am learning my body. Learning to see myself as a sexual and sensual woman. I am learning to feel my body and feel my passion, my nurturing, my soft, warm lovingness and loveability.

A turning point for me realizing that I have always tried to fill the empty space within me with food and it can only be filled with me, with my own loving. As I learn to love and accept myself more fully, more wholly, I have begun to change. I have become more clear about who I am and what I want. I have become stronger and less dependent on validation from outside myself. I still feel insecure about my body weight and fight feeling unattractive every time I leave the house, but the battle is easier won each time I attack those negative thoughts. It is a war, but sometimes I leave my house feeling like I am the beautiful woman I know I am inside, and if someone out there doesn't care to see me as I am, then who needs them. I am teaching myself not to reach for the Oreos and pepperoni each time something feels sad, confusing, or depressing to me, but to stop and spend more time finding other ways to feed myself, to feed my spirit. For me that may mean a hot bubble bath, a long walk, dancing, meditating or laughing.

I still have a long way to go, but I am learning that, when I give myself the love and acceptance that I deserve and desire, I am truly free and nothing is impossible.

Mine

by
Annemarie Succop

———— ⬡⬡⬡ ————

The pictures of my family when I was little make it seem as though I was the only member. Dad always held the camera, Mom was "too fat" to be in pictures, Sue, "too ugly." Me, pudgy, blonde, cute, sprawled across lounge chairs in pigtails and a bikini; me, with my new glasses; me, fat. I was a fat little kid. Mom had a problem with it; I didn't. I liked my bikini—the top covering what would later make me look like a woman, my round belly sticking out above the bottom.

When I was twelve, my sister left home. Suddenly Mom noticed me, really noticed me. Sue had never been what she wanted; now I was even worse, I wasn't even Sue. I was a lanky adolescent, thin and awkward, with every joint and bone curve jutting out. I still liked my body, I still had a sweet tooth, my body and what I put into it were still mine.

I went to visit my big grown up sister. We shopped for clothes; she hated herself in a bikini. She stopped eating for the rest of the week. Sue was doing it, why wouldn't I? Besides, not eating felt like being stoned, another trick Sue had recently taught me.

My battle with food, my body and womanhood had begun.

I went home. I ate only what was put in front of me, and as little of that as possible. No one noticed. Mom had never liked us eating "unauthorized food" anyway. I felt power, control over my food intake, my body, my self.

I was bulimic for years. "But you don't throw up!!" I still can't drink a cup of coffee without thinking about what it's doing to my insides, what it will take with it on its journey out of my body, without wanting to take the post-purge tub baths of my young adulthood.

Years later, I stopped eating entirely. What did I need food for? I didn't need love; why admit to any other weaknesses, needs, wants? My body changed; I looked like my lanky adolescent self again. I didn't need a bra anymore. Men looked at me anyway, said I looked great. Women, concerned, asked where the rest of me had gone. I didn't know; none of it seemed to be mine anymore anyway.

My body craved food, warmth, comfort, support. I greeted every attack of hunger with fear. I would lose control, eating everything in sight, constantly on edge. What need was I not meeting, what need could I not admit to? Every need suddenly had to be met right now, yesterday, last week.

I ate. I ate and ate. My body wrapped itself in layers. Was this one long binge, or the cumulative hunger of the past few years? One day, busy, I skipped a meal, and later saw myself throw my keys across the room in frustration at some minor event. I instantly recognized the irrational flash of anger as my constant emotional state of a few years past. Was I really calmer, happier, more reasonable now "just" because I was letting myself eat? My sanity was more important to me than the shape of my body; I kept on eating.

Without purging, and without a clear line separating hunger from a binge, when would I *stop* eating? Gaining weight could be as scary as losing it had been. I wanted to know that my body, my self, would be the same when I woke up as when I'd gone to sleep, the same a week into the future as it was a day ago. Determined to stabilize my weight at whatever it was where I started, I began the long road of "watching what I ate" without slipping into obsessive control. Through awareness of both my food intake *and* my food-abuse tendencies, my weight has settled into "comfortably fat." I no longer worry about the mysterious disaster that would befall me if I were to gain weight; it's here, I'm living it, and it's not so bad after all.

I wear my stretchmarks like a banner, a bandolier ringing my hips. Food is my companion now, a need I fill for myself. A necessary weakness. I've reframed bulimia as a "stress symptom," an occasional visitor to break the dull monotony of migraines and hyperventilation attacks.

I live in my body; food comes to visit. I cook. I avoid red meat. I've cultivated a liking for some vegetables. Carbohydrates are my friends. Food and I have worked out a complex truce, the record of which is stitched into my skin. My body and what I put into it are again becoming mine.

Toward Fullness

by
Laurie Rizzo

I am a woman. A daughter, mother, lover. An eater. Food nourishes me and you, and you, and you, my loved ones. Eating delights my senses. But I have misused the gift of good, habitually eating to excess. Over the years, I have done battle with my food desires, losing more campaigns than I have won. I try now to make my peace with food.

One glance in the family album reveals that I was the fattest of babies. My mother tells how my newborn helplessness evoked in her a sense of inadequacy. "You poor thing," she said, "depending on *me* to meet your every need." She kept feeding and feeding me—smooth infant cereals, salty ground chicken, creamy vanilla pudding—and I never refused. I imagine myself the contented, placid baby, taking the offered spoon over and over again, receiving and receiving. Do I please you? Yes, I must. You keep offering me more. Smiling and gurgling. I am good. I am full.

Food memories from early childhood are delightfully simple. I had such a good appetite. I ate my broccoli and green beans, my soft-boiled eggs and grape-fruit. I liked everything from iceberg lettuce to devil's food cake. Food pleased me, and my appetite pleased those who were most important to me.

But gradually, my appetite came to elicit a different response from my parents. At a family festivity, my cousin finished his chocolate cupcake, and promptly asked his mother for another. She assented. I asked my father for the same, and was refused. "You've eaten *enough*," he said. With all the intensity of childhood, I writhed as my cousin enjoyed his treat.

Another memory: I am playing with two cousins on a summer day. Hot and bored, I am happy when my mother calls us in for lunch. She serves her specialty—tuna and egg salad on Wonder bread, milk, and canned peach halves. I devour my portion, but it does not fill me. I want the sensation of cold food on my tongue to continue. I don't want to return to the burning swings with my disagreeable cousins.

185

I ask my mother for an extra half-sandwich, another bowl of peaches. She refuses, clearly dismayed by my request. I sulk.

What is the matter with me? Why aren't I more like other children— exhilarated and rowdy, active and thin? In a tender moment, I confide to my father that I can't wait to grow up so that I can do what I want to do. (Eating what I want is a metaphor for doing what I want.) He is genuinely astonished. "Childhood is the best time of your life," he says.

By age eight or nine, my parents—especially my father—begin to fret over my plump body, and try to regulate my food intake. They forbid me the sweet, rich foods that I crave. I resent their interference in this most private matter, and covet the forbidden treats.

I become a food fugitive. A liar and a sneak. While going about my business, I am forever glancing over my shoulder. If the coast is clear, I dash to the bread box and stuff whole Oreos into my mouth, or, in a bolder move, to the freezer where I scoop ice cream with my bare fingers. I then rush back to homework at the table or dishes in the sink and try to "act natural." More often than not, I am caught in the act. And chastised.

In later years, my parents offer to buy me a new wardrobe—all the most fashionable clothes—if I will just lose twenty pounds. They send me to Diet Workshop. To tennis lessons. My father charts weeks in which I must lose two pounds in order to win freedoms. Every Friday evening I take off my shoes and step on the scale before his watchful eyes.

As much as I resent this parental interference, I *want* to lose the weight. I have internalized the idea that my body is "wrong." I daydream a lot. In my fantasies, a thin body fixes everything: I break out of my shyness. I have a boyfriend. I am beautiful. All my hidden talents blossom. I feel worthy. I am wildly popular among my peers, yet my own person.

So, I start diets dutifully: four bananas and three cups of skim milk a day. I eat all the roast beef, mayonnaise, and lettuce that I want, and pee onto a stick which proves, by turning purple, that my body is carbohydrate-deprived. I exercise. I fast. I may lose weight temporarily, but always I gain it back.

In one moment of truth after another, food defeats me. I need the taste of it in my mouth. I am ashamed of my weakness, and I envy those who seem not to hunger. Those who are strong, satisfied, thin. I perceive them to be my rivals and detractors.

For a time during my adolescence my mother loses her hunger. "You're not eating enough," my father tells her one evening. "You're too thin." He brings her a generous bowl of chocolate swirl ice cream. She smiles at him, and begins to swallow small spoonfuls. As soon as my father is out of sight, she pours the remainder down the bathroom sink. "I can't finish this," she says. "I'm too full."

I feel sick with envy. I want my father to tell me that I am too thin. To indulge me. To feed me. Eat, my love. I'll nourish you. I'll answer your heart's every desire. I want the ice cream, and I hate myself for the wanting. I yearn for fullness.

I see women all around me pretending to be full. "It's too much," they say. "I can't eat that much." They are ashamed of their appetites. They pummel their desires. "You must not give in to the ice cream, you sniveling bitch. It shall make you fat and ugly. It shall give you body odors, pimples, and stretch marks. Mosquitoes shall swarm over your body. I order you to refuse the ice cream!"

I am not much good at this false, white-knuckled fullness. If only I could eat my meals and live my life out of a genuine fullness rising from my core.

But how to find such fullness?

When I enter college, a photo ID gives me unlimited access to food. I lose weight, almost without trying. I think it is simple, then, to solve my relationship with food. The overfed baby. The pudgy girl bridled by her critical parents. She has proven over and over again that the size of her body is in her hands, not theirs. Finally free.

It is not so simple. A few years later, I am still battling. Like an accordion, my body expands and contracts. I read feminist critiques. They make sense. It does seem that our misogynist culture has taught me to despise my body, and to hanker after impossible images of beauty. I decide with grim determination that I will forego diets and learn to love my body as it is. But grim determination does not lead to love.

Many years later, I'm coming closer to the mark. I am indebted to a woman whom I barely knew. She stood in a crowded room and said, "Hi, my name is Esther. I'm a heroin addict and an alcoholic." Her face was creased, dark, and beautiful, her voice humble, but full of tenderness for herself. At that moment, something opened inside me.

Just a crack.

The beginnings of forgiveness toward myself and my weakness.

Unclenching the fists of denial and shame for all the years of using food. Culture and parents may have aggravated my food habit, but it is I who have harmed myself.

Food has served as my blanket, my succor. I have used food to dull my feelings. To divert my restlessness. As such, it has choked my growth. More than distorting the size of my body, it has kept me from knowing my deeper hungers. From facing my life squarely.

Now, I may begin.

Weighing the Cost

by
Barbara Katz

—⊙⊙⊙—

I can't remember a time when I wasn't obsessed with food. I grew up the youngest of three children in a household of overeaters. My mother jokes that "goyim drink and Jews eat." Whether this is true or not is immaterial; rather, it shows that my mother, in all her denial, subconsciously made the connection between our family's eating patterns and the alcoholic personality.

I mention my mother because I believe that she is the spark which ignited my eating disorder. It was my mother who enticed me to eat whether I was hungry or not. "Eat, eat *tateleh!*" she cried at every meal, usually encouraging us to eat seconds so there would be no leftovers. And then, in the next breath, she would be telling me I needed to lose weight. "*Oy*, you were such a beautiful baby! You have such a beautiful face, if you'd only lose weight!" My mother despised fat people although she, herself, was rather *zaftig* at the time. I believe that all this negative criticism and fat-hatred created a self-loathing and destructive obsession about food.

From my earliest memories until the present time, I have loved food and counted on it to make me feel better. Food was power and control. Food was making my own decisions about what I would eat, when I would eat, how much I would eat. Food was taking control over what I looked like. Food was solace: it comforted me when I was upset. It seduced me with its taste and with the hypnotic pleasure of chewing and swallowing. It was a complete sensual experience in a childhood devoid of any luxury.

But most important to me now, food was retaliation. When I was angry at my mother, I would eat in defiance thinking, "I'll show her. She wants me to diet and become thin, but I'm going to *eat right now*." Food was a weapon which left no victor. It might have cut down my mother's dream of a thin, popular daughter, but it cut down *my* dreams, too. Food was a sword I turned inward to punish myself for not being that perfect child.

When I was young, there were only breads and starches to binge on in the house. My mother, as the self-appointed food gestapo, kept all sweets out of the house. When I arrived home from school each day, she gave me an apple as a snack while other children in the neighborhood had cookies and milk. I became a secret eater, sneaking downstairs in the evening to butter up four or five pieces of bread and bring them back up to my room. Once, on the holidays, I snuck some red pistachio nuts upstairs and stashed them under my pillow, but was betrayed by the pink stain left on my bedspread. On the weekends, when we were allowed to have pretzels and chips, I sat alone watching TV, munching the entire bag of pretzels hypnotically. This became a practice which I carried throughout my life.

As I look back, certain events come forward in full-blown memories of shame and humiliation: being weighed in by the nurse each year in school while the other kids watched; gymnastics and track and field events where I could never accomplish half the exercises; shopping with my mother each August for school clothes in the "chubby" section; being ridiculed by other kids; and outgrowing clothes before the season even ended.

High school was hell for me. My father had died and my brother and sister had moved away from home. Now, it was just my mother and me sitting around the kitchen table. While other girls began to date and socialize, I turned inward and became reclusive. I stayed home most of the time watching TV and eating. Now my mother and I shopped together and I was allowed to buy my special binge foods for the weekend—usually a combination of sweets and salty/crunchy food. I also started smoking cigarettes about this time and was a heavy smoker from the ages of sixteen to twenty-five.

I was still in "regular" sizes, but I had made my way up to a size sixteen. I went on several drastic, unhealthy diets of my own invention, like eating nothing but lettuce for dinner, or eating only one meal a day. I never lost any significant amount of weight for any significant amount of time. Being a picky eater, I never went to Weight Watchers. Besides, I thought I could handle my food problem on my own. I had no real perception of my size and couldn't have told you if I was thin, medium or fat. Actually, I'm *still* unable to see my size objectively, even today.

On rare occasions, my friend and I would plan weekend-long binges when my mother went out of town. Mom would give me money for food and we'd buy every single binge food we could think of. We even ordered a cake from the bakery and, in a moment of inspiration, had them write *Mazel Tov* on it!

Surprisingly, my weight stayed about the same throughout college, even though I had started smoking pot, which kept me completely anesthetized. I wasn't used to the social scene in the dorms, so I stayed back in my room, smoking dope and eating. I fell in love with my straight roommate, but refused to admit to myself that I was a lesbian. I couldn't binge eat in front of my friends and roommates, so I rarely had the opportunity to do the kind of serious overeating which I had done in high school. Occasionally, I would go on a diet and try to become that mythically happy, thin woman I saw on TV On one diet, I ate nothing but eggs for breakfast and lunch. But nothing worked for long and the deprivation was terrible.

It wasn't until I left college and married my husband that my overeating blossomed into an uncontrollable disease. I was still trying to live a straight life and fulfill my mother's dream, but at a terrible emotional cost. I was overeating, smoking and doing pot all the time. From 1980 through 1984, I must have gained about fifty lbs., settling in at about 230. I would come home from work and smoke dope while I made dinner. After dinner I was so dulled by the pot that I would park myself in front of the TV for the rest of the night, only getting up to go into the kitchen for more food. My husband gave me a popcorn maker on our first anniversary (I guess he thought that would win my heart!) and I would eat large batches of heavily buttered popcorn, smoke dope, and watch TV until it was time to go to sleep. I avoided sex with my husband as much as possible, often claiming that I was too stoned or too full. This went on for about four years, during which time I withdrew more and more from my friends, my husband and myself.

I finally realized what I was doing to myself when I began to notice the early signs of heart disease—shortness of breath, tightness in my chest, a wheezing sound when I breathed and even chest pains. I had trouble clearing my throat in the morning. Because my father had died of heart disease, I was very worried and finally quit cigarettes, after having tried several times before. I stopped smoking pot, figuring it would be hard to keep away from cigarettes if I was stoned.

I gained a little weight at first, but after a few months I found Jane Fonda—not the person, but the workout tape. I got obsessed with exercise. I went on a moderate diet and exercised every single day for the next eight months. Of course, my body changed dramatically and I lost about thirty-five pounds and several sizes. I felt great and thought I had finally licked my "weight problem." I was wrong! I had never dealt with the reasons that I overate, and had simply changed my obsession from food to exercise. That kind of transference does not work. I still had a lot of unfinished business in the way of personal growth, relationships and recovery.

After falling in love with a gay woman at work, I got into therapy and finally learned to accept my lesbianism. I left my husband a few months later. My life was emotionally in turmoil, as I began to deal with being alone, beginning life over again and coming out to my family. With all this going on, it didn't take long to go back to the food. Food was my mainstay, my rock. It had always been the one thing which never disappointed me. I was single now, and there was nobody around to see what I ate. I started bingeing a lot—just about every weekend. By the grace of god, I never went back to cigarettes or pot. Also, I kept up the exercise so I gained weight much slower. It was totally crazy. One night I would eat a ton of popcorn and the next morning, at 7:00 a.m. I would be swimming my guts out doing laps in the pool! My weight began to creep up, maybe gaining fifteen pounds over the next two years.

At the time, I couldn't understand what was going on. My life was the best it had ever been. I was making new friends and had a real social life for the first time in my life. But the food obsession was there, permeating my entire life. I hadn't noticed it, but it had become progressively worse year by year. When bingeing, I would eat 2000 calories or more of food in one evening. Because my apartment was very small, I would bring my food to bed with me and watch TV there. Food became my protector, helpmate and lover.

I had two more changes coming in my life. I started law school in the fall of 1988 and soon after fell in love with the woman with whom I have been living for three and a half years. Everything in my life was different again. Being in a relationship where I was really emotionally involved was new and scary. So was law school! Once again I turned to food to quiet my feelings. But this time, I really put on the weight. Because I was busy in law school, I stopped exercising. Once that happened, there was no chance of keeping my weight or size stable. I put on about eighty pounds in three years. Actually, I would have put on about one hundred pounds, but I tried to diet a little and took off a few pounds here and there.

I'd like to make it clear that my problem was *compulsive overeating*, not being *fat*. The weight gain was just a symptom of my disease. And I no longer hated myself for being fat. I had come to believe that people are naturally different sizes, just like we are different colors. I had grown to accept and like myself as a big woman. But I went way past big. I finally had found enormous.

My weight peaked during the summer of 1991. I wore a size 24 or 26 depending on the fit. It was humiliating to have to shop in big woman stores again, where well-intentioned saleswomen would help you find the more "slimming" styles. And the clothes were either boring or gaudy.

Besides the clothes, however, was the much more serious physical and emotional effects of the weight. I felt horrible. The food kept me tired and dull. At times, I would eat so much that I had trouble waking up in the morning. I started having this extra heart beat—kind of like a "thump" (this reminded me of my father again, who had had an arrythmia, or abnormal heartbeat, just before he died). My blood pressure, always about 110/70, was now 130/90. My period even became irregular. I started skipping entire months.

I really reached bottom during that summer. I was working in the city and had a one and a half hour commute on the subway to get there. I was horribly obese and had no new clothes for the job. I would start to sweat just from the walk to the subway and I never cooled down, even though the subways were air-conditioned. While normal-sized people stood around me seemingly comfortable, I found myself with sweat trickling down my face. People would look at me disdainfully as I wiped the sweat off with a tissue. But the worst indignity of those rides was that I did not fit in the subway seats comfortably, at least not those with contoured seats. If someone got up to leave, I would not take his or her seat for fear that I wouldn't fit or that I would sit on the person next to me. And people avoided having to sit next to me because I overflowed into their seat.

The psychological pain of these experiences was devastating. My life was totally out of control and I barely felt human anymore. I started having anxiety attacks when I had to make oral presentations at school, or when I had job interviews. My self-esteem was so damaged by my physical appearance that I didn't believe a prospective employer would see the "real me" inside my frame. And as always in my life, my mother continues to add insult to injury, often calling me up just to ask me if I'd "gone on a diet yet," or "when are you going to lose weight."

Throughout these years of confusion and pain, my partner has always stood by me with love. She has had to work hard to convince me that I am still attractive to her. With her support, I walked into Overeaters Anonymous ("OA") on September 25, 1991. I weighed 282 pounds. I got a sponsor right away and committed myself to a food plan the very next day. I have been eating "three meals a day, nothing in between, one day at a time" ever since. No, it has not been easy. After giving up cigarettes and pot, overeating was my last addiction, but it was the most pervasive. It was very hard to eat my dinner and know that I wasn't going to eat anything else that night. I had never done that before, and, at first, I didn't know how I was going to make it through the evening. But I finally realized that if you have patience, you can get through anything. Evenings come to an end and I don't die if I can't binge.

It has been hard going emotionally. I no longer use food to cover up my feelings. Consequently, I have been feeling a lot more. I've been very angry at my mother and sometimes dump my anger most inappropriately on my partner. But I'm beginning to sit with my anger or fear. I'm learning that it is okay to feel those feelings and that I don't have to *stuff* them with food.

Today, I am celebrating my eight-month anniversary in OA. I have lost seventy-five pounds so far, and last month I menstruated on schedule for the first time in a year. My heart "thumps" have stopped and the anxiety attacks have decreased. By the grace of god, I will go forward, one day at a time, until my body is healed.

Wisdom To Know the Difference

by
Kriste Fredheim

Bag of potato chips,
Ben and Jerry's chocolate,
Pizza,
Crackers and Cheese,
Double-fisted.
You never arrived for our date.
Business meeting, of course.

In bed together, making love, you grab my belly…
Knead it between your fingers,
Squish my thighs against each other…
Tell me you like plump women.
Bathroom light on, faucet running,
Fingers down my throat,
Tears from the pain,
Heaves for familiarity.
I don't like plump women.

Wonderful smells in the kitchen; it's our anniversary
And you're cooking dinner.
Cherry pie in the fridge for dessert.
But remember, I'm on a diet.
He does, hands me a salad, no dressing.
The pie still tastes good at midnight when he's asleep.

Five miles a day, aerobics, weight lifting,
Exhaustion.
You don't notice.

Laxatives, pills, starvation, nothing works...
Except, of course, the brownies my son made.
Told him the dog got to 'em.
Hope he didn't see the crumbs on my dress.

Looking at the skinny young girl sitting at the table beside us
In the restaurant.
Order me a scotch.
This may work as well as my fingers.
Thought I saw you wink at her.
Gulp, gulp.
You go to the restroom,
She's left her chair and heads to the ladies'.
Smile on your face when you return...hers too.
I notice.

Lambchops,
Potatoes au gratin,
Another scotch,
Asparagus coated with butter,
Garlic bread,
Cheesecake,
Another scotch.
My turn for the bathroom.
I use a lot of soap on my hands.

Dresses in store windows.
Size seven on my wedding day...
You didn't like pinching my stomach back then.
Then again, I didn't have one.
Bikinis.
Mini-skirts.
Summertime.
They say tight shorts are in fashion now.
You wish I would wear them,
Instead of everything baggy.
Baggy always fits.
So do hot fudge sundaes.

Heard your car pull in tonight...2 a.m.
Stuffed the gin and pretzels under the bed,

Ran to the toilet,
Wiped my face, brushed my teeth.
Listerine.
Tried to look pretty.
Lit a candle in the bedroom.

Strange smell on the sheets.
One I don't remember.
You never make love to me anymore.
Wrapping my arms around your warm, thin body…
I remember the gin underneath.
Push me away.
Business meeting wore you out?
I understand.
You just don't like plump women anymore.

Tears.
Gin and Scotch and whatever's in the liquor cabinet.
Twinkies for Ben's school lunches.
Soap operas and popcorn.
Two bags.
Beautiful actresses, beautiful lives,
Beautiful marriages.
Popcorn and kitchen sink.

Infidelity

by
Claire S. Chow

I am eating more
and doing less, these days.
I sit on buses reading recipes,
the novels go untouched.
I memorize meals
and spend more time in supermarkets
than you could understand.
These days
a well-turned roast
or a loaf of home-made bread
satisfies more than just my appetite.
One thing I am learning:
There are foods that you can count on,
they never let you down.

Do You Diet?

by
Karen Twenhofel

"Do you diet?" asked a friend my freshman year in college, as I was stuffing a third homemade chocolate chip cookie in my mouth.

"Do you know how many calories there are in that one cookie?"

Stopping to think for a moment as she and two other friends stared at me, probably wanting to ask me the same question, I realized that I really didn't even know what a calorie was.

All my life I was thin. I never had to worry about what I ate. I snacked and ate sweets, but I was an active child. I'd rush through dinner, inhaling just enough on my plate to satisfy my mother and then run out to join my friends to play until dusk.

I stayed thin until my senior year in high school. Although I didn't even realize it at the time, I did gain about fifteen pounds that year. I just continued to eat like I'd always had, only at seventeen, I wasn't as active as when I was a child.

When I went off to college, the weight gain only got worse. Without having my mom there to cook every meal for me, I thought I would lose fifteen pounds the first month.

How wrong I was! Actually, quite the opposite happened. By November I had gained the fearful "freshman fifteen" and then some.

This brings us back to the beginning of my story—that very moment that will remain in my memory forever—the moment my friend spoke those three words to me (now thirty pounds overweight), "Do you diet?"

From that moment on, my life changed. I not only learned what a calorie was, but just how many were in every food I'd ever heard of, and how to put as few as possible in my body.

From that moment, I'd taken on a new enemy, one more powerful and destructive than any human can be. One that nearly fought me to the death—my death.

Practically overnight, my daily caloric intake dropped from 2500+ down to well under 1000. I went from eating three full meals a day plus in between-meal snacks and late night pizza runs to barely one full meal at all.

Not only did I cut down on food, I also became an exercise fanatic. I went to my dorm's aerobics class every night religiously. Then, after the first fifteen pounds came off, I had enough courage to be seen in a swimsuit at the olympic size pool to add thirty laps to my daily exercise routine. The more weight I dropped, the less I ate. The more compliments I received on my new slimmer appearance, the less I ate—and the more I worked out. It was a rigorous, vicious circle.

Food became an obsession with me. I'd sit in class and plan my meals (if you could call them that) and figure out exactly how many calories were in every bite I put in my mouth each day. Every day it got fewer and fewer. 700-600-500-400. I'd eat a small bowl of cereal at breakfast and a small salad (no dressing) for lunch and maybe another salad (consisting of only a few leafs of lettuce and a tomato) for dinner. Nothing else. No snacks—not even a saltine cracker.

I just couldn't eat food anymore. I was so obsessed with it that I thought about it every second. I thought that I couldn't eat anything or I'd gain a pound—an ounce. If I did splurge and eat some extra mushrooms on my salad, I'd plan two hours of exercise to work it off. I remember one night sitting in my room studying with my friends. One of them made popcorn (no salt, butter or oil) and gave me a small bowl. I couldn't eat just one small kernel—not one. These voices took over in my head, "Don't eat it, Karen. You'll get fat. Don't do it."

There literally was a battle going on in my head. A battle encompassing me so greatly I thought I was sure to lose. In two months, I'd lost thirty pounds. I know this because I was weighed at the doctor's office where my worried friends dragged me after my period completely stopped.

Everyone kept telling me I looked great. Boys started looking when I walked past them. Everything fit and looked great when I went clothes shopping (I was a size five now). But the more people told me I looked great, the more boys who looked and the more size five clothes that fit, the more weight I wanted to lose, the more I worked out, and the less food I ate. When I looked in the mirror, I still saw this overweight person staring me in the face. I couldn't get it in my head that I had lost the weight I wanted and now I could begin to eat more, as long as it was healthy food.

Starving myself and exercising rigorously continued for the next few months. My dropping weight also continued. I remember going shopping for some bib ski pants for a ski trip I was going on with my friends. The only ones I could find to fit me were in the boys department—size twelve.

I really didn't realize that anything was wrong with me. I thought I could just keep on going like I was and I'd never gain any weight again. The problem was that I wasn't maintaining my weight at one level but that I was continuously losing. There were also physical things occurring in my body other than not having my period anymore. My hair was falling out and was getting thinner. It was breaking off more easily, too. I would constantly get head rushes every time I stood up. I didn't have much energy anymore, although I did push myself hard enough to do my thirty laps and my aerobics class everyday. I also started to get very withdrawn and kept to myself a lot. When my friends would all go out to dinner or to a party I stayed home quite often, afraid that I might have to eat something, and afraid that my friends would find out that I didn't eat.

I was fooling myself all the time, though, to have thought my friends didn't know what was going on. They were very much aware of what I was doing to myself and, after a while, they finally alerted my parents who were naive to it all. Once my parents got involved, I couldn't hide anymore. The more I snuck out to the pool and the more I pushed my food around on my plate to look like I ate my whole dinner, the more often my best friend was on the phone to my parents reporting it all.

When I went home for school breaks, my parents would drag me to doctors who always said the same thing. They would give me a chart on the "four food groups" and tell me to eat more. Of course, this was all in vain. I didn't listen to them. I do see now, however, that my parents thought they were helping. They never even knew what an eating disorder was before this, so I can't blame them for not knowing what to do about it.

The one immediate thing they did do was to put me in counseling. I saw the college shrink twice a week for the rest of my two years at Virginia Tech. I guess she helped me, but at the time I hated going to see her because I really didn't think there was anything wrong with me. She made me think there was though. I guess that's what her job was—to try and snap me out of it, to get me off this downhill slide that was destroying me.

My dad made me weigh myself everyday and fill out a chart for him so that I (and he) could actually see if I was still losing weight. We found out that I was, about a pound every few days.

When school let out for the summer, I gained a few pounds to satisfy my parents that I was better. This was to convince them to let me move across the country and transfer to a different school to start fresh and get away from the eating disorder. I learned later that it wasn't something I could run from, but that it was inside me.

Once I moved, it only took me a month or so to slip back into my same old routine. It started all over again. I joined a gym where I began to work out one to two hours a day, plus I went back to eating fewer than 500 calories. And by Christmas, my best friend was back on the phone to my parents telling them all about it. I was put back into counseling and had to report my weight to my parents again. This lasted for the next two years to finish out my college career. During the summers, I would gain a few pounds to keep my parents happy when I went home to visit, but when school started again, my weight went back down.

After I graduated, I moved into a studio apartment by myself. At the time I thought it was the best thing to do in the world, but now I look back and know it was really a big mistake.

I really don't know if it was due to living alone or what, but at this point in my life something happened. I had enough of starving myself so much that I just went in the opposite direction. I began eating too much. It all happened the summer after I graduated. I was job hunting which was very stressful. I went out and hit the pavement with my college degree expecting every door to just open up in front of me and opportunities to drop right at my feet. How wrong I was. First of all, I really didn't know what type of job I wanted. I ended up applying everywhere for all types of jobs thinking my college degree would get me right in, which of course didn't happen. Every "no" I got or every "I'm sorry but you're not qualified," or "I'm sorry but you are over-qualified," drove me into the greatest depression I've ever experienced.

I began to eat, and then make myself throw up. I went from starving myself, to eating normally and throwing it up, to over-eating and throwing up. It all changed so fast. I really can't even remember exactly when it all happened. All of a sudden I was eating again, actually eating real food I had forbidden myself never to eat again. Then after I'd eaten it, I'd start to feel guilty, so guilty that I'd run to the bathroom to get rid of everything I'd put in my stomach.

I realize now that this eating disorder, bulimia, was far more harmful to me than starving myself was. This is because it can be hidden so easily from everyone. I could eat healthily in front of people and then retreat to the bathroom to throw it all up without them even knowing it. I told no one that I was suffering from bulimia because I was so ashamed that I had it. I'd heard of the disease before, in fact one of my best friends had it, and I always thought of it as an ugly, disgusting thing. Before I could never understand how anyone could actually make themselves throw up, let alone eat a lot. Because no one knew, I received no counseling, no opinions from doctors and no support or concern from my parents or friends.

And living alone, I could eat as much as I wanted, because I'd know I could easily go in my bathroom to throw it up with no one around to find out.

Like before, I became addicted to this eating disorder. The more I threw up, the more I couldn't stop. This went on, progressively getting worse, for at least two years. I started off throwing up a few times a week, then once a day, then three to four times a day to finally, after everything I ate. No one knew, and I never got help.

I really wanted to stop, but I just couldn't. And I wasn't skinny any more either. I had gained weight throughout this whole two years. The throwing up after I ate did not make me lose all of the calories I'd just put into my body. Several times I called clinics to get help, but never actually went to see any counselors. I was still too ashamed and I thought I could make myself quit.

I did finally stop, and in fact today I'm actually well enough that I'm having my first child, but it was a long hard battle I was strong enough to win. I really owe it all to one person. I owe a lot to this person, for he made me feel loved and accepted for myself and made all my insecurities disappear. This acceptance of myself, I believe, is what I was somehow searching for in the eating disorders. The less I ate, or in the other case, the more I ate and threw up, the more I felt it would make me a better person or better-looking so I would be accepted by others. It was the only thing I felt I could control in my life. But when I met this person, who is my husband now, he changed my life. All of a sudden there was someone who loved the real me, the inside me as well as my outside. I didn't have to pretend or hide anything from him; he accepted me for who I was. I'm not saying that my parents did not do this also, but here was this stranger who actually felt this way about me and it made me feel wonderful.

The day we moved in together was actually the last day I ever made myself throw up. My self-esteem was improving and I didn't need to control my life with an eating disorder any longer. Soon after we got married, and now, I'm pregnant and feel the best about myself I ever have. I was really lucky I met my husband when I did, because I'm not sure how long I would have made it, throwing up as much as I was. I know that it was very dangerous that no one ever knew and that I received no help. To this day, the only one I've ever told about the bulimia is my husband, and that was only a few months ago, after we were married.

Almost five years of my life were wasted on eating disorders. Five years I lived in shame, in my own little world, keeping secrets and telling lies to everyone I loved.

Now that I'm all better and can look back, I see how lucky I am that I was able to get well and be here today to tell my story. I know there must be some, maybe many, who aren't so lucky.

I think of myself as recovering still, because the eating disorders were addictions like any drug can be. I am afraid sometimes that I could slip back into one of them again, although it has been a full year since I've been well. For now, though, I can be thankful, relieved and even a little proud that I was strong enough to overcome something that encompassed my whole being for so long.

The Rueful Dieter

by
Marilyn Coffey

Tonight's carrots
waterlogged

spinach
overcooked

spirit of meatloaf
broken by filler

gravy too like glue

coffee weak

And this the meal
I dreamed of
all day long?

"Are You Thin Yet?"

by
Jennifer Semple Siegel

—— ⌘ ——

"Are you thin yet?"

Those words, arriving one day—cloaked in a birthday card and sizable check from a great aunt in California—will remain forever grooved in my mind. So will the words that followed: "I hope so because, if not, you'll have to spend your birthday money on fat clothes, and we know how ugly *they* are. And you have such a pretty face."

Happy thirteenth birthday.

I'll never forget the pain from that cruel and cutting message, perceiving, somehow, that love and acceptance were doled out according to how close I could get to my ideal body weight, that fat was a sacrilege, a dirty family secret to be eradicated like a communicable disease, even if it meant sacrificing a little girl's self-esteem.

At thirteen, I was a shell-shocked veteran of the diet wars, having already embarked on reducing regimens, ranging from the downright fad diets ("eat sugar and lettuce for every meal for one week") to the downright dangerous (amphetamines prescribed by my family doctor who himself weighed a whopping 300 pounds).

So I was an expert in attack strategies required for tackling those extra pounds, having begun several years before the vicious cycle of food deprivation, weight loss, bingeing, weight gain, guilt, more food deprivation, more weight loss, more bingeing, more weight gain, more guilt, a cycle that has stalked me throughout my adulthood.

I started picking up unwanted pounds when I was eight. At first, my family teased me about being "pleasingly plump" and "a whole lot to love." Yet, as I look back on old pictures, I wasn't overly obese; perhaps I was simply going through a stage where my height hadn't yet caught up with my weight.

I'll never know, however, because my family would not accept me as I was, and (with the best of intentions, I'm sure) started me on my diet merry-go-round.

First they tried "scare tactics": "If you eat those potato chips, we'll need a derrick to get you to school." Then it was "let's-hide-the-food-from-the-kid-and-maybe-she-won't-notice" approach.

I noticed all right and took steps to compensate by raiding my piggy bank and sneaking down to the corner grocery store for Reese's Peanut Butter cups; I could always depend upon my good friend chocolate to fill that empty spot in my stomach. Once, when I was home alone, desperate to fill that void with something warm and soothing and yet too frightened of food to light the pilot light on the stove, I heated Campbell's Chicken Noodle Soup in the electric percolator.

So by the time I had received the fateful birthday message, I was still not thin, even though my family and doctor had tried just about everything, including thyroid pills, even though my thyroid was (and still is) perfectly normal.

By now, the verdict from my family, peers, and media was obvious: I was not okay. I was fat; therefore, I was stupid, oafish, somehow sub-human, unfit to play with "normal" children. And they let me know about it, too, calling me "Fatso," "Heifer," "Fatty-fatty, two-by-four, couldn't-get-through-the bathroom door."

I hated myself, and, even though I was raised in a staunch Catholic family, I once considered selling my soul to the devil "if only I could eat all the peanut butter cups in the world and still lose weight." Instead, with my mortal soul intact and my self-esteem shot to hell, I began, in earnest, my self-imposed cycle of food deprivation.

By high school, I still was not thin, but my regimen now included days of total fasting, followed by sheer bouts of gluttony. I was completely out-of-control, and, except for periods of self-imposed exile into "dietland," remained out-of-control on into adulthood.

In 1986, I embarked on my last regimented diet, a grueling journey through the Optifast Program, currently the hair shirt, the sack cloth and ashes of all programs, The Ultimate Food Deprivation Diet, the Just Punishment for the Fat, my last crack at formal self-flagellation: for twelve weeks I ate no solid food, limited to drinking 70-calorie milk shakes six times a day. During those three months, I became totally obsessed with food; I counted the days when I could finally put one bite of poached chicken breast into my mouth; I had sexual dreams about food, bacchanalian banquets where the line between good taste and raunchy sex blurred; my senses sharpened, my eyes grew gaunt, my temperament developed a steely edge.

So was I thin yet? Of course not, because the minute I stuck that first bite of *real* food into my mouth, I was fat again, no matter what the scale told me. In a matter of weeks, I *was* fat again, simply reinforcing what my head had known for years.

I finally gave in to my old enemy food, eating whatever I wanted, feeling guilty after every bite and every binge, hating myself more and more. I was mired in a four-year feeding frenzy.

August, 1990: I found myself facing forty—and still not thin yet. For the first time in my life, I actually considered suicide; however fleeting the thought might have been, the possibility was frightening enough to send me scurrying for professional help. I know this revelation will shock my loved ones, including my husband, but I have to tell my story like it is.

Two months later, after receiving some excellent psychotherapy in conjunction with a workshop on overcoming food obsession, I'm finally coming to terms with my love/hate relationship with food. Most importantly, I'm discovering that I need to learn how to love and accept myself—no matter what my weight is and no matter what others (including my family) think about me—unconditionally and without reservation. I'm not quite there yet, but for the first time in my life, I feel hope, *real* hope.

Sometime in late September—I'm not exactly sure why or how—I made a decision to toss away all the diet baggage I've been carrying around for all these years. Now I ignore all the diet gurus and their snake oil remedies and have vowed to get on with the rest of my life.

Also, I have given myself unconditional permission to enjoy the foods I love, in whatever quantities I desire, and whenever I want—guilt-free. Moreover, I have called a moratorium on foods I never really liked in the first place but felt I had to eat because they were "thin" foods for "unthin" people.

In essence, I have thrown out all the old diet rules. After all, generally speaking, people who are naturally slender and have a positive self-image don't put themselves through a lifetime of agony over food. And, now, neither will I.

Am I thin yet? No, but, hey, I'm a heck of a lot happier now than at any other point in my life. Even at slightly under 200 pounds, I am able to look at myself in the mirror and see someone I could genuinely like—even love.

Letting Food Off The Hook

Losing the Passion to Lose Pounds

by
Linda Weltner

———ⓘ———

I finally lost five of the ten pounds I put on this winter. It wasn't all that difficult. I have a formula for successful dieting which I'm perfectly willing to share.

Don't eat.

You think I'm kidding, don't you? You think I lost this five pounds eating cottage cheese and green beans without butter, and fresh steamed vegetables and fruit. That I didn't touch bread, or cake, or ice cream, or anything with sugar or fat or salt. That I cooked my chicken without any skin, that I didn't let a morsel of fried food touch my lips. Well, you're wrong. You can't lose weight that way. That's how I'll eat to maintain the weight I'm aiming for. To actually lose pounds, I have to quit eating.

What exactly do I mean by that? Coffee for breakfast, exercise for lunch, and for dinner a soup whose ingredients I found on a sheet of paper titled "The Secret Diet of the Secret Service" which was left behind at a Xerox machine. This soup, which contains tomatoes, cabbage, onions and zucchini, supposedly has fewer calories in it than you use up eating it, and so I can have as much of it as I want. I snack on halves of unsweetened grapefruit. For a real treat, there's always a sliced apple, sprinkled with cinnamon and zapped in the microwave.

Keep this up long enough and you'll lose weight too. As long as you walk at least two miles a day, ride your bike everywhere, and spend twenty minutes three times a week with your aerobics tape. When all ten pounds are gone, I get to go back on my maintenance diet. Out of prison. On parole. With an occasional dessert for good behavior.

It's gotten so that I feel reluctant to go to parties where there's sure to be high-calorie hors d'oeuvres. I don't look forward to eating at restaurants where I'm always tempted to order something delicious and fattening. It's easier to stay home where there's nothing in the breadbox or the refrigerator. It's also a lot less fun.

That's why this question keeps popping into my mind and won't go away: Is there ever an age when a woman can let herself go?

Let's face it. I'm fifty-three. I wouldn't mind living in a culture that thought it was about time I got rounder and thicker, that still used words like "voluptuous" and "curvaceous." I wouldn't mind looking more maternal—big breasts, a soft round stomach—if everyone agreed I still looked beautiful, if I were considered cuddly and pleasantly plump, *zaftig* as they say in Yiddish, and could forget about trying to remain sexually attractive. (See how brainwashed I am. What I meant to write was "and still be considered sexually attractive.")

I want permission to enjoy eating again.

Everywhere you turn there are articles about the tyranny of thinness in this culture. Girls, it seems, routinely start dieting in fifth grade, and so many female college students have eating disorders that bulimia and anorexia are not only devastating, but commonplace. Everyone's alarmed at what amounts to a nation-wide eating phobia in young women, but what about the older woman trying to resist the way her body naturally thickens at the waist, the way her skin loosens and flaps below her upper arms, the way fat collects upon her stomach?

Every day the battle gets more difficult. It takes time and energy, and worst of all it takes space in my mind, filling my head with calorie counts and broken resolutions. I want to eat without thinking about it.

Yet that's what I did all winter until I saw the numbers on the scale and observed the bulge of my belly. And no matter what I said to myself—*My husband doesn't care about a few pounds more or less...This is the way women are supposed to look at my age...It feels good not to have to watch every morsel I eat...No one's feelings for me are based on how much I weigh*—I still felt self-conscious. I know how crazy-making it is to live in a society that expects an older woman's body to be as slim as a young boy's, but still I fussed and fumed buttoning my slacks. The picture of the "ideal" shape was so deep in my psyche that, against my conscious will, I disliked my curves in the mirror.

It didn't help to blame my unrealistic standards on the culture. I couldn't stop minding the way I looked. In the end, it seemed easier to lose weight than to accept myself as plump.

There are rewards for being thin: the look of disbelief that flits over people's faces when they hear I have two daughters in their twenties, and the frequent comment, "You don't look a day over forty." I can wear last year's summer clothes for another season. I don't look bad in a bathing suit.

But how much longer can I keep this up? Isn't there some point in a woman's life when this long fast is over? When I can eat a decent meal without feeling guilty? When I can take a vacation without having to starve myself for weeks after? When I can walk into a room of older women and think how soft and huggable we all look with our padding?

It's bizarre to spend so much time thinking about food. And I don't binge; I don't vomit. According to the literature, I don't even have a problem. If this obsessive preoccupation is normal, what is it like to have an eating disorder? I can't bear to think about it.

Do I have to stay thin until I die? Am I supposed to look forty when I'm sixty? Why must I try to look like Linda Evans instead of Edith Bunker? Who says so anyway?

Five more pounds to go.

Is there food in the afterlife?

Lesbian Stew

by
Lee Lynch

———CCO———

At dinner the other night, a friend suggested that lesbians have a unique relationship with food. What I took to be the essence of her thoughts was this pithy observation: we fuss over food. It is another of the innumerable issues that make us so loveable.

There probably is not a lesbian in the world who would not, at the slightest sign of interest, tell you about her personal history with food. For some, food has been a joy; for others, a struggle. I spent my earliest years swallowing great quantities of evil-tasting stuff called *tonic* in an effort to fatten my skinny frame. One of the most humiliating moments of my childhood was the time my father, rather than take my hand to cross the street, encircled my wrist with his big fingers and laughed at its slightness, like he'd found a pitiable lone toothpick in an otherwise empty jar. We were crossing a busy street in Boston at the time; to this day I can't think of the school, the VFW post, the apartment building on that site without a sense of shame. All those years of nauseating tonics and I still couldn't measure up.

As an adolescent, I wished food could be served powdered, in a capsule, and that the social rituals around it would be banned by the World Health Organization. Dinner Out was the only thing worse than Dinner At Home with the nuclear family. Why in the world groups of people gathered around tables and talked to each other while stuffing their mouths was beyond me. I had what the doctors called a "nervous stomach." They gave me little blue pills, bitter white pills, tiny peach-colored pills. In college, after a little blue pill and some gross imitation of nutrition, I could just barely stagger back to the dorm to pass out. I spent a good part of my first thirty-five years sick to my stomach. Literally. I thought *everyone* went through what I did, and, like me, was just too polite to mention it.

Now I know I faced two problems. The first was solved fairly simply: I had food allergies. Some of the most common table foods actually make me ill. The second was much larger and more complex: a need to control my life. It was this latter problem which I suspect is at the bottom of the unique lesbian relationship with food.

Everyone, it is said, is born into this world kicking and squalling. The lesbian child, whatever other strikes she may inherit against her, enters life with two. The female condition has been well documented. But who has talked about butch infants striding around their cribs with clenched fists? Of femme fatales plying their early little charms on every aunt, girl cousin and housewife-neighbor who peers into their playpens?

I always thought that I came out at fifteen. Last year I delved into a box of family photographs to find images of Little Lee (clothed in a more feminine appellation) dressed in three-pieced corduroy pants suits, in flannel-lined dunga-rees, in overalls. Images of my pre-adolescent self in flannel shirts and jeans, hair slicked back. Or just-adolescent with my sleeves rolled up to my paltry biceps, and unlit parental cigarette hanging from my sneering eleven-year-old lips. "Holy shit," I thought, I was gay even back then.

"Holy shit," I say now, no wonder so many of us have food issues. If food, as we've learned from research on anorexia and bulimia, is a way of controlling, often the only way of controlling our young lives, no wonder lesbians wield it like a weapon. Scrawny Little Lee was rejecting everything her innocently straight parents were offering her. "This is the life we want you to live," they told me in a thousand different ways, offering me marriage, and my very own family; offering me boys, dresses, homemaker skills; offering me a highly socialized role that my gut knew was dead wrong for me. I rejected their social nourishment—of *course* I'd reject their carrots and spinach and steak. In fact, I suspect my food allergies are no more than a systematic, automatic response my body developed to those foods which most obviously represented to me family life and the golden platter of heterosexuality. I gagged on it.

Enter potlucks, vegetarianism, feminist restaurants, growing our own food, collective cooking, music festival foodlines.

Enter health foods, allergy testing, rotation diets, organic foods, food co-ops, *The Political Palates*, and *Red Beans and Rice*.

Enter this concept, shared with other alternative cultures, of taking control of our lives through food. Creating our own rituals around eating. Determining for ourselves what to feed us, how to feed us, with whom we would feed.

Once, after leaving a lover and moving into my own place, Barbara Grier, then editor of *The Ladder*, urged a recipe on me to forestall malnutrition I was likely to have suffered. She told me to cook up some green peppers, onions, rice, hamburger, and what all in a great big old frying pan, and then to freeze individual packets of the stuff in foil. Dutifully I took a packet of what I'd dubbed Lesbian Stew from my freezer each day before work and each night when I came home I pushed it around the frying pan. I think that was the first time I'd ever fully understood that there was a connection between food and sustaining life—between putting this stew in my mouth and being able to write stories and articles for *The Ladder*, or make love to women, or dance all night.

My cooking repertoire has grown. I've even come to enjoy long solitary nights of baking cookies, the smell of garlic frying in preparation for a rice dish, the way a well-sharpened knife can make paper-thin slices of tomatoes look pretty all soaked in rice vinegar under a sprinkling of minutely chopped scallions. But more, I've come to almost like digging in with friends, comparing recipes or writing styles or the day's events over a casserole topped with bubbling just-toasted cheese. No longer does anyone serve me promises of motherhood, skills for keeping a husband happy, or Emily Post's recommendations on hostessing.

My body has learned what foods poison it; my queer soul has found tablemates to nourish it; I take great care in deciding what I ingest, having been force-fed from an alien menu for too long. Where once the little girl stood accused of fretfully fussing over her food, now, lesbian-like, I fuss joyfully over what I know I need, body and soul.

A Fat Dyke Tells All

by
Marianne Banks

———— ⚭ ————

Food is too important to eat. Could there be a more ignoble ending than being chewed, digested, converted to shit and flushed away?

Fill the bathtub with Hollandaise and luxuriate. Decorate the house using rack of rib end tables and meringue lamp shades. Build monuments to great meals of the past. Elect officials on the basis of their ability to bone chicken or make lumpless gravies. Surely, these are the things that matter!

Food is a funny commodity. All the time you're eating it, it is eating you. Actually all foods don't eat you. Some are too self-absorbed to take the time to make you feel guilty. Salads will not. You can eat all the lettuce you want, secure in the knowledge it will never take a nibble out of you. But who cares? Who wants to be eaten by lettuce, even if it happens to be radicchio? Fruit won't eat you either. Neither will vegetables. You get the idea. Foods low in calories and high in crunch are not even remotely interested in you. So, I ask, why should you be interested in them?

There are, however, far more interested-in-you foods, waiting for your attention. Waiting for the opportunity to inspire guilt. Potato chips, for example, will snack on you as you snack on them. French fries have huge teeth and can be dangerous because they travel in packs. Chocolate will kill you. It is thought that all varieties, from semi-sweet to milk, exhibit psychopathic tendencies. A champion of disguise, chocolate wraps itself in silvery foil and colorful paper so it often gains access to your home before you realize what you're dealing with.

I find it an interesting dichotomy: food that eats you doesn't make you disappear, while food that doesn't does. For the longest time, that was my goal. To disappear. No matter what I ate or didn't, how much or little, I never was able to vanish. My self-esteem did. Rushing out the door, it tripped on the stairs and lay, unconscious, on the front walkway. I had no power of my own except that loaned to me by salads, grapefruit sections and low-fat cottage cheese. But never enough power, enough strength, to refuse a bag of Wise barbecued potato chips or turn away from Fluffernutter sandwiches on spongy, soft, stick-to-the-roof-of-your-mouth white bread. Vowing as I ate to fast the next day to prove my worthiness at worthlessness.

Through it all, I remained a physical presence. A physical presence who enjoyed counting the vertebrae of her spine in the bathroom mirror and feeling her hip bones as they threatened to push through her skin while she lay in bed at night. A physical presence who wondered why she wanted to disappear. Wondered why she was afraid of food. Where did the fear come from? Appearing to grow out of her stomach, she knew that it didn't start there.

It took years to realize what was going on. Years of keeping a running total of each day's caloric intake in my head. Years of eating cottage cheese, carrot curls and radish rosebuds before I heard a word that named the nagging fear chewing away at me. Queer. Lezzie.

I tried it out. Whispered to myself, "I'm a Lesbian." Even the hushed words scared me. I hunted down books on the subject in my high school library. Thick, heavy books that used words like 'psychological trauma' and 'sexual deviation.' Becoming more frightened, I went to see the school adjustment counselor. She didn't adjust much except for her glasses, behind which were the most beautiful blue eyes I'd ever seen.

If I expected things to get easier after I figured out that I was a Lesbian, I soon discovered differently. Hardly anyone is excited by the news. Least of all, one's family. The fear of what I was had been replaced with the fear of people finding out. It was exhausting. I thought about suicide, but I really didn't want to die. I just wanted to be a dyke who could go to Kentucky Fried Chicken once in a while with a clear conscience.

Eventually (if eight years can be called eventually), I accepted myself. Learning to enjoy my Lesbianism, I grew more comfortable and finally was able to relax. Once relaxed I began to eat. Food. Not just Fluffernutters and barbecued chips but bread, pasta and potatoes. Those things I had denied myself for years, the years between twelve and twenty-five. Those years when food was everything to me, though you'd never have known it by looking at my plate.

Gradually I got fat. Actually I think I always was. But locked into a constant, self-abusive battle, I fought against what I was: *a fat dyke*. It proved easier to emerge from the queer closet than the closet of fatness. Self-acceptance regarding my size became a far greater challenge than my sexual orientation ever was. For my family as well.

They simply don't bring it up. But it's there between all of us. At least I sense it. Not so much by what is spoken but because I still remember what was said about my Fat Aunt Helen when I was a kid. She stopped being a person; becoming instead a large piece of furniture that needed to be replaced but was too heavy to move. So now I sit, a sleeper sofa my parents wonder about and excuse away. I suspect they feel that if I have to be a Lesbian the least I could do is being a thin one. Or if I feel a compulsion to be fat, couldn't I quit with the queer stuff?

Now, at thirty-three, I strive to be a healthy fat woman. Accepting my fat was the first step. Although I still have days when I'm convinced I need flashers and a 'wideload' sign, I have just as many days when I feel successful. Part of my success is allowing myself to exercise—something I used to do only when I was thin enough not to need to. I stopped using my exercise bike's handle bars as a clothes hanger, riding it instead, three to four times a week.

Food? Food and I have a love-hate relationship. Like a lover you're convinced is everything you ever wanted except she drives you nuts. So you continue to look. In the past it seemed I was forever wanting what I couldn't have. Now I eat whatever I want. It's strange but since I don't diet, I can't cheat. Nothing is off limits. I try to eat good-for-me foods, but when I don't, I simply don't.

Finally I realize that my size and what I eat have nothing to do with contentment, intelligence, humor, creativity, sexual desire or desirability. Curiously, once I accepted myself and food, all of those increased.

Letting food off the hook, I extended myself the same courtesy. No longer do I allow what I eat to create my power. I stopped using food's presence or absence as a gauge to measure my self-worth.

Food is just something to eat.

Re-figuring Ourselves:
Two Voices on Eating Disorders

by
Kim Lorton and Elena Levkin

——— ⌘ ———

Kim: My mom put my picture on the fridge, not my smiley schoolgirl face, but a close-up of my round rump bent over in tight blue sweats. She sang, "You are what you eat, you are what you eat." I refused. My stomach would not be potatoes wrapped in dough. My legs would not be fat and blood stuffed into opaque sausage casings. But, I did eat.

I ate and ate. And I put my chin to porcelain. I flushed and ate some more. Sometimes I vomited sixteen times a day. That was three years ago, but now I can say that all the books that say once you have an eating disorder, you always have one, are wrong.

Elena: I wanted to disappear and almost did. Five years ago, I went on a "diet" that lasted a year and a half. During that time (and, to a lesser extent, for three or four years after), I was so obsessed with controlling and limiting what I ate that my life revolved around counting and restricting calories. Though I was around food a lot—taking care of and feeding my sister and my grandmother, and sometimes preparing food for my father—I considered most food off-limits to me. Losing sixty-five pounds was not my original goal, but as I lost more and more weight I began to not have any goal at all: I just continued dieting and losing—until I weighed about eighty-five pounds.

As two women who spent portions of our lives obsessed with food and weight, we would like to share our stories, which are different, but share certain commonalities.

Kim: Practically every book or article I looked into said my "dysfunctional relationship" with my mother was central to the cause. According to the mainstream literature, mothers of food obsessive daughters are exceptionally controlling. Looking back at my experience, I would say that my mother did play a central role in my eating disorder. However, to say Mom was the essence of the problem is not the whole truth. To say that Mom is "over-controlling" is ludicrous.

My mother always wanted me to be happy. Unfortunately, her definition of happiness was skinny, pretty, married, and rich. She wanted for me what she wanted from herself. As weight is a "controllable" beauty feature, she not only did aerobics and complained about her own body, but pushed me to do the same. Her effect on my body image was tragic. However, from the perspective of love, it only makes sense that she would want me to benefit from what she saw as beneficial. In other words, we are looking at a phenomena beyond my mother: the social ideal of woman.

Elena: In my case, my family was a major factor in my becoming anorexic. In my pre-teen and teen years, I felt that being fat made me a source of shame for the family. My mom told me that a friend of hers had commented on my weight, and that my weight made her ashamed in front of the friend. I was constantly told I should not be eating this or that, should go on a diet, should stop eating so much, etc. My dad would often focus on my fatness and slowness, telling me he was teaching me not to be lazy. For example, when I was twelve or thirteen, on "vacation" with my father, sister, and a friend, walking to a beach about one or two miles from where we were staying, my father decided that I was being too slow and that he needed to teach me not to be lazy. He made me run, even though I was wearing thongs, threatening to hit me if I was too slow. As I was running, the thongs cutting into my feet, afraid of receiving a blow any second if I slowed down too much, I felt disgusted with myself and wished I could be more like my thinner sister, who was allowed to walk behind without the threat of being hit. Although my father's beatings generally were not based on my being "overweight" (my sister, who was much thinner, experienced them as well), at times I felt that my weight made his hitting more justified, and wished I was small. I grew up hating my body, so I guess it shouldn't come as a surprise that I wanted to get rid of so much of it.

This is not to say that these pressures occurred in a social vacuum. They took place within a social context (which is not limited to U.S. society—my parents had spent most of their lives in the Soviet Union). A society that devalues large women and that pressures women to be thin affects the messages parents send to kids. Families that accept these pressures devalue those within the family who do not live up to these standards, and see fatness as a stigma. Within a context that portrays fatness as shameful, my mother saw my weight as something of which she should be ashamed, and passed this shame on to me. Also, those who learn from their own families and from the culture in which they live to control and punish their bodies and see parents as having the right to control and punish children may pass on this authoritarian attitude about the body and about children to those over whom they feel they have control.

Although family did play a part in both of our eating disorders, the extent to which we see our families as responsible varies from person to person. A pitfall in clinical interpretations is the tendency to see eating disorders as having one cause: the family and especially the mother. These interpretations tend to overlook the fact that many problems and pressures within the family are inseparable from social context. However, views that ignore the role of family pressures and/or abuse in favor of the media as the sole cause can be harmful as well: such views can be used as excuses to shift the blame from perpetrators of abuse to an intangible and elusive society. Social pressures are not separable from the family. Both claims that "society has nothing to do with it" and that "the family had nothing to do with it" overlook the fact that the family is part of society.

The "experts" who claim to know what's going on inside our heads have painted us as having some sort of distorted mirror disorder: we are skinny women who think we are fat and aspire to be the model on the cover of Seventeen. *But this picture does not fit our experiences.*

Elena: The whole time it was happening, I never considered myself anorexic. I had heard and read about anorexia, but I didn't think it applied to me, because I thought that I was only anorexic if I still considered myself overweight. When I was getting below 100 pounds I didn't see myself as fat but as afraid that if I let go of my diet I would become fat. At one point, the issue for me became not so much that I wanted to avoid being fat, but that I wanted to be as small as possible. My anorexia was not an effort to conform to a feminine beauty ideal; I didn't wear makeup and didn't shave my legs. While I can't definitively say what caused it, I do know this: both when I was starving myself, and when my father hit me, I wished to be as small as possible and physically present to myself. By being anorexic, perhaps I was attempting a "disappearance act" for which I had so often wished. And being small seemed ideal in a family where it was best not to be noticed. It seems to me that my family played more of a role in my eating disorder than did the skinny models.

Kim: Although I hate to admit it now, I did want to be on the cover of *Seventeen.* I had stacks of magazines and carefully cut out the pictures of the skinniest and, in my mind, most beautiful models. This, by the way, was a diet incentive trick that I learned in a book by Cheryl Tiegs. And what a trick it was.

My conceptual system became one based on comparison and contrast with other women. In a way, I had perfectly clear vision: the ideal of beauty, represented by a fashion model, was not the figure I saw in the mirror. I often complained that I was "fat." However, the idea that I looked into the mirror and saw an overweight figure is an oversimplification.

When I was thin, I knew I was thin. With satisfaction I would wrap my hand around my ankles, my middle finger and thumb easily touching. I loved to lay down and see my hipbones jut out, to watch my jeans grow rather than shrink with every wash. The greatest compliment was, "Oh my God! You are soooo skinny!"

What I did see was the potential to be fat. As if there was a line separating fat and thin, I was terrified of stepping over that line. The fashion models represented "thin." The things that made me different from them signalled danger, signified that I may belong to the other category: *fat!* Among these signals were my double chin, a belly that protruded beyond my hipbones, and any increase on the scale.

Eating disorders do not have one source for all who have them. Kim's was related to glamour and Elena's to an effort to become as small as possible. Although one of us wanted to stand out and the other to become invisible, both of us aspired to the female roles prescribed or required by our families. Controlling our bodies was a way of dealing with the family and social pressures we faced.

Kim: I began throwing up in May, as the pressure of the coming bikini-season began. In the early stages, I ate healthy portions at mealtimes. Then, I would discreetly excuse myself from the table and throw it up. It seemed like the perfect solution: I could eat as much as everybody else and still lose weight.

As I quickly lost weight, however, my body became hungry. It was a frantic hunger, that could only be alleviated by a binge. This hunger throbbed inside my skull as I plundered the cupboards, eating whatever was left from my last binge. I did not want to leave clues that I was out of control, so I tried to be inconspicuous about my binges.

Alone, I'd start with a spoonful of ice cream, then another, carefully carved to replicate the previous spoon-scars that my mother left. At the critical point where I could be accused of making a noticeable dent in the ice cream, I would return the treat to the exact place I found it with the label facing in its previous position. I began a search through the refrigerator and found…left-overs! Stuffing! Perfect! With something like stuffing, I could take a lot, fluff it back up and return it to the fridge. As I ate, I could feel my stomach fill. One wrong move and the food would settle, first in my stomach and tomorrow in my thighs. I needed something else, liquid, orange juice! Orange juice, stuffing, and ice cream! The combination is just perfect, and as I drank from the tupperware container, I could feel it hit the spot below my ribs with an almost orgasmic pang. The binge no longer threatened my body. I could quickly walk to the bathroom, bend over the toilet, and with ease the binge would come up in one mass…one putrid, yet satisfying mass. I was free from its solidification on my body. I was, in the most crazed way, in charge, I could quell the uncontrollable hunger and control the fat that would have possessed my body.

As I mentioned earlier, my mother imposed a certain amount of control over me in her push towards me losing weight. I saw our relationship as one of competition. I wanted to be skinnier than her. I also felt a sense of hatred towards her for trying to control my life and weight. Thus, control meant being more in control than my mother and proving it by being thinner than her. It was such a joy to borrow her jeans and see how they sagged on me in places that they were tight on her.

For a while I felt sly and invincible. But, as the binges and purges became more frequent I knew I was losing control. I needed to regain control.

After abnormal indulgence, I had no clue where to start. I believed I was incapable of control, run completely by habit. In an attempt to stop my habits, I looked to other sources. I had a few anorexic friends, and I saw them as holding a power I wanted…a power to deny food and romance hunger. I began to follow a strict diet.

I lost the largest amounts of weight during this period. I carefully counted every calorie I ate, as well as every calorie I burned. My limit was 1,000 calories, countered by a burning of 1,600 to 2,300 calories a day. I measured a successful day by an empty and growling stomach when I climbed into bed, safe from further temptation. A super-successful day meant I burned at least a thousand more calories than I consumed.

My efforts were supplemented by a liter of diet coke and two or three diet pills. (I also began crushing the pills and snorting them, in hopeful imitation of the quick-acting and powerful drugs such as cocaine and crystal meth).

I granted myself a little lee-way on the calorie intake. 1,200 would be okay, if I did my video workout twice. And, I would allow myself one uncounted sweet treat every three days. However, when the numbers got too high, somewhere around 1,800, I considered the day a failure and a threat to my body. One step over the line, 100 calories out of control, and I felt completely devoid of control. A series of frenzied binges and purges took over the rest of my day.

Part of the reason I preferred anorexia over bulimia is that no one, and particularly my mother, had more control than I did. Binges and purges required a good deal of secrecy which any extra person could thwart.

When I went to college and lived in the dorms, no one kept an eye on me. Mealtimes were the greatest hour of socializing, and the food was unlimited. I would fill and refill my plate, fill and unfill my stomach, about three times in the course of a dinner hour. However, things were going whacko in my body. My body began to cling onto every calorie that got through my digestive tract. My body image was terrible. I had gained twenty-five pounds in that first year, and all my previous control mechanisms began to fail me.

I decided I had to quit being bulimic and went to a nutritionist. She (Trish Ratto) was helpful in telling me what was happening to my body (my metabolism was tweaked), and gave me suggestions of normal eating patterns. The plan was very general, which was good because strict plans only set up a dichotomous line of success and failure. She told me that I would inevitably gain weight, and after a while my metabolism would normalize. She was right, but the experience was incredibly painful.

I, a person completely obsessed with food, body, and control, had to watch my body grow in a manner that was completely uncontrollable. I went from 103 pounds to 128, then 140. Although I was eating an average amount of food, my body hung onto every calorie in fear of another bout of starvation. Having a full and protruding stomach was a hellish feeling, but knowing that throwing up would only mean I'd need to eat again and feel disgusting again, I tried to let the food settle. I watched it settle on every part of my body. Dealing with the disgust of my own body and the heaviness of food was an active and painful fight not to throw up. I felt that my weight, which was approaching 160 pounds, was the cause of all my unhappiness.

I tried to quit for three years. During this time I gained weight and lost self confidence steadily. At 165 pounds, I had no idea when and if I would ever stop gaining weight. When I got the most frustrated, I would give in to a binge and purge.

There were three things that changed my thinking about weight. The first was getting to know women who were happy, even though they might be considered overweight. The second was an introduction to feminism, which questioned the beauty ideals I'd always taken for granted. The third was a change in my view of other women. I began being attracted to women, rather than seeing them as competition. Rather than hating my own body and being jealous of other women's bodies, I began to hate the social structure that was the source to my unhappiness: a structure that said women should be thin and pretty and in competition for men. I also began to see that, although my mother had put pressures on me, she was actually on my side.

The changes inside me and my mother's support became apparent at a family soccer game. My uncle—a misogynist creep who thinks he's such a stud because a Taiwanese prostitute wanted to marry him when he was in the navy, and who refers to his wife as "thunder thighs"—pushed too far when he yelled at me, "Hustle, Lorton! Burn off some of that fat you got up there in Berkeley!" I hustled, right over to him, told him to fuck off, and punched him hard. I was so angry that I didn't even think of what the rest of the family would do. My mother's reaction was the most surprising of all! I turned around and saw her jumping up and down, yelling, "Go, Kim! Yeah, Kim!"

My mom always supported me, sometimes in the wrong ways, but she always supported me. For me, the emphasis on mothers as the locus of eating disorders was not only incorrect, but harmful in any attempt to repair my relationship with food and my body. The focus on my mother as the main cause blinded me to the actual cause which was the patriarchal order, embodied in jerks like my uncle. Worse yet, as I mentioned earlier, I saw her as an obstacle to my own control and was constantly in competition with her for that. When I realized that relationships with other women, including my mother, could be based on love rather than competition, I had a powerful tool and saw support that outweighed the pressure all around me.

I began to focus my energies on feminism. Although my body was comparatively large, the system I was up against was even larger. I figured that if I was going to put up a fight, a strong body with legs as solid as trees rather than as small as bird ankles were an asset for me. Being proud of my body, in whatever form it was, was the tool I needed to truly regain control. After accepting myself and quitting my diets and purges, my body began to trust me again. After reaching 165 pounds, slowly and without dieting I lost about forty pounds. Skinny is a comment that I can take as a compliment when I think of the strength it took for me to let my body do what it wanted to do. Strong is a much higher compliment.

Elena: When I was anorexic, controlling what I ate was a central part of my life. I couldn't eat an apple without weighing it. I limited myself to 500–800 calories a day, often going as low as 300.

Eventually, I stopped because I was threatened with hospitalization, which I really wanted to avoid: I measured my self-worth on the basis of my grades as well as my weight, and hospitalization would involve withdrawing from school (and a perceived failure on my part). Also, I planned to go to a research program in another state during the summer, but my father told me that, unless I gained weight, I could not go. Continuing with my "diet" would have caused me to lose all control (by being hospitalized), and would have prevented an opportunity to temporarily get away from my family. So I started eating more. But I did not let go of control over what I ate: I increased the number of calories I allowed myself to eat, but kept it at a defined and set number—1200 a day. Eating and body image is something with which I have struggled (and am struggling) even after I was no longer anorexic. In fact, I did not stop regularly counting calories until last year. My involvement with feminism helped me overcome some of this rigidity. As I was becoming more and more involved in feminist activism, and as I was coming out as a lesbian, I found myself not caring about keeping to a set number of calories a day. Now, when my mother tells me that I have gained too much weight, I feel angry instead of ashamed. And, like my involvement in feminism, my allowing myself to feel angry towards my parents for what they had done to me has helped me channel this anger away from my body—where it never belonged in the first place.

For both of us, feminism served as a major impetus to change. We began to see the contradictions in our lives—how we fought against the control over women at the same time we perpetuated control over ourselves. We began to get angry at this woman-hating and body-hating society, and at those who try to draw us into it. A campus scale-and-TV-smashing rally made it apparent to us that other women were also internalizing anger back at its source, and served as an empowering experience. Society's control over women's bodies, both through the mainstream media and from within our families, no longer caused us to direct anger and disgust at our own bodies, but rather at those who hurt us and at a framework that oppresses us.

Barley Soup and Other Battles

by
Carolyn Gammon

———— ⊕⊕ ————

I must have won an early victory over the barley soup. I don't remember how; only when the whole family was eating my father's barley soup, I was eating Campbell's canned tomato. I must have been very young. Maybe I threw up into the soup. Maybe I passed out. Maybe I said something I wasn't supposed to. But somehow I gained the right not to eat it, a right which was never questioned again. It was my only clear victory.

One minute late for meal times, you got beaten. Didn't finish all the food on your plate—another beating. Meal times were a war zone and my two older brothers, my sister and myself were the hostages. But even hostages can maneuver. Stuffing my cheeks with cold mashed carrots I managed an "excuse me" and headed to the toilet.

Sitting next to Granny was a godsend. She was in her eighties and could leave food on her plate. My sister and I on either side, sometimes she ended up with more than she started with.

My father called himself "a product of the depression." He reveled in telling us how they ate stewed tomatoes two weeks straight, every meal. How his mother hid their poverty from them by saying: "Tomatoes are in season, can't let them go to waste." His father caught mackerel and perch from the dock. They ate a lot of fish. And they ate everything on their plates.

I pushed cold lumps of potato to the edge of my plate. As he went to rest, my father made my mother promise to strap me if I didn't finish. Knowing my mother never would or could, I shovelled the pile into the garbage and headed to my bedroom minutes after he left. "Help me get her, Peter," I heard her say. My brother held me in the kitchen as my mother administered the beating. I fought the whole time.

My sister and I bond over our gooseberry terror. Picnics had their own particular violence. Jen and I looked at each other, our plastic cups half full of canned gooseberries, our mouths filled with the other half. In an unseen moment we made a quick move to the garbage can. We were about to spit when the command came: "*Don't* you *dare* spit those out!" He could move fast. "Swallow," he ordered as we guiltily turned from the garbage can. "*Swallow!*" he bellowed. I swallowed. Jen swallowed. Part way down my esophagus I felt the mush coming up. "*Swallow!*" I heard again. I swallowed. Again and again I ate the same gooseberries.

Stew on Sundays, salt cod fishcakes on Saturdays. Tongue every second Thursday, turkey once a month. Potatoes, always potatoes. My mother shopped once every two weeks. It was the sixties, and bread in plastic, ham in cans, milk in powder was the cheapest and the best. Margarine not butter, thin skim milk. When I first saw the inside of a green pepper in my twenties, it frightened me!

Peter liked chocolate donuts and he was greedy. He wolfed my half. I yelled too loud. The judge handed down the sentence swiftly, gave Peter the money and sent him to the store. We all stood as witnesses as he carried out the punishment, downing one after the other, one dozen chocolate donuts. Probation terms banned chocolate donuts from the house forever.

My father stopped speaking to my ungrateful brothers in their teens. They met only at mealtimes. "Carolyn, tell Geoff to pass the gravy." "Geoff, pass Daddy the gravy." "Carolyn, tell Peter to stop slurping his soup." "Peter, quit slurping." Nine months.

On birthdays we had our choice of cakes, angel food, gumdrop or fruit-cake. My father made them all. I chose gumdrop but in later years found it too sickly sweet. But Carolyn was gumdrop cake so I never chose another.

He made all the Christmas treats: plum pudding with hard sauce or brown sauce, snow pudding with custard sauce, dark and light fruitcakes, molasses cut-outs, oatcakes sweated thin, delicately patterned rosettes fried in hot fat, mock mince pie. For New Year's, finely spiced wassail with a floating clove-poked orange, eggnog and flying hens. The kitchen became his territory; we were not to enter except to pass through. I gave up my warm spot by the stove.

I was the only child in sports and needed money for meals for the overnight trips. But no child was to receive an allowance and there were to be no inequities. Mum had only her grocery money. I packed lots of lunches and, in restaurants, learned to order soup. Teammates obliged with leftovers. I loved leftovers and learned to be funny by eating everything from chicken wings to cheesecake. Once they collected sundae toppings for me and I ate twenty or more maraschino cherries.

Hark! The twelve o'clock news, every weekend noon meal. And none of us, not even Granny, said a word.

I'm not sure when he last struck me, but at age thirteen he came at me with the intention to do so. I stood and faced him. He saw in my eyes that a blow would meet with a defending arm or I'd run. I was getting into athletics and he couldn't catch me. He still had his mouth however.

Older, I did most of my eating outside meal times. Found excuses not to be at home. Sports were perfect. Practice at six tonight, sorry, practice till eight, sorry. Sports, sports, sports. Mum kept homemade TV dinners in the warming oven. I ate alone at ten p.m.

I ate alone and I ate a lot. I ate and ate. Apple crumble, chocolate mocha pudding, carrot cake, muffins, frozen ambrosia. Four- and five-course dessert-meals at ten p.m. I never went out. I stayed in and ate.

The Diplomat Hotel had the biggest pieces of coconut cream pie in Fredericton. Jen and I had two pieces each. Back home after dark we took warm water and mustard out to the backyard, stuck fingers down our throats. Gagged. "Jennifer!" my father's voice. "A call for you," then, "what are you two *doing* back there!?" We threw glasses and all into the bushes.

Running over the train bridge to the other side of the river, back over the Princess Margaret bridge, through the Participark, equals 1200 calories. Two hours of basketball equals 1000 more. Cycling a mile up Regent St. to the gym equals 400 more. That means I can eat a Mars bar, a McDonalds shake and maybe a bag of cheesies.

We're at my father's workplace. I meet him for lunch. "What will you be having for dessert?" the waitress asks. "Nothing for fatty here," my father replies. "Pumpkin pie," I reply.

At the YWCA where I've taught weight training to women the past few years, I train my staff to never encourage weight loss, to recognize the most urgent signs of anorexia, to promote all sizes and shapes in women's bodies. I risked my job defying the Calvin Klein clone fitness industry. I counsel women to be strong and healthy, to think of food as a gift, not calories, to nurture their bodies for themselves, not for others. I figure if I can convince them, maybe I can convince myself.

I'll never know what battle I won over the barley soup. But it must have been a big one. I sailed pieces of Kraft processed cheese over my tomato soup like ships, sinking them victoriously with my spoon or watching them slowly melt away.

No Simple Feast

by
Deonne Lynn Kahler

Before high school, I ate to survive.

Then something changed. I'm not sure exactly when it began, but about once a week after school, I would consume as much ice cream, cookies, and potato chips as I could safely get away with. Enough to make me full to the point of nausea. I had to be careful to cover my crumbs—tracks?—so that my mother wouldn't notice anything missing from her cupboards. I never finished off a carton of ice cream or a bag of anything. I ate enough to satisfy my desire, but not enough to make a noticeable dent in the supply.

Initially, I didn't think much about it. The eating. I didn't consider it "bingeing." I was simply a typical teenager, eating too much junk food. After the first few months of this weekly ritual, I admitted two things to myself: no one else I knew ate this way (or admitted it anyway), and no one else must know that *I* ate this way. I would have been mortally embarrassed if someone were to discover that I participated in this ritual eating, and that I had no control over the episodes of bingeing. So began the compulsion that would control my life for the next ten years.

All that went wrong in my life, all the small disappointments, the anger I felt, any emotion I could neither express nor understand, I would blanket with food. What changed between middle school and high school to start this pattern? When I was younger, I would simply cry, rage, complain to my friends and family, and (usually) be comforted, or at least commiserated with. I was an only child and had no siblings to rely on for support, although friends my own age and those of my parents were willing to listen and empathize with me. Why then in high school was I no longer able to appease my demons? Was there increased pressure from parents and teachers to be more mature and therefore less vocal about my anxieties? "You're not a kid anymore," and "Don't cry, or I'll really give you something to cry about," were my parents' favorite admonitions. The message I received was that it was no longer okay to share emotion or be upset about life's inevitable ups and downs.

Perhaps it was a growing fear of my quickly developing body. Suddenly I had breasts, toned legs, shapely buttocks. Was I trying to cover this Lolita with fat so I wouldn't have to deal with men's advances? Men were outwardly confident and swaggering in high school—very frightening. And they were paying attention to me—help! I had always been able to flirt and enjoy the minor attentions and flattery of the boys in my classes. Now, I was becoming a body to be reckoned with, or rather, a body that was potentially desirable and sexually appealing. Maybe I was looking for ways to regain dominion over an increasingly out of control situation. I could direct my food intake and physicality like I couldn't direct those around me.

Food didn't talk back, criticize, or eye me with steel blue looks, as if to say, *how could you be so stupid? What a disappointment you are.* This was the extent of my father's attention to me, aside from his iron-fisted strictness. He was either punishing me or ignoring me. I so desperately wanted his attention, respect, adoration. I would have settled for a question about a musical I was performing in or a game I was cheerleading for. I got none of this from him, and instead only received petty criticism and whispered disappointment. I fought inwardly to beat him at his game: I would give him the cold shoulder and ignore his few comments to me; he didn't notice. I confronted his pointless criticism—he grounded me. My mother watched all of this in silence.

Like clockwork, the binge recurred once a week after school. My weight fluctuated between 118 and 128—at 5'4" this was "normal," but when you're obsessed with food and the scale this is not acceptable. I would run the track at lunchtime so that I could eat my sandwich, chips and apple I had brought from home. My mother commented about my weight—have you gained some? Maybe you shouldn't eat so much junk—do you really need to eat those cookies? Are you eating too late at night? My father never commented on my appearance, but suddenly, because of my mother's attention, my eating was no longer private. My binges were showing up in public, and my mother, who had always thought me to be perfection, had abruptly taken me off my gilded pedestal. She was a Perfect Size Six.

I was raised in San Diego, a city that worships the suntanned and lithe bodies that line its beaches. There was an unspoken rule among my high school girlfriends that it was okay to eat too much and maybe vomit to get rid of the offending meal, or to use drugs (over the counter or illicit) to aid the battle against an apparently invisible weight gain. Once in a while I would glimpse packs of diet pills buried in purses, amphetamines, or an almost empty bottle of laxatives on a medicine cabinet shelf. I even caught one friend retching after lunch in the girls' bathroom, and she explained that she "just got sick once in a while."

I sensed that bingeing was condoned, as long as you didn't gain unacceptable amounts of weight (more than ten pounds seemed to be the standard). Because of both youthful metabolism and only a weekly binge, I managed to keep up the superficial appearance of the ideal San Diego high school student. I was active in drama and music, made the cheer squad two years in a row, had a steady boyfriend and was well-liked by my teachers and peers.

I went away to college at the age of seventeen and often looked back on my high school years with both wistfulness and relief to be away. Outwardly, as always, I appeared to be happy, healthy, and progressing. I joined clubs, made friends, kept up with my studies, and ballooned to 150 pounds in six months.

I was either eating or thinking about when I would eat again. I didn't vomit afterwards, but instead adhered to an incredibly rigid self-imposed diet the day after every binge. Since I binged regularly, this turned into a pattern of one day eating everything decadent, bad, and guilt-laden, while the following day I would eat whatever food categories were left—mostly vegetables and fruit. I had memorized calorie counts and could recite values for most basic foods as if they were were multiplication tables. This cycle of one day on, one day off repeated itself over and over for years. I was like an alcoholic if I "fell off the wagon" by eating foods I perceived as not being on my good list, I would go into paroxysms of guilt and eat until I felt justified that I was indeed a bad person. I lived in constant fear of when I would binge again, and yet I craved eating like an addict craves the needle.

This behavior kept me from enjoying my college years. I was either secretly eating, or sick from eating so much that I couldn't go anywhere. I would eat furtively, like a squirrel, hurrying to get the binge over with so I could then continue my day's more acceptable activities. Seeing other women who were slim and popular increased the magnitude of my compulsion and unhappiness with my rounder body. I remember sitting on the floor of my dorm room with a carton of butter pecan ice cream and a bag of Soft Batch chocolate chip cookies (my binge of choice), praying that my roommate wouldn't come in and find me sitting amidst the empty containers. I stayed home that night to eat, instead of going to a championship hockey game that everyone but me had been looking forward to for days. It was easier for me to stay home and bury my anxieties in sweets than deal with the sight of other people being happy, thin, and seemingly well-adjusted. I held a job at the Department of Education doing secretarial work, continued to go to parties and sporting events, and had a couple of boyfriends that year. As always, I appeared to be a high functioning, happy freshman. In retrospect, I rarely enjoyed anything because I was always worrying about when I would binge next. I lived in fear of myself.

Sex and eating had the same guilt level for me. The pleasures that most normal people enjoy caused me to obsess for days about whether or not I should have eaten those cookies or fooled around with that boyfriend. I enjoyed the moment I was immersed in the activities, but afterwards would berate myself for slipping into the mire of decadence. A rigorous mental self-flogging would follow, and I would search for ways to atone for my sins. You can't say that I learned nothing from eight years of catechism.

My self image continued to plummet and I was convinced I could never control my eating. I went into therapy for the first time, only briefly. I couldn't admit the extent of my bingeing to my therapist, who I suspected was a lesbian and therefore made me uncomfortable. Was she thinking I was desirable, with me being a woman and all, although probably a little too chunky for her tastes? Counseling lasted about three sessions, and I didn't get anywhere near the real issues—which were a mystery to me as well, at that time. I didn't admit that her sexual persona was a problem for me, but instead explained my cessation of therapy by stating emphatically that "my problems really aren't serious enough to warrant seeing a shrink."

I continued the same repetitious pattern of eating/not eating. I would inwardly shudder if a friend asked me to grab a bite before class. Ordering a salad and pretending that was enough to satisfy me, while mentally plotting how I could eat a bag of chips with dip when I got home. If anyone commented about my weight gain (usually an older relative), I would blame it on drinking too much beer and getting too little exercise, when in reality I wasn't drinking more than usual, and I was compulsively exercising, as well. If I missed a day of exercise I was bad and had to be punished. I was a goddess in my own little world, meting out punishments and rewards for evil and virtuous behavior. So continued the seemingly endless cycle.

Embarrassed to be seen eating in public, I would eat only if absolutely necessary and if the foods were "healthy." I believed that others would be disgusted that I, an overweight woman, would be eating anything "unhealthy"—as if I didn't deserve to eat anything other than lettuce. The compulsiveness of it all wore me out. I was constantly on the hunt for hideouts where I could secretly nibble snacks, stores with good junk food, or a diet soda machine. Diet sodas were another of my "safe" foods to consume in public—I was never without a Tab or Diet Coke. Perhaps I was just keeping my mouth busy to avoid eating.

There is a happy ending to this story. After years of secret crushes and vivid fantasies, I allow myself to realize I am a lesbian. All those years of wonder become reality. "But I adore men!" I say. Wrong. I adored convention and the ease of attracting nice men who would keep me in serial, unsatisfying monogamy for years. With that ever-popular hindsight, I see now that my truest relationships (friendly and erotic) were always with women—and those with men were primarily a cover, a diversion. Maybe I had finally gained enough maturity and frustration with my Mobiüs loop lifestyle to deal with the real issue of my longing to love women openly and honestly.

I enter therapy a second time, to "deal with this issue" (as my mother put it) of me being a *lesbian* (ssssh!), and only end up staying a few sessions. My binges stop, dead in their tracks. I am dumbstruck. I tempt myself with chips and cookies. I enjoy a few and put them away. I read a book instead. My weight drops to its natural level of 120 pounds. My self esteem soars

My relationship with my father improves. As he mellows with age and I am bolder and more self-assured, we have conversations. We talk about goals. He says he is proud of what I am accomplishing in my life. We argue about Ayn Rand's objectivism. I tell him the tie he is wearing makes him look like a used car salesman, and we both laugh. My mother sits by, stunned and happy.

At last I am finding peace, and can fill a void with what I had really been looking for all along. Not trashy food and mediocre sex, but the loving of women and my own self-allowance to wholeheartedly enjoy it. I am born again.

It breaks my heart that I, and thousands of other women, are unable to look beyond our eating and see what it truly represents for each individual. For me, increased maturity and letting go of fears about who I really am marked the beginning of the end of an era involving much wasted time, money and energy. As the one member of my own personal food cult, I could at last lay it to rest and continue my life as the same person, but with the honesty and joy to live my life in the public realm, as well as in the private. Ended was the double life I had been leading since high school—and I was fused back into the woman I was born to be.

Now, I still eat ice cream, cookies, and chips. Even a lot of them at times. But the thing that has changed is my attitude about eating. I no longer dread my next meal, or hide while eating. I revel in my newfound ability to enjoy food, to share this communion with others. When the waitress comes to our table with the dessert tray, I am able to say "I must try the chocolate fudge cake." And, with a smile, ask for ice cream to go with it. This may seem minor to many, but to those of us who have known the fear and shame related to binge behavior, this is indeed no simple feast.

When I Eat It Is Not Like on TV

by
K Kaufmann

—— ◯◯◯ ——

When I eat it is not like on TV.

It is not like the restaurant commercials for all-you-can-eat soup-salad-pasta-taco-dessert bars where people walk around with plates loaded with more food than one could or should eat and everyone is smiling.

It is not like commercials where ice cream makes children happy and saves the party or candy bars satisfy you or actors eat whole boxes of crackers or bags of corn chips without feeling guilty, let alone sick.

It is not even like in the newspaper where restaurant reviewers have enormous meals twice a day and describe in sensuous detail the flavors and textures of every gourmet morsel they put in their mouths, or in the comic strips where compulsive females pigging out on junk food are supposed to be cute and funny.

When I eat I do not taste a thing. I cram food into my mouth, a pint of ice cream with caramel sauce, a bag of cookies, a half dozen bagels, a half pound of margarine, candy bars. I cram it all into my mouth, stuff into my stomach until it is physically impossible for me to eat more, until my stomach is distended and hard there is so much food in it. And I stay up all night watching TV because my stomach hurts so much and I cannot lie or sit in one position for too long and I spent the next day on the toilet shitting long heavy turds, sometimes so much it clogs the toilet and I can't flush it down. I feel hungover and exhausted and spend the day watching more TV because I am too tired and depressed and ashamed to do anything else. I watch the soaps and the talk shows and the sitcoms and TV movies and all the commercials and I wonder how I ever got the idea that eating was supposed to be fun.

Some Questions of Etiquette

by
Angela Peckenpaugh

Who is cooking?
Is she cooking?
Is it usually her cooking?
Who is eating?
Is it usually him?
Is he helping with the dishes?
Is he doing the shopping?
Who is serving? Receiving?

Who is eating?
Is she in a restaurant,
looking at the menu?
Or is she the one with the pad
ready to hear an order?
Are you aping the chef
on television?

Does the one who is seated
usually sit?
Is one the one
who jumps up to get it?
Is one the one who wipes the table,
cleans the refrigerator,
toilet?
Is one the one who is fed,
now aged, decrepit?
Who is licking the spoon?
Can he afford it?
Is he rich, is he a child,

is he a Republican, a corporate boss,
a Russian, Iraqi, Somalian,
Japanese businessman?
Who will get to eat in Haiti,
and who will be given more food stamps.
Who will work to eat
who is serving the dessert.

Will that be medium or rare?
Will that be pot luck?
Shall I RSVP?
BYO? Is the gentleman paying?
Is the woman
wearing the apron?
Is the man wearing the pants?
Is the woman expecting?
Is that father
picking up the tab
for their wedding?
Is that couple both men?
both women?
Who is carrying the tray?
Who did you say was dieting?
Starving? Bingeing?
Who is picking up
the tip?
the virus?
the care package?
Who is cooking?
lying down?
standing and waiting?

Confessions of a Food Junkie

by
Ruth Hinkle

———⟨∞⟩———

I am a food junkie. Give me stress, and I will run for the snacks. Give me cookies or ice cream, and I feel better immediately. Any kind of chips—plain, barbecue, corn, taco, chips with ridges or without ridges—will pull me through the tough times. Never mind the weight gain or the cholesterol levels. I figure I can worry about that later. Right now I need a snack.

Snacking makes it easier to handle the stresses of life, like when the cable goes out on my TV for the evening, or when it rains for the fifth weekend in a row. More dependable than a best friend, food will get me through. Everybody needs to find their own way of coping in the world, and snacking works for me. Even my dog agrees. He is always right there to help me with that piece of cheesecake or that bowl of ice cream.

I revel in the *convenience* of using food for stress relief. I don't have to change into jogging clothes or even leave the house. I don't have to clear space in front of the television to work out with the exercise video. It is so simple just to go to the cupboard or refrigerator and get out the food and eat it. And at work, those fabulous idols of the lunchroom, the vending machines, are always ready to drop whatever I could possibly want into the tray below.

In my more rational moments, I realize that the consequences of this kind of behavior may cut my life shorter than it has to be. Who wants to die early? So I clean up my act for a while and lose a few pounds and feel much better about myself. During these times I use other ways to deal with stress, but they are just not the same. Eating is so much easier and takes less thought. So why bother? I make my choices in life and I like to eat. Besides, why should I have to worry about heart disease and high cholesterol? I am only forty years old. That stuff is for older people.

They say exercise is a good remedy for stress, but exercise is such a drag. Couch potato fits me better. Just give me a bag to open—that's exercise enough for me. I have heard of more idiots dropping dead from jogging than from opening a bag of potato chips.

Food is my friend. It cheers me up when I am depressed, celebrates with me when I am happy, and calms me down when I am nervous. Food will not betray me, so give me food. Give me pizza. Give me french fries. Give me ice cream, corn chips, and whatever else might make me feel good. Food will be my friend until death do us part.

Now if I can just get my tongue out of my cheek, I will go have a Twinkie.

Foods for Life

by
Nancy Poland Heisel

———— ⊛ ————

Eating is my answer to all of life's varied situations. Food is: a sympathetic shoulder to cry on when I am sad or melancholy; an antidote to boredom; a friendly companion when I am lonely; a lover when I need to be held and caressed; an energizer when I am weary; an upper when I am depressed; a sugar-coated pacifier when I am angry; a reassuring hand when I am anxious and afraid; a brass band parade when I want to celebrate.

Food is the drug of choice when I need to be anesthetized against the onslaught of unacceptable emotions, emotions that I don't want or know how to handle. Somewhere in my growing up, I decided that many emotions must be controlled, to be kept in check. My world would be a safer place if I was restrained, appearing to be in control. Emotions that run rampant would leave me vulnerable and that is intolerable.

Different kinds of foods minister to me in different situations. But sweets predominate.

My anger is pacified by chocolate. Anger, my own and others', causes a fearful reaction in me. Conditioned to believe that anger is a negative emotion and even a sin, I avoid it at all costs. Swallowing my anger has been a pattern all of my life. Instead of confronting, speaking my piece, or just blowing up, I seek out chocolate. Anything will do in a pinch but the ultimate, most effective anger soother is a hot fudge sundae, lathered in whipped cream, decorated with bright red cherries and pecan chips. Vesuvius may rumble inside but my lips smile in grateful appreciation.

Loneliness can overwhelm me at any time, even when I am not alone. Then I gravitate to any food available. At parties and gatherings, where numbers of people crowd into festively decorated rooms, I can feel isolated, unconnected. Then I graze, moving from one hors d'oeuvres table to another, connecting with one familiar friend, food.

At family gatherings, I am often filled with an unexplained anxiety. I should be more, do more, relate more. Candy relieves my anxiety, but only temporarily, and I continue to stuff myself with sugared confections—caramels, gummy bears, chocolate-covered anythings—even after I go home or the guests leave. I've wondered what would happen if we took the food and drinks out of entertaining.

Could we converse at all without a cheese cracker in one hand and a drink in the other?

In recent years, I have experienced sad feelings. I assume it is my age. Life is swiftly passing by and I can't put on the brakes. Endings and deaths seem to be all around me. Crying is a natural response but one I find most difficult to do. An axiom I've tried to live by is "keep a stiff upper lip." Tears imply weakness, vulnerability, and I must be strong. I choke back the tears and eat. Pie, cookies, bakery goods, even a dried-out Twinkie will comfort me for a while.

Many times when I need to be held, to be comforted, to be caressed, to be loved, there is no lover in sight. Instead, ice cream caresses. The soft, delicious, rich taste can almost take the place of a lover's embrace.

Boredom finds me rummaging in the pantry, ferreting out potato chips, salsa and nachos, peanuts, even driving a few miles for a chili three-way. While reading an interesting novel, watching a favorite TV program or relaxing at a movie, I want food. Chocolate-covered raisins, popcorn, pretzels—any junk food will do.

I equate tiredness with weakness. I do not allow my body to be tired, especially in the middle of the day. It must continue to go, go, go. Resting is legitimate only in the evening when the daily routines and work projects are completed. When my body screams at me to nap at three in the afternoon or at least to take some quiet time, I respond with peanut butter. Mixed with canned chocolate icing, peanut butter is "awesome," but plain or crunchy does the trick. No bread needed. Peanut butter by the spoonful is the great picker-upper I know.

Fear and anxiety leave me uptight and empty. A huge cavern in the pit of my stomach yawns, demanding to be filled. I throw food into the gaping hole, whatever is on hand. It fills the void for a time but soon it opens wide once again and I am on the prowl for more food.

How do I celebrate? A good check up at the doctor's or winning the state lottery will find me at a bakery or an ice cream parlor looking for something extravagant like an amaretto cheesecake or turtle pie. No celebration is complete without an extra-special, totally unique and scrumptious dessert.

In spite of all the emotional eating that I do, I am only a few pounds overweight. Maybe a good gene pool can account for that. I know when my eating is out of control and I consciously try to master it. Diet workshop and sharing my eating dilemma with friends have helped me to take charge of the food I shovel into my mouth. I attempt to deal with my emotions and life situations in more positive ways. But sometimes the only way I can take care of myself and protect myself is through food. I know what I am doing and I choose to eat. And it is okay!

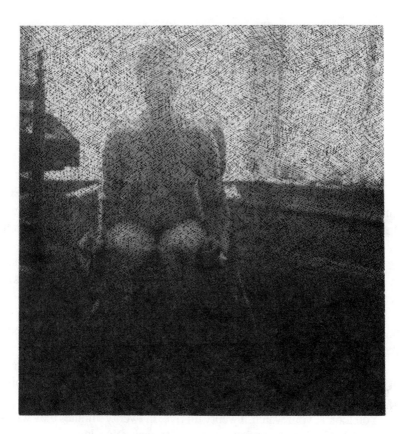

I Found Myself Attracted
To Chocolate

Temptation

by
Jo Nelson

———— ⟐ ————

So, here you are, standing in front of the pastry counter in the Epicure department of Neiman-Marcus. They are brewing gourmet coffee to give as samples. The aroma has put a ring in your nose and pulled you here. Your stomach gathers itself to make a complaint. It growls.

Your diet of several weeks is finally working. You've lost six pounds and you're over the cravings of that first week. You no longer feel deprived of sweets. You want bread!

Behind the glass, precious as diamonds, lie the croissants. They snuggle on a napkin of forest green. You count them. Nine, there are nine. Out of habit, you pick the six you will take. The biggest, of course.

Never mind the hard rolls, or the loaves of French and rye. Forget the danish, cherry and apple, catching the light like rubies and citrines. The croissants are the jewels of choice in this display.

You look at your watch. Twenty till five. In twenty minutes they will mark everything to half price. Just twenty minutes to wait. You know how well they freeze, and how often are you here, just at five?

You pass some time looking at items on the nearby shelves. A bottle of vinegar from France contains the stem of an herb. The label on Ultra Fine Olive Oil looks like a Botticelli. God, this floor is hard.

Your feet hurt and your legs are tired. You look at your watch and find two minutes gone. Resolutely, you head for the escalator. You sigh as you step aboard.

They've placed the sales racks where you have to see them during your slow descent, but you studiously look at your feet. You're saving for that trip to Santa Fe, and, besides, your own clothes will fit if you can just maintain this diet.

A few quick steps put you on the next conveyor. First floor, coming up. But wait, what is that smell? One glance confirms the worst. Against the side of the escalator bank, you see the dreaded candy counter. The gleaming curved glass reaches out to snare you as you step onto the marble floor. Chocolate stretches as far as your eyes can see.

You put one foot firmly in front of the other. In the first section, Fudge Loves nestle in their bright red boxes. Then there are the Bachman's. You turn your head away and swallow. Next are the Godivas, beautifully shaped like seashells and acorns. That's it, keep going.

Oh, but now you see the Truffles. Those egg-shaped delicacies of pure chocolate with nuts hatching out of their tops are the last temptation. Your steps slow, you breathe deeply. The heady fragrant of chocolate hovers around the case as thick as opium in a den.

A small golden tray balances delicately on top of the case. On a lacy white doily, they have placed some samples. You hand reaches for the largest piece. You pop it into your mouth and sprint for the door.

How We Fare

by
Edith Pearlman

―――― ◯◯◯ ――――

There's nothing to eat. Nothing safe, that is. There's not a crumb in the larder that isn't saturated, over-preserved, lipidized, pesticided, or otherwise baneful. The canned tuna has too much mercury. The raw tuna has too many organisms. The bottled water contains cleaning fluid and the shortbread contains calories and the Brie clings to our vessels like mobsters to their mouthpieces; and the oat bran, shearing off our intestinal polyps on its mad dash to the sea, trails an oily substance which causes those polyps to pop right up again, all smiles.

We mustn't eat rice. Rice paddies are heating up the planet as they flood the atmosphere with carbon dioxide. We mustn't eat endangered species, either. Grapes and chocolate bars are boycotted. If poisons won't starve us, politics will. Alcohol makes us feel guilty.

To add to our troubles comes the news that the free-range chickens have gotten into the hashish. And a recent study suggests that vegetables grown organically take on the sociopathic qualities of their human caretakers, and sometimes mutate into full-blown criminals. Last month several turnips held up a package store.

How are we handling the crisis at our house? How are we dealing with the bad vibes that come over the wire and the lists of noxious foodstuffs that slither through the transom?

By ignoring them, that's how. By eating anything and everything we like—immoderately, lustfully, with both hands. By refusing to consider media reports, packaging labels, dietary warnings, family histories; the numbers on the scale, the sizes on the clothing, the blimps in the mirror. We convene in the dining room at seven—my husband and I, the children, Uncle Irving, assorted *schnorrers*. We enjoy a rich and dangerous repast. We rise from the table—those still able to rise—at about nine. By then the air is fragrant with cigar smoke and triply-caffeinated brew. We are replete, happy, and probably moribund.

But we are *not* disorganized. To replace the vitamin charts that formerly decorated the pantry, and to compensate for our disregard of the old food groups, we have developed five new categories of nutrition, one for every working day of the week.

1.) The one-color appetizer. Orange is a favorite, since it allows so many culinary adventures—salmon Maraschino, peach-and-pimiento salad. But green has its own visionary possibilities (fiddleheads suspended in lime jello); and nobody has achieved a more shimmering opalescence than the house-guest who moussed some tofu, added sour cream, and adorned the resulting cold fusion with a crown of water chestnuts.

2.) Meals honoring a state. Such dinners often include entertainment. Success has been mixed. The celebration of Wisconsin, famed for wholesome products like apples, corn, and soybeans, cast a pall on the assembly; and the discussion of populism that followed ended in a fist fight. By contrast, Louisiana provided us with pecan pie as a main dish and sweet potato pie as a side interest. Uncle Irving did his justly famous imitation of Jean Lafitte.

3.) Initial-letter meals. C is popular (anything that can't be Creamed can be Caramelized), as is L (Lobster and Linzertorte). K seemed at first to present a problem; but Kielbasa and Kumquats turn out to be tasty in combination, especially when followed by Kourambiedes (Greek butter-and-brandy cookies—we are militantly multi-cultural).

4.) Food that has figured in stories we've loved. Often the books we choose are childhood favorites. We've feasted on honey from *Winnie the Pooh*, and creamy clotted cheese from *Heidi*, and applesauce-and-powdered sugar sandwiches from *The Moffats*. *The Adventures of Peter Rabbit* suggested the succulent Lapin a la MacGregor. We've also borrowed from Mann's *The Magic Mountain* (roast beef, pumpernickel, a Gruyère cheese dripping moisture), and from Dickens's *Martin Chuzzlewit* (heaps of oysters, platters of pickled cowcumbers, and pints of foaming beer).

5.) Food of the Week in Review. And why not? By the time Friday comes around, the remains of several banquets are cluttering up the refrigerator. Cook declares a night off; and we make do with whatever is left of the Purple appetizer (Borscht with plums) and the Rhode Island clam cakes. Zucchini Ziti goes around again, as does the Zabaglione. We relive a supper from *The Great Gatsby*: "glistening hors d'oeuvres, spicy baked hams crowded against salads of harlequin designs and pastry pigs and turkeys bewitched to a dark gold...champagne...in glasses bigger than fingerbowls."

Fitzgerald published *Gatsby* in 1925. Cholesterol was still called Cholesterin by the handful of scientists who knew of its existence. Bran was what you fed the pigs. Champagne, in any kind of glasses, made you feel *good*.

(It still does.)

The Mind-Tongue Connection:
If It Tastes Good, You Will Eat It

by
Elizabeth Alexander

———— ∞ ————

No one has ever accused me of being too thin. Indeed, my affinity for the fifth major food group—the one without a name—manifests itself, on a regular basis, in a recurring tightness in the fit of my blue jeans.

Ah, the fifth major food group. Kahlua mousse. Glazed crullers. Zabaglione. German chocolate frosting. I eat it in fourth helpings. I eat it for dinner. In the case of chocolate chip cookie dough, I eat it raw—as long as there is room for a shirt tail between me and my blue jeans. When my jeans won't go on—even after I've wiggled on the floor, even without my underwear, even despite a willingness to consider a fit that goes under the curve and into the crack as "going on"—then it's time to buy a pair that will. No. No, no, no. It's time to diet.

I have been on well-balanced diets. One-thousand calorie diets. Seven-hundred-fifty calorie diets. Low-carbohydrate diets. Hard boiled egg and plain lettuce diets from hell. Admittedly, these get the job done. After a week or so, my blue jeans zip again. But, meanwhile, I have become emotionally unzipped. I am fit to be tied. Ask the man who has sat across the table from me for seven years eating everything he wants. Okay, so he doesn't want German chocolate frosting. But if he *did* want frosting, he would eat it. By the canful. With no discernible effect on the fit of his blue jeans. It makes me sick.

There are many diets that have a bad effect on the attitude, not to mention the libido. Diets that, by the end of the day, don't facilitate your greeting the man across the table in Saran Wrap, à la Total Woman. Diets named after enclaves of the rich and thin, like Scarsdale or Beverly Hills. Diets with few or no selections from the fifth major food group. Diets that suggest that woman can live by nutritious calories alone. In short, diets that ignore the fact that if it tastes good, you will eat it.

For some baffling reason, mothers regularly ply the most dreadful programs for weight control on their teenage daughters, the world's most vulnerable and least truly needy group of dieters. My mother, an afficionada of the well-balanced diet, proclaimed in 1972, "It's not hard to lose weight. You just eat no sugar, no carbohydrates, and half of everything else."

At which proclamation, my little brother made himself useful for the first time in his life. "But there is nothing else," he said.

Where has the paradigm of the Diet as Deprivation, espoused by my mother and other string bean determinists, gotten us? Into a nasty humor.

The key to successful dieting is not nutrition. It is fun. The tighter your blue jeans (the longer your diet), the more fun dieting must be. "Fun?" you may ask, "Give me just one example of a fun diet." There are three: the Dessert Diet, the Breakfast Diet, and the Personal Injury Diet. These diets anticipate sabotage. They *assume* that if it tastes good, you will eat it. They are built around that inevitability.

You can't live on these diets. But you don't need to. They work fast. For improving the fit of the jeans they are *sine qua non*.

Sine qua nonnest is, perhaps, the Dessert Diet. It consists of: coffee with cream or tea with sugar early in the morning; one double-dip ice cream cone or one frozen yogurt sundae as soon as the will has awakened and wants to cheat (try to hold out until 11:00 a.m.); one bagel with cream cheese in the late afternoon; and, in the evening, one lite beer. I lost five pounds in five days on this diet in 1980.

("But did you *keep* them off?" the voice of my mother rises in my mind. "Go away.")

As you get older, the Dessert Diet becomes harder to follow. The late morning infusion of sugar rushes into the bloodstream. You collapse before anyone else in your office has gone to lunch, and the bagel doesn't really bring you back. Hence the modified Dessert *Meal* Diet for those over twenty-two.

Unlike the full-blown version of the diet, The Dessert Meal Diet includes one genuinely healthy meal—four ounces of chicken with green beans, say, or a container of yogurt. This is to buffer the effects of the sugar consumed in the title meal. The Dessert Meal. Go for it—especially if someone is taking you to a restaurant where they serve dessert souffles or tiramisu. The Dessert Meal Diet, like the man across the table, was born to eat out.

In college, I expanded so much that I couldn't pull my blue jeans up *on* my butt, never mind over it. I attribute this to a profusion of foods from the fifth major food group and a lack of sex. Only the Breakfast Diet saved me from expanding all the way out of Laura Ashley.

The Breakfast Diet, designed for institutional living, consists of all the breakfast you can eat—and nothing else. It gets the impulse to gorge out of your system early in the day. By evening, the bloatedness wrought by the enormous breakfast you consumed in the morning has fallen away. The stomach is concave. This engenders, as others eat dinner, a triumphant feeling of ensuing thinness and an incentive not to cheat.

The Breakfast Diet works best if you keep it to around 750 calories, but it works no matter what. You can eat one bowl of fruit, two large pieces of blueberry coffee cake, and one bowl of cream of wheat with milk and sugar and still lose weight. I mean, how much can you really eat at 6:00 in the morning?

During a period when a badly sprained ankle made walking a very bad idea for me, I discovered the Personal Injury Diet. Naturally, my blue jeans were quite loose at the time, so I didn't really *need* to discover a new diet. But there it was. Opportunity to fine-tune the Personal Injury Diet arose just a few weeks following my recovery from the sprained ankle, when I dislocated my right kneecap (so much for the Jogging Diet).

The Personal Injury Diet uses immobility or near-immobility wrought by physical catastrophe to stem caloric intake. I don't recommend that you slam your foot in a door to go on this diet (it's not *that* good). Think of the Personal Injury Diet as a way to wrest some benefit from the injuries that arise "naturally," in the course of exercise, muggings, working with chainsaws—whatever.

You don't have to think much about what is or is not allowed on the Personal Injury Diet because you can't get to anything anyway. The one meal, lunch, that I had to make for myself, consisted of as much as I could carry in two fingers from the local convenience store to my apartment: one can of Diet Dr. Pepper, one eight-ounce container of vanilla yogurt, and one red delicious apple. And a Milky Way.

The man across the table prepared dinner. It consisted of real food, which I don't like. By the time I was off crutches, my blue jeans wouldn't stay up without a belt.

Like the Dessert Diet, the Breakfast and Personal Injury diets are eminently compatible with traveling. With one caveat: When visiting people who have embarked on a lifetime of good eating habits, bring your own chocolate eclairs.

The nutritionally zealous host and hostess will object. Pay no attention. Although they may live longer than you, they will lead gastronomically squalid lives. And fat ones. Look closely. The nutritiously zealous eat their official food at breakfast, lunch, and dinner but dabble secretly in the fifth major food group at all other times. They're into denial. They do not want to accept the sordid truth: although you may be able to get it down if it's good for you, if it tastes good, there are no two ways about it. You *will* eat it.

Chocolate in the Closet

by
Sharon Weinstein

If chocolate went public,
Could be eaten in daylight—
Not in the dark—
Would we choose it for breakfast
with toast?
For lunch with mayonnaise?
For dinner with baked potato?

Or would we shove it
In a bag for later?
Stuff it between our legs?
Squish it to mud with our palms?

Faced with chocolate
on our plate
Would we be appalled,
or free,
at last?

Bittersweet

by
Amber Coverdale Sumrall

———— ∞ ————

Every Saturday night when I was growing up, my father would buy a half-gallon of chocolate, chocolate chip, chocolate fudge ripple, or rocky road ice cream. My mother would take the thin chocolate ice-box cookies from the freezer and we would prepare for our weekly ritual in front of the television, watching my father's favorite show, *Gunsmoke*. As Matt Dillon challenged evil wherever it reared its ugly head, we lifted spoonful after spoonful from the cardboard tub or scooped the ice cream out with our cookies. My mother finally stopped setting bowls out; we preferred spooning, passing the carton around and around until it was empty, our fingers sticky sweet.

In my first year at high school I would devour an entire box of hand-selected See's chocolates while reading *Jane Eyre* or *Gone With The Wind*. The fact that my face broke out afterwards seemed a small price to pay for such unadulterated pleasure. At the cinema, my friends and I ate bars of Milky Way, Snickers, Three Musketeers while watching the doomed lovers, Warren Beatty and Natalie Wood in *Splendor in the Grass*. Afterwards, we sat at Woolworth's counter drying our tears and consoling one another with creamy chocolate malteds in frosty metal tumblers. After heavy petting sessions with my steady boyfriend in his midnight blue '57 Chevy, I would order a hot double fudge sundae from the carhops at Bob's Big Boy. Sex was sinful, but chocolate did more to assuage my guilt than ten rosaries after Confession. When my dress size when from a nine to thirteen, completely bypassing eleven, I swore off chocolate, determined to curb at least one of my rampaging appetites. My resolve lasted until I experienced my first marijuana brownie.

Later, it was the forbidden chocolate bodies of men I craved: their skin glistening in the hot sun, their dark bodies melting on the white sheets of my bed. Their mouths soft, sweeter than a hundred Hershey's kisses.

Chocolate Kisses

by
Lori Horvitz

———⦿⦿⦿———

I flirted with Anna in a Salamanca cafeteria. We didn't exactly make eyes at each other from across the room; we threw food at each other from across the table. You see, we were both enrolled in a Spanish class and the arrangement included room and board. The board consisted of god-awful greasy ham-flakes and tin-flavored string beans on a good day. Instead of eating the food, we played with it—shaped it into odd forms, mixed it and color-coordinated it, made up surreal scenarios to describe it. Needless to say, the other diners weren't too impressed with our behavior.

I noticed her from the very first day—built like a pit bull, head up high, her long blonde hair flowing from shoulder to shoulder as she spiked a volleyball across the net. On break from her law studies in Munich, she decided to pick up another language (her eighth). Our food fights got worse as my attraction to her deepened.

At the end of the course, she invited me to travel to Portugal with her. "What are you going to do there?" I asked nonchalantly, holding back my excitement, screaming inside "Yes yes, I can't believe she asked!"

"Oh, drink wine on the beach and watch the sun go down."

"When are you leaving?"

"Tomorrow afternoon."

In her little blue Fiat, we rounded narrow corners on winding Spanish roads, passed massive oil-tankers, listened to Tracy Chapman and Eartha Kitt. By early evening, we reached the Atlantic. Anna immediately stripped down and wrapped herself in the pounding, cold waves. Splashing and screaming like an over-excited water spaniel, she motioned for me to join her. I declined, worried I might turn blue and die of hypothermia; I mean, my blood isn't that thick.

So there we were, drinking wine and watching the sun go down on a windy Portuguese beach. We set up our sleeping bags side by side on a grassy dune. Under a full moon, Anna gazed at me and remarked, "I'm so glad you decided to come along with me...anyway...sweet dreams."

How was I supposed to sleep? I lay awake for most of the night, couldn't help myself from moving closer and closer to her. I took it as a good sign when she didn't move away. By the time Anna woke up in the morning, our sleeping bags were touching. She yawned and then recalled her dream.

"I had this kind of erotic dream, what do you call it, a wet dream?"

I played it cool…if that wasn't a dead giveaway, then what was?

While driving through a small, colorful town, old women in black attire sauntered next to tired mules. I tapped my food to Lisa Stansfield's, "This Is the Right Time"; Anna commented that the song reminded her of a crazy woman she met in a "Lesbian Discotheque." Hmmm…

We finally got together in the middle of a silent corn field where we stopped to take an afternoon siesta. We held each other tightly, both of our hearts pounding with agitated passion. She claimed that she hasn't suspected I was "one of them," had never thought this would happen. Hah, I had sensed it would and thank god it did. The tension was so thick, you could easily bang your head against it and get a concussion.

My lonely, miserable year prior, since my last lover and I split, was finally justified. Anna and I toured spell-bound cathedrals, stole kisses in public gardens, exchanged ambrosial back massages on empty beaches.

During one of our many voluptuary luncheons, we ate olives, cheese and fresh bread in a sweet grape vineyard. After we exchanged succulent Port wine kisses, she pulled off her shirt and laid down on a spread-out blanket, baring her graceful breasts to the Portuguese sun. "What's for dessert?" she murmured in her charming German accent.

I picked up a container of chocolate pudding, scooped out a glob with my finger and slowly licked it off. I scooped out another fingerful as her seductive brown eyes signaled for me to come closer. I sat down next to her bronzed body and tenderly spread some pudding over her erect nipples as she let out a hearty laugh, "It's so cold!" I leaned over and slowly tongued the pudding off her hard delicious chocolate-covered tits. We caught each other's grin from time to time as I continued to clean off each breast.

Now it was my turn. I pulled off my shirt; my white bust waited for a cold shock. She carefully dabbed the pudding on as I let out a soft thrill. Then she went to work. Oh that feeling, that cold, sensual feeling! The soft tongue circles glided over my most sensitive spots. Tingles ran up and down my body, stopping at each pore, each cell, throwing a surprise party for each neuron. My kidneys tickled inside while the brilliant midday sun warmed thousands of leaping goose bumps.

We packed up and drove to a pension in Porto where we washed the ingrained chocolate off each other in a well-deserved steamy shower, had a delicious blackened fish dinner with potent Tawny wine, slept tightly in each other's arms.

After an insanely romantic week with Anna, we parted for a few days with plans to meet in Madrid, the night before I had to fly back to New York.

She stood in front of McDonald's at Plaza del Sol waiting patiently for me. Walking with each other arm in arm through the crowded streets, we laughed when we passed the "Museo de Jamon" (Ham Museum) where cured slabs of meat hung from a gold-plated ceiling. She told me she had a little surprise for me, I told her the same. We discovered that we each had an identical surprise—a container of cold, creamy chocolate pudding.

Chocolate

by
Jeanne Simonoff

———⚭———

When I was a kid I'd steal candy bars at my dad's grocery store and go into the back room, where years later hundreds of UNO candy wrappers were found as I disappeared. I was never heard from again. I ran off to the place filled with the flavor of chocolate. I'd take a bath in it, bathe you in it and lick it all.

When I'm alone I eat chocolate. It's a healing potion. I want to bite down into you like a bar of chocolate, trace the tracks of each bite and throw away all wrappers. You are much like that and I have to have you or I'll die.

When it's a certain time of year the kid down the street comes to my front door selling Girl Scout Cookies. In 1947 Jews couldn't be Girl Scouts so I was never allowed to join. I buy the chocolate mint-filled cookies and eat each and every one of them. I tell myself it's a cannibalistic ritual. I always want to eat what I couldn't be.

You are like that, just around the corners of my mouth, enticing and addictive, ready to mainline you, to keep you in my system. You'll never leave me.

I have a special relationship with chocolate. It's like a final dessert. I will be buried with it, wrapped in a thin chocolate shroud, coated and treated, and then I'll be ready for the hereafter.

The candy maker will make chocolate figures of me so that all my mourners will be able to have a taste of me and one extra to take home. I'll never be forgotten. If requested you'll get an extra supply to help you grieve through the long cold winter. Spring rains will be cocoa tainted and you can stand out in the middle of a shower to catch all you can that is left of me as it rains down and covers you.

I like that, thinking of myself falling one grain at a time.

Lurid Tales of A Chocoholic

by
Carole L. Glickfeld

With the curiosity of many a six-year-old, I would rummage periodically through my mother's dresser. I had to be careful, though. My mother was chronically neat, folding not only blouses and slips but panties and corsets—the kind with whalebone. I didn't know what I was seeking; long before I became a writer, though, I knew there was more to people than what was visible.

One day, under the corsets, I came across a major find: a little cardboard box about three inches square, and no more than half an inch deep. Inside I found a surprising treasure, a foil-wrapped chocolate bar. Nothing about my mother, who discouraged her children from eating candy—begrudging us only an occasional nickel to buy Hershey's and Nestle's—would have led me to believe she secretly enjoyed a stash of sweets.

The chocolate was deeply scored into little squares, dark, a bit powdery on the outside. One of the squares was missing. I could hardly understand why my mother had only eaten such a tiny piece. Those rare candy bars she allowed me were demolished post-haste.

Some time later, when I returned to check on my find, a few more powdery squares were gone. Unable to resist, I helped myself to one. It was dry, a little bitter for my unsophisticated taste, but all the same, it was definitely chocolate. Not long after that, I tried some more, and after a bout of diarrhea, my mother figured out what I had done. She cautioned me, gently, not to eat any more Ex-Lax.

My next unlikely find was on a subway platform in Manhattan, the Dyckman Street station. My father gave me a penny to put into a vending machine and—voilà—there was a tiny rectangle of Suchard chocolate! The wonders of chocolate tumbling from a machine (this was in the mid-fifties) was probably my first experience with synergy. Thereafter, pennies increased in value. I hoarded them, ever ready for the next subway ride.

Chocolate from a vending machine, below or above ground (we also took the elevated IRT subway) was *sans pareil*, which brings to mind that delicacy of delicacies, non-pareil: chocolate encased in white sugar dots. Later these came in vending machines, too. Getting back to penny Suchards, what also made them special was their double wrapping; the environmentalist in me would only burgeon later! And part of the delight then was getting my "fix" under the time pressure of a train roaring into the station. Insert a coin, push the plunger (or was it pull?), get a response! By such things I understand the innocence of another age. Perhaps later it was really chocolate I expected when I found myself in Reno, my hand Permabonded (it seemed) to the arm of a slot machine.

During my teens I found myself attracted to chocolate in the form of sprinkles (the scoop of pistachio ice cream and the sugar cone being incidentals). And the chocolate soda of black-and-whites (the white being vanilla ice cream). When I lived in Boston, I went for the Jimmies right away, and found a form of chocolate soda in Brigham's so potent it didn't need the ice cream.

During my junior year of college, I moved out of home and was self-supporting, a feat I managed by clerking in Macy's and spending only fifty cents a day for food. Dear Reader, I confess, I spent half that on a quart of milk and the other half on five 5¢ chocolate bars. After three months, my gums bled. Fortunately, the woman from whom I rented a room took pity on me and fed me good nourishing food, in exchange for doing household chores. I now had disposable income to spend on, you guessed it!

These days, when ninety-nine times out of a hundred, I choose what's supposedly good for my health, I'm still pleased with the fact that I used to indulge myself. Those were the days before we heard of addictions and bingeing, before weight and health were national obsessions. I doubt that I was compensating for anything. I simply loved the taste and texture and smell of chocolate. Me a chocoholic? Nah. Not even when I found it nearly impossible to bake chocolate chip cookies. I had to, quick! pour the chips into the batter before I poured them down my gullet. What was strange about eating just the outsides of chocolate-covered ice cream pops or the chocolate frosting on cupcakes? The realization came belatedly. One night I suddenly found myself craving something, I don't know what. I looked in the fridge, the freezer, the cabinets. Whatever I seemed to want wasn't there. Then my glance fell upon a tin of cocoa—unsweetened. Chocolate? Yes, the very thing! Unsweetened? Better than no chocolate at all, I thought, coughing as the powder tickled my throat.

"*What* are you doing?" my husband asked, incredulous.

I was spooning tablespoons of unsweetened cocoa in my mouth. Doesn't everyone?

I'm not on the wagon. I've handled my addiction by becoming a connoisseur: having an occasional binge but only of chocolate of the best kind. Truffles are my current addiction, hand-dipped, of course.

Not long ago, when the urge for a truffle was strong, I chose to miss a bus that ran infrequently, so I could stop to binge. "You won't believe this, but…" I told the person I was supposed to meet. She took it personally; "Second place to a truffle?" Oh well.

Naturally I don't keep chocolates in the house. I couldn't. However, I do have some baker's unsweetened chocolate in the cupboard. For baking, of course, and…well, you never know…

Time Out

by
Tryna Hope

I take an orange and a large chocolate bar in to my bedroom. The fan is on. I pull back the covers exposing cool white cotton sheets, the only thing I'll lie on in the summer. Pushing aside my coffee cup from the morning, I find a place on my night table, within my reach, to arrange my food. I plump up my pillows and get in bed.

My son Jonah is at his friend's house. Miriam's at school. No one to need me. My friends know that between 1:00 and 4:00 on Tuesdays and Thursdays is my time. I work hard for this, exchanging child-care, fitting shopping, appointments and car-pooling into all the other hours of the week.

I call it my Sabbath, doled out in three-hour segments. This is My Time For Myself. Alone. At first I didn't know what to do. I invited over everyone I knew. We'd talk and laugh, drink coffee and watch TV. But when the kids came home I'd be drained, hardly enough left to feed them dinner and put them to bed.

So I stopped inviting anyone over. Miriam and Jonah knew the phone code so I'd only answer if I knew it was them. I had projects to do like making a present or writing a letter. Lately, though, I get into bed with my favorite food and hang out. Bed was my home within home. Whenever I needed to think, space out or recover, I'd take to my bed. Like today.

I close my eyes and reach my hand over the night table. I play a game with myself. Whichever food my hand falls on, that's what I'll eat first. I touch the cool skin of the orange. I move to the preferred chocolate and bring it onto the bed.

From the time I was thirteen until last year, I ate no chocolate. Chocolate gave me pimples. Only cancer scared me more than pimples. All those years, I dreamed of eating chocolate, of smelling it, smearing it all over my body, swimming slowly and endlessly through an ocean of chocolate.

In the fifties, I'd imagined stocking a fallout shelter with wall-to-wall chocolate. If the Bomb was dropped, I'd gorge myself on pounds of chocolate, safe because the world was coming to an end. I'd frighten myself with thoughts of a false alarm, having to live with pimples the size of potatoes.

Last year, though, I decided to try it in tiny bites. When nothing happened, I ate more. And more. I ate chocolate in desserts, on sundaes, and straight up. I tried it on chicken, peasant bread, and rice cakes. All I got was joy.

Now I take off the paper wrapper and unpeel the silver lining. I hold the little squares to my face and inhale. I break off a piece, put it on my tongue, and wait. As the thick candy melts, it drips down my throat. You can get addicted to this stuff, I think to myself. My mother is addicted. She starts eating it and doesn't stop. She always gets pimples. And she keeps eating it.

I'm like my mother. I will eat chocolate forever. I want to become very good at it. I suck the chocolate, letting the candy cover my tongue with brown, sweet syrup. I lick each finger then pick up the orange, still cool from the ice-box. I take little bits of rind off and put them on the window sill.

The orange is juicy, tastes good after chocolate. My eyes close and I drift off. The breezes blow over the peelings on the sill sending me dreams of women dancing in the sky, held up by giant bandanas, floating, floating until they land on tip-toe in fruit trees, their gigantic handkerchiefs trailing red and blue behind them.

Yes I Will Have A Waffle

My Good Food Foot

by
Robin Bernstein

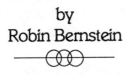

This is true, I swear it. This is how I eat a fried vegetarian samosa, or pool of matzoh ball soup, or a platter of slippery lo mein. Or sometimes just a good sandwich just right—turkey and mayo and lettuce breaking cold water. This is how I eat the foods I love.

First bite, and my eyes slide back and a little groan smokes out the side of my mouth. Oh, it's so good. Oh, it's so good. Swallow. Can I repeat that? Another bite. Oh, still so good.

As the food slips down my throat, my attention slides down my body, until my mind curves into my left foot. Then I notice something: that foot is rotating in wide, gentle circles. I don't do it deliberately, it just happens. I coo and explain to everyone who hasn't heard: "That's my good food foot. That's what my foot likes to do when I eat the best. Maybe someday I'll be a restaurant critic and I'll rate everything by how many rotations it gets." Once I've noticed, I can stop the turning if I want; it's not like hiccupping. But if I don't pay attention, it'll twist and curl all night.

If I keep eating that fine food, it'll activate another part of my body. This is true, I swear it: I feel it in my crotch. I swear to god and back, I feel my vulva get fat and flush, feel that electric line of my clitoris from hood to root, feel that fine milk and sweat.

Depending on who my company is, I might announce this development, or I might not. Usually I don't have to, because by now I'm leaning back in my chair, moaning and thrashing and crooning *"Oh yes oh yes it's so good."* I've been accused of doing this merely for attention, but that's not right. You should see me when I'm alone!

When someone witnesses this for the first time, she usually asks two questions:

"Your foot...does it also do that when you're..."

Yes. Yes, it does.

"And have you ever actually...you know...just from eating? Food, I mean."

No, but I've come close.

Oh! My friend's mouth opens, dazzled by possibility.

Love Food

by
Lynore G. Banchoff

Yes, I will have a waffle.
I don't want to regret in August
the food I denied myself in July.

Yes, I will love you today
and not look back in September
with an empty heart.

Why put myself on a diet
when I do not know
if I will ever eat again?

Meat

by
Audrey Ferber

—⟨◯◯◯⟩—

After another hot summer afternoon of punchball and potsy, I opened our screen door and was greeted by a lovely vision. My mother, in a starched half-apron, bent over the broiler. The kitchen was full of the aroma of cooking lamb. She was grilling lamb chops, just for me. I put my arms around her waist and watched as she sprinkled the chops with garlic powder, paprika, and celery salt. She swatted my wrist as I tried to put my finger in the bottom of the pan to touch the hot orangey grease.

The table was set for one with a light-colored raffia place mat. Most of my friends were allowed soda only on special occasions, but I had it every night. My mother had already poured my cold ginger ale into a tall, thin glass etched with stars, and had folded my napkin into a triangular shape.

"Food should look as good as it tastes," she said, arranging my chops, mashed potatoes and peas with a carrot curl for eye appeal on one of our new amoeba-patterned plates.

She sat with me as I ate. The fat crackled around the edges of the chop as I cut in with my serrated knife. I knew from watching friends and my older brother eat that not everyone loved fat the way I did. Secretly, I thought of those other people as prissy, the trimmers who spent so much time cutting and discarding, that by the time they got to their meat, it was reduced in size by half and ice cold. Once I was in the flow of eating a lambchop, I didn't stop.

The potatoes were bland. I ate a few forkfuls, just the parts that had absorbed juices from the lamb. The peas were wrinkled. It was hard for me to get excited about other foods in the presence of meat.

After cutting some pieces from the eye of the chop, as few as it took to convince my mother that I was civilized, I picked the bone up in my hand. No knife was as effective as my incisors for locating the tastiest bits of meat. The lamb was tan and brown and pink and grey, a meat rainbow, and had the feel of wadded flannel against my teeth. Runnels of grease dripped down my fingers. After I had gnawed the bone clean, I tongued the marrow. My mother didn't approve of this "hands on" eating style in public, but on nights when we were alone, she never criticized my manners.

"Will you have lambchops for dinner too?" I asked smiling up at her, the hardened fat around my mouth cracking like paraffin.

"Yes. I'll make a steak for your father, but I prefer lamb," she told me confidingly.

I knew it. I had sensed my love of lamb was something special between my mother and me, something we shared. Maybe it was because we were women. Maybe it was because we were smart.

And there was something else about lamb. It had a winey, almost uric smell that I connected to love, to dark, grown-up sensuality, and to my period, which I expected to start any minute in the next three or four years. Steak was tough, masculine. My father probably needed the blood meat so he'd have the strength to take the subway and work all day standing on his feet.

I turned down my mother's offer of dessert. Fruit cocktail would have disturbed the salty, garlicky harmony of flavors in my mouth. We sat in silence. I was sated, and could feel her pleasure in my having eaten so well. My fingers left smudges on the chrome strips around the dinette table. Outside, the day had turned to dusk in meaty shades of pink and grey.

Entre Nous

by
Lisa Heldke and Anne-Marie Gronhovd

---⟨⟨⟩⟩---

October 16, 1991, In the air over Minneapolis
Dear Anne-Marie:

Today you had surgery on your stomach. I just talked to you on the phone, and you told me that you are feeling okay and that the procedure went well.

Once you'd assured me that all was well, the next thing I asked was "How long before you can eat again?" Naturally this would be uppermost in both our minds right now, given how much we both love to eat, how much we enjoy eating with each other, and how worried we were about how serious and lengthy the interruption to our eating would be.

When I think about our friendship, my thoughts of you are inseparable from thoughts of food. The loaves of homemade French bread I send back with you to Minneapolis on weekends, and the bar of chocolate you bring back from France each summer for me (and which you enjoy vicariously, because you're allergic to it). The vinaigrette dressing you taught me to make. The lunches in your office and the dinners at my house. The lunch-and-walk-around-the-lake-and-ice-cream parties you host every spring to celebrate term's end. The Women's Studies pot lucks. (Oh yes, and the dinners of gummy Creamettes spaghetti, and breakfasts at Country Kitchen. It hasn't all been *decent* food we've eaten together.) Just think of it! Two women in the U.S. in the late twentieth century who love to eat. And who *talk* about loving to eat! Uncanny.

I sometimes think, only half kiddingly, that one of our most outrageous acts of feminist resistance is the fact that you and I love to eat and that we do so publicly. We've talked about this aspect of our relationship often. You've told me how odd it is for you that Americans in general, and American women most particularly, associate eating with guilt, will talk about overeating as a moral failing. You've commented about how frustrating it is to hear women say "I shouldn't have eaten that," much as they might say "I shouldn't have stolen that stop sign, the removal of which resulted in the death of five innocent people." For you growing up in France, overeating was a source of physical pain, perhaps, but never moral pain. While growing up, if eating *was* at all a form of resistance for you, it was because you attempted to refuse the meat your mother made you eat every day. "Having an appetite" was normal, nothing to suppress.

Now, having lived in the United States for a long time, I know you've come to understand American women's eating malaise well; you have a daughter of your own, you've taught many women students, and you are a women's culture-watcher. Given all this firsthand experience, it would be impossible for you *not* to realize that you and I are engaged in resistance—in a refusal to comply with the requirements of proper feminine comportment—every time we clean our plates.

What I don't think you know is that my public consumption of food is a personal accomplishment, that it is an achievement for *me* to say aloud "I love food." To go back with you for seconds at Faculty Forum dinners. To say, loudly and unapologetically, "I'm *hungry!*"

Of course you know that I used to *weigh* more (there it is, the word I've avoided), but do you know I used to be among the vast number of American women who have some kind of eating disorder? "Nothing dramatic," I find myself rushing to explain. "It's just that, for several years, I could never eat anything without firmly believing that I shouldn't. That's all." So that's In My Past, and that's part of why I take such tremendous, such *profound* joy in the fact that you and I, my dear friend, *eat.* That we love to eat.

I love the pleasure you take in your food, especially when it's food I have made for you. I love the detailed stories you tell of pastries eaten on your trips back to France, of food you made for your family on your weekends in Minneapolis. I love the fact that you share my indignity over the barbarity of bad food, of food extruded from machines, prepared by robots, made from plastic and asbestos. And, most of all, I love coming to the table with you, knowing that, for the next two hours, all there is to do is to eat and talk with you.

When can you come for dinner?

Love,

Lisa

May 27, 1992, In my study (a room of my own),
thinking of our precious friendship

My dear Lisa,

I did not know how to start this letter. "My dear American friend" was the first sentence that came to my mind. Considering the cultural context in which this epistolary exchange was going to take place, it seemed appropriate. Then I thought of Wim Wenders' film "The American Friend," and I realized that this beginning could be suspicious or ambiguous, and I did not want this to happen. Contrary to the film, our friendship started very well and we did not wait until later on to share the pleasures of our cultures in a very respectful and attractive way. I guess what I wanted to say with the epithet "American" is that you are my true and best American friend with all that this declaration implies. But because of Wenders' film which, after all, is mainly a man's thing, I opted for another beginning.

It is indeed true that we have shared the pleasures of food like Roland Barthes shared the pleasures of the text, giving it this privileged moment of true jouissance that some people seem to reserve only for sex. Food is a sensuous experience if we give it the time, the knowledge and the renewed attention that its desires arouse in us all.

Your letter is one of the most beautiful love letters I have received in a long time. I thank you for addressing it to me and making me aware of this real friendship that we have shared through literature, philosophy, food and other wonderful things in life. However, I must confess that I still cannot see eating in public or in the privacy of one's house—and admitting that we profoundly enjoy it—as an act of feminist resistance. In theory, of course, I am compelled to, as I witness the atrocious pain of my female friends and students denying themselves the pleasure of food and the desire for it. In France and Italy (both of which I consider my countries of origin), people diet only for health problems under medical supervision, and only after having questioned repeatedly their physician's diagnosis.

I would dare to go as far as to say that it is a sin to diet in the land of plenty when our sisters and their children are starving in a world of no water, no food, and no home. I believe it is an abominable bourgeois statement to say "I should not have eaten this food," or "I am so full," when you leave the table of your host or your own. Nobody eats to be full, but to feel good about satisfying a need and a desire for something pleasurable. It is to satisfy a bourgeois image of women in our society that these women respond to an anonymous but nonetheless imperious social code of oppression, repression and denial of food through anorexia or deprivation imposed by cruel diets.

Technology has invented a great intruder to the concept of the delight of food; the microwave oven. It is an offense to food to use such a utensil to cook it. You kill it. Something that should bake for fifty minutes, tease and caress your nostrils and taste buds with its good smell while in the oven, should not be deprived of its foreplay. Just like sex, you are not going to do it in five minutes just because, after all, we need sex to stay alive. Nonsense. We do not need sex to stay alive, we need love, the love of sex, food, good discussions, etc. The reason given by microwave users (which is a reason abused by many) is to save time. Nonsense again; take the time to cook instead of going to watch TV later on for hours. There is always good bread and gruyere and a good glass of Beaujolais. It is quickly prepared and quite enjoyable and satisfactory for an evening or two in a long working week.

It could be said, then, that eating is associated with guilt in this country, but it could also be said that eating is associated with time. Eating is important enough that one should take the time to prepare food, eat it and enjoy it. Those are acts of love that take time, like many other acts of love.

As you wrote, dear Lisa, my resistance was to reject food I did not like; meat, for instance. I must have known when I was little that it was a feminist act to reject meat for political or ethical reasons. Although I must admit, I have never liked meat; I was probably a vegetarian already in the womb.

It is interesting that women are the ones who deny themselves the pleasures of food more than men do. The tremendous suffering involved in being anorexic in order to fit in to a capitalistic society is due to the extreme importance of looking fit even if in reality it means you do not fit at all the proportions of your own body, of your own mind. As if your body and your mind did not speak to you anymore, but to the others, the media who oppress you to the point of not being able to make the difference between your own desires and those of a gritty economy that has left behind those who do not retain enough power to respond.

Well, sister, you better let those lips welcome the good food, and yes, I will come for dinner any time.

Love,
Anne-Marie

Potato Passion

by
Louise Condak Liebold

I have often said, "*If* I should ever contemplate suicide, it would be by potato."

After the listener has asked the question, "But, how?" I tell them, "Simple. I would die by jumping off a cliff into the world's largest mound of fluffy mashed potatoes—what a way to heaven!"

But, there's a happy ending because I wouldn't die—I would eat my way out of the mashed potatoes with my low spirits lifting all the while. Some fantasy. I can easily be comforted by just the sight of a potato—even if it's still dressed in its jacket. My earliest potato recollection is when I would come home from a hard day's work in the first grade and my mother would be waiting for me at the door and the sweet smell of frying oil would pull me into the house. Smiling she would ask, "Guess what I made for snack for you today?"

Even though she knew I knew, I played her game. "What?"

"Your favorite, French fried potatoes."

There was a method to her potato madness—she also loved potatoes so much so that when she was a young woman in France, they nicknamed her *pomme de terre*. I was a chip off the old potato. Silence would prevail as the two of us grabbed our forks and dug into those mouth-watering fried spuds—lots of salt, but no ketchup (that came later in my potato years). I was ready to face anything—even homework—after that. And, so it went through the years. If a date wanted to impress me while we strolled the boardwalk at Coney Island, he would buy me a bag of french fries—not ice cream. He would have to get his own bag—I was not, and never have been, a great sharer when it comes to potatoes.

I haven't met a potato I don't like (except perhaps anything instant). Ask my family and friends. Scalloped, au gratin, baked, roasted, dumplings, soup, salad, cake, stuffing, stew, fried, omelet, skins, knishes—and, of course, my favorite, mashed. My eyes light up when a member of the family suggests, "Mashed potatoes tonight?" The light in my eyes turns to pure potato passion—and no one, no one else

269

is allowed to lick the electric beaters after the mashing. I am not the best masher in the world, although I am considered a more than average cook. I think it has to do with my ethnic background, which is Armenian. My mother's mashed potatoes were of the lumpy variety—but I ate and loved 'em. She used real butter and real milk, not light margarine and skim milk as we do in our house these days. The best mashers I've met were my late mother-in-law (German descent) and one of my best friends of Irish descent. These two nationalities—based upon my personal research—are the best mashers and gravy makers. Then, there is this great authentic French bistro in Manhattan which serves a simply wicked plate of mashed potatoes with their *coq au vin*. To die for.

My husband doesn't share my potato passion—her prefers to get his potato kick from his vodka on the rocks. Since we live on Long Island, we get our fair share of a variety of potatoes since the east end of the island has been producing potatoes for hundreds of years. My favorite time of the year is September when we drive out to the North Fork and I practically buy out the potato supply at the local farm stands. We have russets baked one night, and mashed another, and red bliss boiled, saladed and home fried the rest of the nights. It's incidental what other food accompanies our potato meals. *The* potato is the leading star at our dinner table most nights. Sure, I admit, I do concede to rice pilaf and pasta often, but it's the potato that brings out the lust in me. I get potty over potatoes.

Ode to a Boardwalk Fry

by
Elayne Clift

—— ∞ ——

Beach bums, like old soldiers, never die. During the winter they may fade
a bit, but come Memorial Day they can be counted on to return to the sea, lured by
sun, sand, and surf. In my own case, the lure is salt. Not the foamy kind that comes
in with the waves, but the sprinkly kind that gets shaken over boardwalk fries, just
before they pour the vinegar on. I am, you see, a beach bum of the junk food variety.
What brings me back to the seaside time after time is not the fantasy of a golden tan,
or the sound of the waves rhythmically lapping at the shore (although I do like that
part), or the garishness of boardwalk nightlife. It is the junk food I have known and
loved since the days of my youth, which fortuitously occurred an hour from the
New Jersey shore.

Even now, I need only be within a few miles of Ocean City's Ninth Street
causeway before I begin to salivate for a double Taylor's Pork Roll with cheese,
followed of course by boardwalk fries, or a hot pretzel with mustard. It has always
astounded me how soon after ingesting that very treat that my system can crave a
Kohr's soft ice cream, so gracefully wound into the cone in slightly lopsided
fashion. Give me enough time and I can guarantee you that the smell of a slice of
pizza will make me lurch my way to the nearest carry-out in the boardwalk.

My earliest beach days were spent in Atlantic City, and I can still remember the joyous sound of the ice cream man as he stepped gingerly over the burning
sand with the cold box slung over his back. "Ice cream! Fudgsicle! Get your i-i-i-ice
cream!" Like a living mirage he would come closer and closer while we jumped up
and down with a dime in our hands. When we were very clever, we could time it just
right so that we'd just had a hot dog, smothered in mustard and relish, from the
nearest beach stand. It was worth waiting an hour to go in the water because "you
just ate," and to this day, there isn't a hot dog in the world to compare.

Now during my annual visits to Ocean City, one of the best treats of all is
still breakfast on the boardwalk after a bike ride. It's one of the few events in life for
which I am still willing to get up early. That is because if you want to be hungry for

271

a steak sub at lunchtime, you'd better have breakfast at a reasonable hour. So after a modicum of exercise which leaves me disproportionately ravenous, the time-honored tradition of breakfast at the Boardwalk Cafe includes bacon, eggs and toast with coffee, which barely holds me over till sub time.

The food rituals continue even as we depart. While I can usually control the temptation to "stop for deli" (absolutely no one outside of Jersey knows the meaning of "thin sliced"), who can resist stopping at a farmer's market to load up on fresh corn, peaches, blueberries, asparagus and fresh eggs? The stand I like best just happens to be located next to a Carvel's soft ice cream stand (which also sells boardwalk fries), but once over the causeway, I begin to decompress, and with a concerted effort and a renewed distaste for gluttony, I usually manage to resist.

Fortunately, vanity and a busy schedule usually preclude more than an annual visit to the Jersey shore these days. But like an old soldier returning to the battlefield, those visits are full of sensual remembrance. Luckily for the beach bum, unlike the soldier, they are easily explored again, for old time's sake.

Winter Evening

by
Wynne Busby

—⦿⦿⦿—

I run cold water into the sink and drop in the potatoes, one by one, their colour brightening in the water. I let them soak while I take the cutting board and slice four onions, also red-skinned.

"The onions have lots of skins, it will be a hard winter," my grandmother used to say. These have only three skins. It will be a mild winter where they come from, wherever that is. I have no way of knowing.

Now I rub the potatoes clean of earth and eyes and dry them. I slice them evenly. I used to help my father dig the early potatoes in the big old-fashioned kitchen garden which was his pride and joy. I would gather up the tiny potatoes in my small hands, the smell of the earth rising to me. You could still taste the good earth on those potatoes after they were scrubbed and cooked with a little mint.

I arrange the slices of onion and potato in alternate layers in a casserole. Between each layer I sprinkle a little pepper and salt and some grated cheese. The dish is almost full—just one last layer of potato to finish off. I arrange the slices, each overlapping its neighbour, in concentric circles on top of the dish. A half cup of white wine poured over and a last sprinkle of cheese and it is ready for the oven. I start it in a low oven; this dish is best if cooked slowly.

As I prepare this meal for Lucille, Nancy and Maureen, my present-day family, I reflect how as a child I never learned the custom of giving thanks before a meal. I realize now that I missed a lot. Over the years I have come to understand that food is a blessing as well as a necessity and that to prepare food in the awareness of this blessing is a grace. It is a kind of prayer; not prayer using words, recited, like those mechanical grace before meals prayers, but a prayer of being. The action is the prayer—the seeing of the red skins of the potatoes, the clarity of the water, the curl of the cheese falling from the grater, the seeing of these with full attention and awareness.

It has taken me a long time to learn this. I have learned very slowly by practical experience and with a few good old recipes handed down. Mostly I have had to make such wisdom as I have from scratch, without any mixes or packets. It is the same with my cooking.

I clear away the onion skins and put the cutting board and knife to soak in the sink. I turn up the oven temperature a little to 300°. I'm not sure what time the others will arrive, late afternoon or early evening, but this dish will not spoil and the fish can be cooked when we are ready to eat. I am looking forward to their arrival. It is a special occasion. Since Lucille and I bought this house in the hills above the "Happy Valley" last October, I have been living here but she has been still working in Boston and spending just weekends here. Now she is moving here permanently. Maureen and Nancy are part of our "family of choice" which overlaps (sometimes) with our birth families. They will be here to give their blessing to our shared life in this new home.

The light fails early these winter afternoons. I carry some logs into the sitting room and kneel to make a fire. I put two logs across the andirons and then some paper and kindling. I have some pieces of birch bark, which is wonderful for getting the fire going even if the wood is a bit damp. I put two smaller logs across the top and strike a match, putting it to the paper. Slowly the flame travels along the paper. The kindling catches and the birch bark flames up. I watch the fire take hold of the logs, the life of the tree transformed. I kneel and watch, awed at this gift, this life given to sustain mine. "Thanks be for fire," I pray silently. But the words are not it really. The words are not prayer. I am prayer as I kneel, receiving the life of the tree. "Will I be ready to give mine back when the time comes?" I wonder.

Back in the kitchen I boil water and make tea. The water spurts onto the crisp dry leaves. The sun has gone down leaving the sky green and the darkness falling. I sit near the fire and sip the tea. When it is quite dark I switch on the porch lights so the others will see their way. I have become used to the darkness of the country night now, but they are coming from the city, where the black night is never allowed to fall, never allowed to wrap the city in sleep.

I can smell the potatoes cooking. I turn the oven up to 350° and take the lid off the dish so that the top layer of potatoes will get brown and crisp.

Lucille, Maureen and Nancy arrive, tired after their drive, exclaiming in delight at the bright welcome of the fire. As they sit and enjoy the fire and a glass of wine, I heat the broiler for the fish. I take the salmon steaks out of their wrapping and season them with pepper and salt and a little dry mustard. I place them on the broiler pan with a small dab of butter on each. As they cook, the butter melts and browns. I turn them over. They are fresh and juicy. The flakes of the flesh show like the layers of life in the logs. "This is my life, given for you. Take, eat and be thankful."

There was a time, not long ago, when I would not have eaten fish or any meat, certainly not prepared it in my own kitchen, not even accepted it when offered to me elsewhere. That was during the time when I was leaving my marriage and exploring what was really me in a carefully constructed persona. I refused to accept the gift of life if it came in certain forms. I was conscious of the huge consumption of meat in our "civilized" countries and I wanted no part in it. I could not carry the burden of taking life.

Now, though, I have come to see that as a kind of spiritual arrogance from which I suffered at the time. (What arrogance to refuse the food offered to me in the sacred gesture of hospitality.)

Nor did I appreciate what privilege lay behind my power to make such choices in a world where the majority of people have no choice whether they eat or die of hunger.

Did I think I could escape from the never-ending cycle of birth, growth, death, each feeding the other, each transformed into the other? Now I am beginning to understand that cycle and my part in it and I believe there is wisdom in full recognition.

As the fish finishes cooking I remember a revelation of five years ago which taught me so much. I was walking along a stony shore in Kent. It was cold as a spring day in England can be. The tide was at its height with huge waves crashing on the shore. The beach was deserted. I walked along with a bent head, for I was looking for some of those flat cockle shells called pilgrim shells. My boots scrunched along the stones. I had just made a major decision. I had been offered a place to study in Boston for a year and I had accepted—although I had no idea how I was going to pay for it. I was beginning to learn though that sometimes life requires us to launch out not knowing how we will reach our destination. So I had accepted.

There were hardly any shells on this beach, but as I walked along with the wind at my back one pilgrim shell, miraculously unbroken in those rough seas, was washed up at my feet. I picked up another and another; they were coming in with the tide which was at its highest point. I found ten in all. A little further on something white and shiny landed a few feet ahead of me. It was a fish, the life dashed out of it by the stones. I stood and looked at it for a long moment, then bent and picked it up, putting it in the bag with the shells. I am still in awe as I remember that day for as I walked on seven fish were flung at my feet and I gathered them up.

Eventually I turned and walked back along the beach, the wind blowing fine sand into my face. I was reluctant to leave. I felt as though some powerful spirit was present, and was laughing in a gentle loving way at my amazement. As I walked away from the car I turned back again and again. That evening I cleaned the fish carefully and ate them for my supper.

The next day I had a letter to inform me that I had been awarded a small grant from a Quaker education committee. It wasn't anything like enough but I sat down and cried anyway. That evening my sister called. She and her husband wanted me to take the opportunity offered and not to be stopped by lack of funds. They would lend me the money—to be paid back if and when I could.

I am thankful that I had the sense to accept the gifts offered. I learned from that experience that everything I need will be provided, but not necessarily in the form I expect. I am learning, slowly, not to put preconditions about what I will accept. This only closes doors. Gifts come in unexpected forms. I am learning to be alert to see them, to stoop to take up the ones which fall at my feet.

These lives were given to me, given for me. "This is my body, given for you…" I could never connect with the Christian eucharist, with its talk about the god-man whose body is to be eaten. "The bread of life" they say, but all you get is a dry wafer which sticks to the roof of your mouth, not bread, not food at all. I have listened as the white-robed priests—men or women it makes no difference—say the words to consecrate the "bread" as if the food we receive were not already sacred.

I believe now that all life is sacred and that life given to feed me is transformed into new life, my life. My task is to hold that sacred and then to pass it on in the next stage of transformation. It does not end with me. I must be ready to give my life back, to pass the gift on when the time comes.

Now I sometimes eat meat too. At least I do not refuse it if others offer it to me. But I am mindful of the violence carried in the meat, the death-in-life of the factory farms. I try to find meat from humanely raised animals. I do not want to take that violence into myself and perpetuate it.

"We are ready to eat!" I call the others to the table.

The potato dish is sizzling hot, brown on the top, the salad glistens in a glass bowl. I serve the fish on individual plates decorating each with a wedge of lemon. Maureen pours the golden wine for us. In silence we join hands around the table, our eyes meeting in a circle of loving glances. We are prayer.

Song For Ten Scallops

by
Lesléa Newman

Who were waiting
in a Chinese fish market
to be scooped up, weighed
and wrapped in wax paper,
to be carried home, unwrapped
and sautéed with soft mushrooms
and beads of brown rice
to be slid into a wooden bowl
sprinkled with tamari
and lifted with chopsticks,
to be chewed, swallowed and digested,
to become part of my body
to become part of the earth.

Fat

by
Janice Eidus

———⟨◯◯⟩———

When we scratch the surface of this obsession with weight and food
we enter the hidden emotional life of woman.
—*Kim Chernin*

Very very until I was fourteen.

My birth was upsetting for Mother, not because I emerged wet and gookey, like all infants, but because I was so damned *large*!

"Are you sure she's mine?" she swears she asked.

The doctor attempted to reassure her; he had seen bigger, undoubtedly.

She wondered if the fact that the doctor himself was overweight had something to do with my appearance.

When my thin, wiry father unsuspectingly entered the delivery room, she demanded to know whether he had ever been stout before they'd met.

He admitted to having had two such periods: at eight, he was called Dumbo and was dressed up as an elephant by neighborhood hooligans; this sufficiently traumatized him into remaining slim, until age sixteen, when he deliberately chose and cultivated overweight as his form of adolescent rebellion.

Mother felt betrayed. "You never *told* me!" she wailed. "Our marriage is a *sham*!"

Father admits that quite a few years passed before she warmed up to him again. "Lean years," he chuckles. "But when she finally did give in, it was well worth the wait."

I didn't do well in school because all I wanted to read were cookbooks. What use had I for Willa Cather, James Fenimore Cooper, for American History texts, for Biology Review pamphlets?

Oh, but I could read all night long about Baked Alaskas:

1 8-inch slice of Sponge cake
1 1/2 pints vanilla and strawberry ice cream mixed

5 egg whites
dash salt
5 tablespoons sugar
dash vanilla
3 glacé cherries

And I could study recipes for Apricot Tarts, choosing a winner:
1/2 cup Sugar Dough (recipe in Chapter 3)
2 cups Jeannette's Almond Cream (recipe in Chapter 6)
20 canned apricots, halved
4 tablespoons sugar
Apricots and almonds liberally to your taste

My seventh grade English teacher sent me to the school psychologist. "I am frankly prejudiced against overweight girl-children," he said during our first and only meeting. "Therefore, I'll be brief: Keep A Neat Loose Leaf, And Study In A Quiet Well-Lit Room."

When I was fourteen, I was sent to a summer camp for fat girls. That year, I fell in love with Beatles George Harrison and Paul McCartney, and I quickly noticed that George's blonde girlfriend was skinny as a rail, as was Paul's auburn-haired love. Their photographed arms seemed skinnier to me than one of my real-life pudgy fingers. Even the fiancé of my least favorite Beatle, Ringo Starr, was emaciated. And I lived solely for George, for Paul! They were everything to me! Drastic measures were called for; my body had to quickly shed its excess. I would make the greatest sacrifice ever, for George, for Paul!

And so, at camp, I ate only a third of the measly diet portions of food, did three times as many exercises as required. When the exhausting softball games were finally finished, I jogged twice around the field; when our morning calisthenics were through, I rapidly did thirty-five extra jumping jacks. The other girls were all in awe of me. Except for Dahlia.

Dahlia was the fattest camper there, and my best friend. Most of my food went to Dahlia's plate when the counselors weren't looking, but even without me she had her ways: a cousin in New Hampshire had been bribed to mail her disguised boxes of chocolates, caramels, sugar doughnuts, fudge cookies.

I swore to her that it was only for George and Paul that I would starve myself so.

"I do not judge you," magnanimous Dahlia said.

At summer's end, I was awarded the three most coveted medals: *Most Pounds Lost, Firmest Thighs*, and *Baby-sized Appetite*.

Dahlia was chosen *Most Sociable*, which she was not.

"That cow," I heard one counselor say to another, as Dahlia accepted her award.

And I did remain thin, although I never got to meet George and Paul. Since I no longer glutted myself on cookbooks, I began doing well in school. And so, to my mother's enormous delight, I grew up into a tall, thin, cultured brunette.

My mother was proud when, at family gatherings, I'd merely swallow one olive with a bite already taken out, or when I'd spend most of the party sipping one glass of Diet Cola and chewing (over and over) a soggy pineapple chunk. She frowned when she saw me swallow a quarter of the last quarter of a stale blueberry muffin left on the buffet table by an obviously satiated guest.

Over the years, many men wanted me, and finally when Stan and I met last year, I allowed myself to become engaged. He says that he loves me, that he lives only to breathe my slender, wan essence. "You are more beautiful," he says, "than the Vogue cover girls!" I like him a great deal; he has what people call "personality."

Stan is thin. He works hard to stay that way. Even during the coldest winter, he runs six miles a day; at his health club he's a frequent user of the pool, the courts, the sauna, the exercise room, and the masseuse.

We are, we've been told, a beautiful couple, a handsome couple, a perfect couple, a model couple, an ideal couple and an enviable couple.

But Stan is ashamed of his family. They are fat! His father is a businessman whose huge belly flops over his leather belt, whose round sweat stains spread underneath his arms, forcing him to carry an extra shirt to work every day.

Stan's mother dresses sedately in an attempt to hide the pounds, which seem to increase at a weekly rate; black tunic tops ineffectively conceal her ever-spreading hips.

His parents are proud of their son's athletic body and thrilled by his model-like look. "Such cheekbones," his mother once marveled. "If I didn't know better, I'd swear your back teeth were gone."

But it is Stan's sisters whom I love!

Gigi adores pastries and crumb buns, and whipped cream on anything!

Madeline wears horizontally-striped terrycloth jumpsuits and glittering high-heeled shoes, always in colors chosen to loudly clash with her sparkling mauve eye shadow and polished lime green fingernails.

They shop in a specialty store called *Proud Poundage*, which carries dresses in their favorite colors: *Plump Plum Purple*, *Wide Whale White*, and *Big Baby's Blue*.

And, thanks to them, things are rapidly changing for me! Thanks to them, I'm happy again, at last! Two nights ago (the night that Stan left to go visit his old college roommate), Gigi and Madeline invited me to go see "Georgy Girl" with them at our local art cinema. On the way to Madeline's apartment, after the movie, they kept stifling smiles and laughter, but I didn't pay much attention. But then, as soon as we stepped inside, I saw the surprise: a feast! Not olives and anchovies and clam dip for sliced celery and carrot spears, not bite-sized frankfurters, not home-made egg salad! Oh, but Baked Alaskas, Apricot Tarts, Napoleans, Eclairs, Boston Cream Pie, and Strawberry CheeseCake! Had they found and read my teenage diary?

At first I was immobile, frozen. But Gigi took a moist apricot tart and wiped the icing all over my hands, on my arms, my neck...she was gentle, professional, tender..."You'll be fine," she whispered.

My first bite of Napolean was chilling; I swooned. Yes, but by the time I was biting the Boston Cream Pie, I was drunk, hooked, ecstatic! "Tell me, tell me, all about the custard!" I cried.

"Luscious, creamy, thick..." chanted Gigi.

"Melts in your mouth, smooth," sang Madeline.

And then, miraculous impulses, I looked Dahlia up in the phone book! Oh, Magic, Magic! Not only was she listed, but she didn't live far away at all! After so many years, I called her up...She drove right over and arrived in minutes, bigger than I'd even recalled, or expected!

Stan, of course, knows nothing. He'll be gone for two more days. On Saturday, when he returns home, he'll find this note on his desk:

"Stan, I am returning to my happiest state, my state of birth and joyous pre-pubescence! I curse George, I curse Paul! My thighs will spread, will wobble, will shake! Cellulite will build up, daily, diligently. Nothing I now own will fit in just a month or two. Or even less if I'm lucky! Gigi, Madeline, Dahlia and I are all living together. At any time—night or day—you will find us in the kitchen, reading recipes aloud (we have choreographed dances to a few), cooking, baking, eating, always eating! Perhaps you would care to come join us? We will be happy to allow you to partake! If not, I grant you my blessing in finding another fiancée; there are many thin women in our city."

I signed my letter with fondness and a smeared red kiss. "P.S.," I wrote. "My current favorite is Pineapple Cream Pie:

> *1 1/2 cups crushed pineapple*
> *1 1/2 cups milk*
> *8 tablespoons butter*
> *3/4 cup sugar*
> *3 cups cream cheese*
> *5 tablespoons cornstarch*
> *3 eggs*
> *3/4 Pie Dough*
> *1 cup heavy cream, whipped*
> *salt, vanilla, lemon extract, to taste*

"P.P.S." I wrote. "Do you understand? Can you picture it? The heavy cream is whipped, whipped, whipped!"

Eating Cheesecake on the Edge of a Cliff

by
Peggy J. Mawby

————— ⦻ —————

By the 1990s, the American people had become flabby, listless, irritable fast food addicts. The President feared that there was no one to stand up and defend the United States in the event of war. In the name of national security, the government took control over one of life's basic necessities—*food*.

As a result of this government take over, there were no more grocery stores as we once knew them. Everyone was assigned a station for food supply pick-up. One week rations for three balanced meals a day were sold. Items included tofu, brown rice, whole grain breads, and most fruits and vegetables. Dairy products were limited and other fruits and vegetables were banned altogether. For example, the avocado was no longer acceptable because of its high fat content.

Meat was another story. Red meat was banned. This caused great panic among the beef cattle farmers. The problem was resolved when the government decided that it was acceptable to export all the beef the farmers could raise. Each person was allotted four ounces of fish twice a week and three ounces of poultry once a week.

Cakes, pies, candy, and other sweets were still available in very limited quantities, at very high prices. Many of the companies who created those sugary treats either changed their focus to more healthy goods, or sold to foreign markets. For Americans who could not kick the cupcake craze, there was always the black market. For most of us, however, those sinful snacks, such as the Twinkie, became distant, sweet memories.

Those restaurants which served greasy, fatty foods were set up by the government to unload the billions of tons of processed, prepackaged, preservative-full foods which were already produced when the diet law was put into effect. No one wanted to destroy the environment by throwing all those chemicals in the ocean or by burying them in the Yellowstone Parkway.

The solution—feed it to all those hopelessly overweight people and kill them off all that much sooner. So, there was a percentage of the population that always ate at restaurants such as "House of Poundcakes" or "Fistful of Fat." Some people began to wonder when the country would run out of the pre-diet law foods. It had been ten years after all. There were rumors that the government was buying from foreign and black markets the very foods it had outlawed.

I belonged to that segment of society which always lived on the Edge. That was why the scales showed up everywhere. If your weight got up there a bit, you were pushed closer to the Edge. The authorities knew about the gain almost momentarily.

There were lines at all the stores and businesses while people waited to find out for what services the scales said they were eligible. Even the library had a scale. One week I gained two pounds and could not check out anything but paperback romances. This stress caused people to skip meals, or jog ten miles a day. I always preferred to eat munchkin meals three times a day and jog five miles every other day.

In the beginning, people got relief from this pressure by traveling across the border to Canada or Mexico. It was great relaxation to go to a restaurant and order cheesecake for dessert. It was so much quicker filling up at the gas station in Windsor. No weighing in. Then the government caught on. You had to weigh out and weigh in at the border. Sure, you could still eat that tantalizing Canadian cuisine, but somehow you just didn't feel like eating dessert.

For all us "Edgies," clothes had always been hard to buy. There had always been plenty of shops that did not sell anything over a size ten. It became much worse. Anyone who weighed beyond the thirty pound oversize limit had to go to the "Tent Shop." "Tent" was just that—canvas. Although it came in a variety of gaudy shades, it was still canvas and marked the wearer as distinctly as the Star of David.

Physical fitness programs were pushed by the government as part of the diet plan. Soon there was a spa for every two hundred people. The first program I tried was low-impact aerobics three nights a week. It was not the best program for me. I found out that aerobic exercise was the unscientific term for Broadway's "A Chorus Line." There was never proof—but I was sure that half the class was planted by the government. None of those women could ever have been within a hundred miles of the Edge! Most wore those skin tight, shimmering leotards. Flab was foreign to them. While they all kicked their legs up in time to rock and roll, I tried to keep the permanent waste pack below my belly button from bouncing. Needless to say, I changed to another exercise program. I won't even discuss the aquatics routine. The fact that I never learned to swim hindered me more than a little.

I finally decided to put an end to all my frustrations. Walking that fine line on the Edge, slice of cheesecake in one hand and stalk of celery in the other, started to take its toll on me. It was only a matter of time before I would fall over the Edge. The cheesecake was getting heavier all the time.

Food

by
Kathleen McGookey

Knowledge is power, and
food is love, as they say. Come

let me feed
you: spinach, creamed corn,

tomatoes, squash. Whatever
you'd like, but let me

in that kitchen, my kitchen, brimming
with what attracts

you to me. My refrigerator
is never empty. The delicacies

you'll find here, I can promise
you, are not to be taken

lightly, nor the fact that I
have assembled this feast

for you. What I want
is food, and something

further—your tongue
touching my silver fork, your hands

wrapping around the coffee
cup, the seat cushion supporting

your weight, the table
creaking under what

I prepare: noodles, sauces, eggs,
the mustards of love, give me

cinnamon, nutmeg. Wooden spoons
and spatulas. Come in

and I will feed
you. Who says I don't have

power? When you're gone,
I stand in my kitchen, I lie

and listen, I listen
to my food breathe.

Contributor's Notes

Anni Ackner is a fat, Jewish, socialist, bisexual, diabetic writer who, though born in New York City, somehow finds herself currently residing in Reading, Pennsylvania, where she does political work, tends an extremely temperamental Siamese cat, and dreams of her mother's stuffed breast of veal.

Elizabeth Alexander is a freelance writer of textbooks for elementary, middle and high school students. Formerly an ordained minister in the United Methodist Church, she has been a port chaplain to seafarers in the merchant marines. She has just completed her first novel, *Everyone Said Yum.*

Kathy Anderson: My writing has appeared in *Sojourner, Common Lives/Lesbian Lives, The Philadelphia Inquirer, By Word Of Mouth* (Gynergy Press), and is forthcoming in *Black Buzzard Review.* I work as a librarian and live in Audobon, New Jersey, where I occasionally enjoy potato chips and Tootsie Rolls.

Nicole Annesi: Born and raised in upstate New York, I am a graduate of Le Moyne College with a degree in English Communications. I am currently working on a masters degree in English. I became interested in eating disorders when those close around me became victims of them.

Lynore G. Banchoff: I have written poetry for ten years and give poetry readings in Rhode Island and Massachusetts. Recently I have begun to submit my writing to publishers. I am a clinical social worker at a counseling center where I do both supervision and therapy, and I have a small private practice.

Marianne Banks: If I were to have a label, it would not read fat-free, low calorie, or 100% cholesterol-free. Instead it would say: fledgling writer, Lesbian, tasty and truthful.

Karyn Bauer: I am twenty-three years old and a graduate of Rutgers University, where I earned a degree in French and also focused on Women's Studies, African-American Studies and English. Currently I work at ORBIS International, a medical organization that fights blindness worldwide, and at a shelter for battered women.

Tricia Bauer's stories and poems have appeared in a number of literary reviews including *Carolina Quarterly, Kalliope, The Massachusetts Review, Black Warrior Review, Hawaii Pacific Review, Fiction Network, The American Voice, Epoch, The Ohio Review,* and *American Literary Review,* and her non-fiction has been published in the *Sunday New York Times.*

Robin Bernstein: I'm a Jewish lesbian, born in Brooklyn in 1969. My work has appeared in periodicals such as *Common Lives/Lesbian Lives* and *The Philadelphia Gay News.* My play, *Selected Shorts,* was produced in Philadelphia in 1991.

Michelle Blair is a writer of both fiction and non-fiction. She is currently at work on a novel about love and sex, specifically about the tension between the romantic ideal and what happens ultimately in reality. She is a native of Manhattan, where she teaches English language and composition.

Becky Bradway: I have published stories in *Sojourner, Other Voices, Willow Review, South Carolina Review, Ascent, Laurel Review, Sequoia, Greensboro Review, Mississippi Valley Review, Soundings East* and other magazines. I work for the Illinois Coalition Against Sexual Assault, where I edit the Illinois Coalition newsletter.

Gayle Brandeis is a lacto-ovo vegetarian writer and dancer living in Riverside, California with her omnivore husband and their still-breastfed son.

Maria Bruno: I am an Assistant Professor of Women's Studies and Writing at Michigan State University and have published fiction in *Ms., Midway Review, Red Cedar Review, Earth's Daughters,* and *The Burning World.* I have also published scholarly articles on Charlotte Perkins Gilman and Italian American Women Writers.

Wynne Busby: I was born in Wales fifty years ago. Now I live in western Massachusetts with my beloved companion, Lucille, and the cat, Artemis. I am a dreamer, storyteller, mother, writer, gardener and cook. In this second half of my life, I am trying to understand the mystery of the transformation of life into life.

Rhoda Carroll teaches writing and literature at Vermont College of Norwich University. Her poems and stories have appeared in a variety of anthologies and literary magazines, including *The Texas Review, The Louisville Review, Slant, Green Mountain Review, Poet Lore, American Writing, Embers, The Northern Review,* and others.

Moira E. Casey was born and raised in Manasquan, New Jersey on the Central Jersey coast. She is currently attending Trenton State College as an English Education major. Her first published work was printed when she was fifteen years old in the quarterly magazine, *Just About Horses.*

Claire S. Chow: I was born in New Jersey in 1952, moved to California for college, and received a Master's in English from the University of Chicago. Currently I am working on my license as a marriage and family therapist, keeping track of two kids, and wondering what to eat next.

Elayne Clift is a writer and health communication specialist in Potomac, Maryland. Her award-winning writing has appeared in over two dozen publications. A poetry chapbook, *And Still The Women Weep,* was published in 1990 (OGN Publications) and her book *Telling it Like It Is: Reflections of a Not So Radical Feminist,* was published in 1991 by KIT, Inc.

Marilyn Coffey has been ruefully dieting, off and on, for decades. Known for her wit, Coffey won the 1976 Pushcart Prize for "Pricksong," called "a wry poem about an obscene house plant." Her most recent poetry book, *A Cretan Cycle,* retells the Greek Myth of the Minotaur from a feminist perspective.

Denise Duhamel is the author of three poetry chapbooks: *Heaven and Heck, Skirted Issues* and *It's My Body.* Her work has appeared in the anthologies, *What's A Nice Girl Like You Doing In A Relationship Like This?* (Crossing Press) and *Mondo Barbie* (St. Martin's Press).

Janice Eidus is the author of *Vito Loves Geraldine,* a collection of short stories, and *Faithful Rebecca,* a novel. She has won numerous awards for her fiction, including an O. Henry Prize. Her work has been widely published in magazines and anthologies in the USA and abroad.

Anita Endrezze has published in ten countries and in seven languages. Her work has been recently published in *At The Helm of Twilight* (Broken Moon Press), *Talking Leaves* (Dell, 1991) and *Harper's Anthology of Twentieth Century Native American Poetry.* She is half Yaqui and half European.

Karen Erlichman: Born July 18, 1962 in Philadelphia, Pennsylvania, I am a Jewish Lesbian activist, writer and social worker. I have been living with CFIDS for almost seven years. Currently I live in San Francisco, California.

Audrey Ferber: I was born in Brooklyn, New York in 1949. I have written children's books, a radio play, short stories and essays and am at work on my second novel, but I especially like writing about food.

Lois Fine: I am thirty-three years old and have recently become a proud co-mother for the second time. I am a Jewish Lesbian activist with a penchange for pie charts and big-bellied women. I hope to instill in my children, among other things, a healthy attitude toward eating, food and their bodies.

Kriste Fredheim is a 1991 graduate of Emerson College in Boston. After a solo trip abroad last fall, she returned to the U.S. in order to launch a freelance career in photojournalism. In her spare time, she contributes to "Women Who Write," a local writers group.

Gladys M. Furphy is the owner of a weight-loss franchise, Diet Center, located in Milford, Connecticut. Prior to this, she worked for thirteen years at a Fortune 500 company in Stamford, Connecticut. She has a B.S. in Business Administration and an M.A. in Communications.

Carolyn Gammon is a Lesbian writer and activist from New Brunswick, Canada. She is based in Montreal, but currently lives in Berlin. Her first book of poetry, *Lesbians Ignited,* was published in the fall of 1992 by Gynergy Books.

Gwynne Garfinkle: I'm a Jewish feminist writer from Los Angeles. My work has appeared in numerous publications including *Sojourner, Mixed Voices* (Milkweed Editions) and *Tales of Magic Realism by Women* (Crossing Press). My first book of poems, *New Year's Eve,* was published in 1989 by Typical Girls Press.

Helen Trubek Glenn received a B.S. and R.N. degree from Cornell in 1961. At mid-life she began writing poetry, and graduated from Vermont College's M.F.A. in Writing Program in 1991. Her poems have appeared in *Yankee, Poet Lore, Northeast,* and other magazines. She and her husband live in Northwestern Connecticut.

Faithe Glennon is an emerging writer who currently lives in Chicago, Illinois, where she is at work on her first novel concerning anorexia.

Carole L. Glickfeld won the Flannery O'Connor Award for Short Fiction for *Useful Gifts,* about a family with deaf parents and hearing children. Winner of an NEA Fellowship, Glickfeld has published stories, poems and essays in literary magazines and anthologies, and is writing a novel, *The Salt of Riches.*

Bonney Goldstein was born in Brooklyn, New York, and currently resides in Boulder, Colorado. She received her B.S. from Mills College, and is currently completing her M.F.A. at Goddard College. Her poetry has been published by *The Mile High Poetry Society.* She is currently teaching creative writing and the history of contemporary American Jewish women writers.

Anne-Marie Gronhovd teaches French Languages and Literature and Women's Studies at Gustavus Adolphus College in St. Peter, Minnesota. She specializes in teaching feminist perspectives on French and Quebecois literature. She writes and publishes on Marcel Proust and Quebecois women writers.

Pamela S. Gross received her M.F.A. from Florida International University. Her poetry has been published in *Echoes, South Coast Poetry Journal* and *GW Review,* among others. She is married with five children and lives in North Miami Beach, Florida.

Susan Hauser's collection of essays, *Meant To Be Read Out Loud,* was the recipient of a 1989 Minnesota Book Award. Other books: *Which Way To Look, What the Animals Know* (fiction), *Girl To Women* (non-fiction) and *Redpoll on a Broken Branch* (poetry). She has an M.F.A. in poetry from Bowling Green State University.

Nancy Poland Heisel has a B.A. in Women's Studies and Liberal Arts from the College of Mount St. Joseph. She is a reporter for *Voices and Visions, Women's Studies Newsletter* and *MSJ Dateline.* She has been married for thirty-five years and has eight children and nine grandchildren.

Lisa Heldke teaches Philosophy and Women's Studies at Gustavus Adolphus College. She writes frequently on food: with Deane Curtin she has just edited the book *Cooking, Eating, Thinking: Transformative Philosophies of Food.*

Ruth Hinkle has been juggling numbers in a Finance Department for seventeen years while working part-time towards her Bachelor's Degree in Psychology and English Communications. With graduation only a year away, she has been drawn into the new challenges of freelance writing as an outlet for her ever-consuming energies.

Tryna Hope has published fiction and poetry in *Sinister Wisdom, The Tribe of Dina,* and *Word of Mouth, Volumes One* and *Two* (Crossing Press). She is also co-host of the lesbian cable TV talk show, "Out and About."

Lori Horvitz lives in New York City. In addition to writing poetry and short stories, she is a filmmaker and musician. Her poetry has appeared in *The Brooklyn Review, Stet,* and *The Little Magazine.* To support her artsy habits, she has worked as a bartender, teacher, photo-journalist, graphic-designer and all-natural ices vendor.

Susan Ito is a writer living in Oakland, California, where she is an M.F.A. candidate at Mills College. Her fiction and non-fiction has appeared in *New Directions for Women, American Way Magazine, Hurricane Alice,* and numerous anthologies.

Sibyl James' publications include *The White Junk of Love Again* (Calyx Books); *Vallarta Street* (Laughing Dog Press); and *In China With Harpo and Karl* (Calyx Books). "Literary Weight Loss" is part of her short story collection, *The Adventures of Stout Mama,* from Papier-Mache Press.

Deonne Lynn Kahler lives in San Francisco, California. "No Simple Feast" is her first published work. She is pursuing graduate studies in Psychology as well as continuing to write about the all-too-pervasive problem of eating disorders.

Barbara Katz: A New York Jewish lesbian by birth, I have just relocated to Atlanta to begin my legal career emphasizing women's issues and lesbian/gay rights. At thirty-three, I still struggle every day to let go of denial and resentment while cherishing my body, mind and spirit.

K Kaufmann is a freelance writer who is, among other identifying nouns and adjectives, lesbian, Jewish, rape survivor and compulsive overeater. She co-wrote with Catherine Dee, the *Women's 1992 Voting Guide* (Earthworks Press) and reviews women's fiction and nonfiction for the San Francisco Chronicle.

Eileen Kostiner was born in 1938. She attended Tufts University and Harvard Business School. She began to write in her thirty-eighth year when the women's movement encouraged her to speak in her own voice. Her chapbook, *Love's Other Face,* was published by Curbstone Press in 1982. She is married and has two sons.

Elena Levkin, a Jewish Russian emigre dyke, studies Psychology and Women's Studies. She also does clerical and computer work, works at a wimmin's coffeehouse, volunteers at a hotline, and is learning massage therapy. After graduation, she hopes to do graduate work in Feminist Psychology and to become a psychotherapist.

Louise Condak Liebold is the author of *Fireworks, Brass Bands and Elephants: Promotional Events With Flair for Libraries and Other Non-Profit Organizations* (Oryx Press, 1986). Her first short story, "The Stick-Up," appeared in the Fall 1992 issue of *Eclectic Literary Forum.*

Ellen Linz is a writer who has only recently surrendered to this fact, after years of denial. She has been fat, thin, and inbetween. Food is the focus of her life, but she also craves friendship, especially with other writers. Originally from New York, she temporarily lives near Dallas, Texas.

Kim Lorton grew up in Southern California where everyone looks like they just walked out of a Sunkist commercial, but moved to San Francisco where diversity is seen more positively. She studied Linguistics and Women's Studies at U.C. Berkeley, and plans to pursue a Ph.D., focusing on the politics of transformation and identity.

Lee Lynch has published ten books with Naiad Press including *The Swashbuckler, Old Dyke Tales, Morton River Valley* and her new collection, *Cactus Love.* She is active in environmental issues and in fighting the powerful conservative movement which is attacking our rights to publish, print, sell or buy lesbian literature.

Ellie Mamber has been published in small reviews and anthologies, including *Connecticut River Review, Beacon Review, Women and Aging* (Calyx Press) and *The Tie That Binds* (Papier-Mache Press). She is a mother and grandmother and develops and administers human services programs in her region.

Peggy J. Mawby: Food has been calling to me for years. The problem is that I always come when I'm called. This is the first time that I have written so blatantly about society and food. Since I have not enclosed a photo, you may never know whether I chose celery or cheesecake.

Kathleen McGookey lives in Kalamazoo, Michigan. She teaches at Western Michigan University, where she is working on her MFA in poetry. Her work has appeared in *The Prose Poem: An International Journal,* and *Black Warrior Review.*

Margaret McMullan: My work has appeared in *Glamour, The Greensboro Review, New England Review, Cleo* and *The Clothesline Review.* I have just completed my first novel, *When Warhol was Still Alive.* I am currently an Assistant Professor of English at the University of Evansville where I teach creative writing and women's literature.

Carol Sue Muth was one of the founding members of *Lake Effect Magazine*, where she was a poetry editor for seven years. She lives in Sodus, Wayne County, New York, where she is an active member of Upcountry Writers. Her poems have appeared in *Yarrow, Creeping Bent, Rhino* and *Williwaw*.

Tema Nason was born in Brooklyn, New York and has worked as a union representative, government economist, and in a factory. She is a research associate in the Sociology Department of Brandeis University and the author of *ETHEL, the fictional Autobiography of Ethel Rosenberg* (Delacorte, 1990).

Rochelle Natt: I've published in many literary magazines and anthologies. In 1991, I received Honorable Mention in the Colorado Review contest and the Judah Magdes award for a poem on the Jewish experience.

Sheryl L. Nelms has had her writing published in many literary and commercial magazines including *Kansas Quarterly, Webster Review, Spoon River Quarterly* and *Reader's Digest*. She has been a writer-in-the-schools for the South Dakota Arts Council and has taught writing workshops at many colleges, conferences and community organizations.

Jo H. Nelson has been dieting for forty years and writing for seven. "Temptation" was inspired by a two-week stint behind the candy counter while employed at Neiman-Marcus where she learned that the scent of chocolate, when encountered daily in large doses, is a cure for the craving.

Lesléa Newman is the author of twelve books and the editor of two anthologies. Her latest works include a novel, *In Every Laugh A Tear* (New Victoria Publishers, 1992), a collection of poetry, *Sweet Dark Places* (HerBooks, 1991) and a children's book, *Saturday Is Pattyday* (The Women's Press of Canada, 1993).

Ariadne Northstar lives in the greater Boston area with her cat and her dreams. Her dreams get lost more often than her cat. Nevertheless, she is thankful for much in her life. While labels worry her, the labels "artist" and "academic" would not be too far off the mark.

Edith Pearlman: I have published more than one hundred stories and essays in national magazines, literary journals and big city dailies. My work has received two O. Henry prizes, two PEN awards, and a Distinguished Story Citation from Best American Short Stories.

Angela Peckenpaugh's books of poetry include: *Letters From Lee's Army* (Morgan Press), *Discovering the Mandala* (Lakes and Prairies Press) and *A Book of Charms* (Barnwood Press). She is an Associate Professor in English at the University of Wisconsin-Whitewater and poetry editor for *Affilia Magazine*.

Mar Preston is a Canadian, yet a long-time resident of Los Angeles. She writes: "Home of the beautiful, Los Angeles may be the most unforgiving place in the world for anyone who doesn't meet the current fashion ideal." She writes an occasional poem, but thinks of herself as a novelist.

Ann F. Price is a freelance writer and music therapist. She has led poetry therapy groups with the elderly for ten years, encouraging the "putting down on paper" of the stories and issues of their lives. She has traveled a similar journey herself, exploring her present and past through music and poetry.

Sima Rabinowitz works as a secretary and a sales clerk. Her short fiction, poetry, essays and book reviews have appeared in *Evergreen Chronicles, Hurricane Alice, Common Lives/Lesbian Lives* and in anthologies from Alyson Publications and Crossing Press. She was eating lunch while she wrote this bio.

Naomi Rachel's poems have appeared in over two hundred publications. She is an instructor at the University of Colorado, and works as a Poet-In-The-Schools. She donates much of her time to activist campaigns to save our last ancient forest ecosystems.

Dana Lauren Ramos is a new writer, with recently published fiction in *The Arizona Mandala* and in the 1992 *Side Show Anthology*. She plans to attend the Masters of Professional Writing Program at the University of Southern California in 1993.

Nina Rapoport is a twenty-five year old recent graduate from University of California, Santa Cruz with a degree in Women's Studies. She has recently published essays in *The Alternative Report* and *Now Hear This*. She is in the process of planning a year-long traverse of the country, during which she intends to sample as many varieties of mint cookies as she can get her hands on.

Laurie Rizzo has worked as a preschool teacher for many years. She writes "on the side." Home has been upstate New York, and Cincinnati, Ohio. She now lives with her husband and young son in western Massachusetts. She considers herself to be a (slowly) recovering compulsive overeater.

Althea Rosenbloom is a pseudonym. I am a Jewish lesbian incest survivor, and this is my first published writing. I live in Washington DC with three cats, one dog, a massage table and too many books! Thank you Lesléa, Olivia, Kathi, Carole and Joanne, for believing.

Hendle Rumbaut was born in Florida in 1949, raised in Lawrence, Kansas, and graduated Phi Beta Kappa from KU. Her photographs and fiction have appeared in newspapers and magazines. She is Associate Editor of *Argonaut Magazine,* the mother of Sasha Maria (aged 20), and she has worked at Austin Public Library for eighteen years.

Dorothy Ryan is a former advertising copywriter. She has done occasional freelance writing. Her biography of Dorothy Harrison Eustis, founder of The Seeing Eye, was included in the reference volume: *Past and Present: Lives of New Jersey Women.* She has also had poetry published by small presses.

Kimberly Sender: I am twenty-one years old, living in Cleveland. I am a college-bound author-to-be who spends her free time in independent study. I believe mental illnesses such as anorexia nervosa are coping mechanisms developd to survive in today's difficult society.

Jennifer Semple Siegel, an M.F.A. student at Goddard College, is currently working on her novel, *Weightlessness: The Story of Samantha.* She teaches writing and tutors in The Writing Center at York College of Pennsylvania. Her article, "Alan Sillitoe," will appear in an upcoming volume of *The Dictionary of Literary Biography.*

Nina Silver's writing on feminism, sexuality, metaphysics and the natural sciences has appeared in *off our backs, The New Internationalist, Natural Food and Farming, Green Egg, Gnosis, Jewish Currents,* and the anthologies *Women's Glib, Call It Courage,* and *Closer To Home: Bisexuality and Feminism.*

Jeanne Simonoff: I work in Los Angeles as a writer and a rehabilitation counselor. The unifying theme is to tell the truth. My grandparents came here from Russia at the beginning of the century to gain freedom to practice their lives without repression. I practice my life here, also, in the same spirit.

Cynthia M. Stacey: I am presently completing graduate work at Harvard and will be entering medical school thereafter. I am a thirty-four-year-old lesbian and suffered from an eating disorder while in college. My career goal is to counsel women and perform medical research on depression.

Heather Stephenson earned a bachelors degree in English *summa cum laude* from Princeton University. She completed "Howl," which was inspired by the poem of the same name by Allen Ginsberg, while teaching creative writing at the Putney School in Vermont. She is a vegetarian and a survivor of adolescent ballet lessons.

Dorothy Stone: Dot and Doll are, as you've probably suspected, two parts of one person, Dorothy Stone. Dorothy Stone is using a pseudonym and has changed a few details of her life story, but most of "Sisters" is absolutely true.

Annemarie Succop is a recovering bulimic fat woman currently living in Seattle.

Amber Coverdale Sumrall is editor of *Lovers, Write To The Heart, Sexual Harassment: Women Speak Out* (Crossing Press, 1992) and *Women of the Fourteenth Moon: Writings On Menopause* (Crossing Press, 1991). She also co-edited *Catholic Girls* (Plume, 1992). She lives in Santa Cruz, California.

Joette Thomas is the Administrative Director of the Center for Eating Disorders in Ann Arbor, Michigan. She is currently finishing her Master's thesis in Women's Studies at Eastern Michigan University. Her subject is the ways in which female visual and performance artists are using the female body in their work.

Lou Ann Thomas spent her first seventeen years on a farm in northeast Kansas. She has been a professional journalist as well as a high school English and journalism teacher. Lou Anne now lives in Kansas City where she writes and provides a home for her cats, Harry and Emily.

Karen Twenhofel: I grew up in Northern Virginia. I attended two years of college at Virginia Tech before transfering to San Diego State University, where I obtained a B.A. in Journalism. I got married three years later. My husband and I now live in Florida and are expecting our first child.

Patricia J. Washburn is a newspaper editor, writer, freelance indexer and part-time actress. She lives in Freeport, Maine with a musician named Gary Beckman, two cats named Annie and Cracker and a rabbit named Rowan.

Dr. Sharon Weinstein is a professor of English at Norfolk State University where she teaches Creative Writing, American Literature, and Women's Studies. She has published poetry, fiction, and critical essays in publications such as *Lilith, Western Humanities Review, Aethlon: The Journal of Sport Literature, Ethnic Studies*, and *The Poet's Domain*.

Linda Weltner's weekly column "Ever So Humble" has appeared in the At Homes pages of *The Boston Globe* for the past eleven years. Winner of the New England Women's Press Association Best Columnist Award, she is the author of *No Place Like Home* (Quill), a collection of her columns. She is the mother of two grown daughters and lives in Marblehead, Massachusetts with her husband, a psychiatrist.

Kara J. West is an unemployed recent college graduate who is occupying herself by sending out numerous résumés and serving as a volunteer literacy tutor. She lives in Richmond, Virginia.

Jan Wienpahl: Thirty-nine years old and single, I have a Ph.D. in Anthropology and an M.P.H. in Epidemiology. I have done anthropological research in rural Kenya and have worked at the National Institute on Aging. Currently I am developing a freelance writing career and living in Santa Barbara, California.

Selected Resources

Books

Autobiography, Memoir and Fiction

Atwood, Margaret. *The Edible Woman.* New York: Warner Books, 1989.

Ephron, Nora. *Heartburn.* New York: Knopf, 1983.

Liu, Aimee. *Solitaire.* New York: Harper and Row, 1979.

Miller, Caroline, Adams. *My Name is Caroline.* New York: Doubleday, 1988.

Millman, Marcia. *Such a Pretty Face.* New York: Berkeley, 1981.

Newman, Lesléa. *Belinda's Bouquet.* Boston: Alyson Publications, 1991.

Newman, Lesléa. *Good Enough to Eat.* Ithaca, NY: Firebrand Books, 1986.

Newman, Lesléa. "Perfectly Normal." In *Secrets,* Lesléa Newman, author. Norwich, VT: New Victoria Publishers, 1990.

O'Neill, Cherry Boone. *Starving for Attention.* New York: Continuum, 1982.

Rubin, Evan. "Preparing Dinner." In *True To Life Adventure Stories, Volume II.* Judy Grahn, editor. Trumansburg, NY: Crossing Press and Diana Press, 1981.

Shute, Jenefer. *Life-Size.* Boston: Houghton Mifflin, 1992.

Sussman, Susan. *The Dieter.* New York: Pocketbooks, 1989.

Weldon, Fay. *The Fat Woman's Joke.* Chicago: Academy Chicago Publishers, 1986.

Non-fiction (including self help)

Bruch, Hilda. *Conversations With Anorexics.* New York: Basic Books, 1986.

Chernin, Kim. *The Hungry Self: Women, Eating and Identity.* New York: Harper and Row, 1985.

Chernin, Kim. *The Obsession: Reflections on the Tyranny of Slenderness.* New York: Harper and Row, 1981.

Kano, Susan. *Making Peace With Food.* New York: Harper Collins, 1989.

Kolodny, Nancy, J. *When Food's A Foe.* Boston: Little, Brown and Co., 1987, 1992.

Lawrence, Marilyn, editor. *Fed Up and Hungry: Women, Oppression and Food.* New York: Peter Bedrick Books, 1987.

Newman, Lesléa. *SomeBody to Love: A Guide to Loving The Body You Have.* Chicago: Third Side Press, 1991.

Orbach, Susie. *Fat Is A Feminist Issue.* New York: Berkeley Books, 1978.

Orbach, Susie. *Fat Is A Feminist Issue II: A Program To Conquer Compulsive Overeating.* New York: Berkeley Books, 1982.

Orbach Susie. *Hunger Strike: The Anorexic's Struggle as A Metaphor For Our Age.* New York: Norton, 1986.

Ray, Sondra. *The Only Diet There Is.* Berkeley, CA: Celestial Arts, 1981.

Roth, Geneen. *Breaking Free from Compulsive Overeating.* New York: New American Library, 1984.

Roth, Geneen. *Feeding the Hungry Heart.* New York: New American Library, 1983.

Roth, Geneen. *When Food is Love.* New York: New American Library, 1991.

Schoedfielder, Lisa and Weiser, Barb. *Shadow on a Tightrope: Writings by Women on Fat Oppression.* San Francisco: Spinsters/Aunt Lute Book. Co., 1983.

Siegel, Michele, Ph.D.; Brisman, Judith, Ph.D.; and Weinshel, Margot, MSW. *Surviving an Eating Disorder: Strategies for Family and Friends.* New York: Harper and Row, 1988.

Wilson, Jan. *Directory of Eating Disorders Programs, Therapists and Services.* Palm Bay, FL: Center Publishing, 1992.

Periodicals

ANRED Alert
Anorexia Nervosa & Related Eating Disorders, Inc.
PO Box 5102
Eugene, OR 97405

Eating Disorders Digest
Center Publishing
2514 Palm Place Dr. NE
Palm Bay, FL 32905

Heresies: A Feminist Publication on Art and Politics.
    Issue #21: "Food Is A Feminist Issue."
PO Box 1306
Canal Street Station
New York, NY 10013

International Journal of Eating Disorders
John Wiley and Sons, Inc.
Journal Division
605 Third Ave.
New York, NY 10058

National Association of Anorexia and
    Related Disorders Newsletter
Box 271
Highland Park, IL 60035

Radiance: A Magazine For Large Women
PO Box 31703
Oakland, CA 94604

Sinister Wisdom. Issue #28: Special Focus on
    Body Image, Size and Eating.
PO Box 3252
Berkeley, CA 9470

Films

Gilday, Katherine. *The Famine Within*. Canada: Kandor Productions, 1991. 90-minute and 60-minute version. Distributed by Direct Cinema, Telephone: 1 (800) 525-0000.
Jaglom, Henry. *Eating*. Los Angeles: International Rainbow Pictures, 1990. 110 minutes. Distributed by Rainbow Releasing, Telephone: (310) 271-0202.

Organizations

Anorexia Nervosa and Related Eating Disorders, Inc. (ANRED)
PO Box 5102
Eugene, OR 97405

Counsel on Size and Weight Discrimination
PO Box 238
Columbia, MD 21045

F.E.E.D. (Foundation for Education about Eating Disorders)
PO Box 16375
Baltimore, MD 21210

International Association of Eating Disorders Professionals
34213 Coast Highway, Suite E
Dana Point, CA 92629

National Anorexic Aid Society
5796 Karl Rd.
Columbus, OH 43229

National Association of Anorexia Nervosa and Associated Disorders
Box 7
Highland Park, IL 60035

NAAFA (National Association for the Advancement of Fat Acceptance)
PO Box 188620
Sacramento, CA 95818

Overeaters Anonymous
World Service Office
2190 190th Street
Torrance, CA 90504

Mary Vazquez

About the Editor

Lesléa Newman has written extensively on eating disorders. Her books on the subject include: a non-fiction book, *Some Body To Love: A Guide To Loving The Body You Have* (Third Side Press, 1991); a children's book, *Belinda's Bouquet* (Alyson Publications, 1991); a novel, *Good Enough To Eat* (Firebrand Books, 1986) and the recently completed young adult novel, *Fat Chance*. Lesléa lives in Northampton, Massachussets and is the founder and director of *Write From the Heart: Writing Workshops for Women*. She frequently travels around the country to give readings from her work and teach a variety of women's writing workshops including *What Are You Eating/What's Eating You* which focuses on the relationship betwen women, eating and food.

The Crossing Press
publishes a full selection of books of
interest to women. Call toll free and
ask for a free general catalog.
800-777-1048